Arbitration of Intra-Corporate Disputes in Turkish Law

Aysel Cetinkaya Uyar

Arbitration of Intra-Corporate Disputes in Turkish Law

PETER LANG

Bibliographic Information published by the Deutsche Nationalbibliothek
The Deutsche Nationalbibliothek lists this publication in the Deutsche Nationalbibliografie; detailed bibliographic data is available online at http://dnb.d-nb.de.

Library of Congress Cataloging-in-Publication Data
A CIP catalog record for this book has been applied for at the Library of Congress.

This book is a revised version of the doctoral dissertation of Aysel Cetinkaya Uyar submitted in partial fulfillment of the requirements for Penn State Law's Doctor of Juridical Science (S.J.D.) program in 2017.

Printed by CPI books GmbH, Leck

ISBN 978-3-631-77572-1 (Print)
E-ISBN 978-3-631-78534-8 (E-PDF)
E-ISBN 978-3-631-81508-3 (EPUB)
E-ISBN 978-3-631-81509-0 (MOBI)
DOI 10.3726/b16656

Peter Lang – Berlin · Bern · Bruxelles · New York · Oxford · Warszawa · Wien

This publication has been peer reviewed.

www.peterlang.com

This book is dedicated to the memory of my beloved father,
Fehmi Cetinkaya (1966–2014)
whose guiding role in my life was, and remains, immense.
For your unflinching commitment to my career pursuits,
you are profoundly appreciated.
Without you, none of my success would have been possible.

Acknowledgements

First and foremost, I am deeply indebted to my supervisor Professor Thomas Carbonneau for his enormous guidance, inspiration, and encouraging comments. I would not have completed this book without his attentive supervision and contributions. It has been an honor for me to have such an experienced and internationally renowned authority on arbitration as my advisor.

I am further grateful to Professors Samuel Bufford and Julie Metzger, and to my dear friend Tatiana Chiribau for being my second family in the US. Living with them, I was too busy making unforgettable memories to ever feel lonely or homesick.

My deepest appreciation goes to my family for their unwavering support and encouragement. The continuous and unparalleled love of my mother Berrin Cetinkaya and my brother Fırat Cetinkaya have enabled me to overcome all manner of challenges. Although we have been separated by thousands of miles, they have been with me every step of the way.

Most importantly, I want to express my sincere gratitude to my dear husband Can Yucel Uyar, who has been with me all this time and made these years the best my life. He has supported me through every critical step of this book with great love and patience. I want to thank him for everything.

Contents

Introduction

Arbitrability establishes the essential boundary between the regulatory authority of the legal system and the contractual process of arbitration. Arbitrability may overlap with public policy and other vital concerns of national legal systems. Today's legal systems may clearly maintain the scope of their authority and resist acquiescing to the trend toward universal arbitrability. States may, in fact, choose to prioritize their sovereignty over other principles of law such as freedom of contract in some certain circumstances. Protecting and maintaining the legal apparatus supporting the social, political, and economic order of the State may require such an approach. Certain areas of law including criminal law or family law can demonstrate this point.

The contemporary era, however, has seen a diminution in cardinal legal values and the exclusivity of legal authority. While legal systems might reevaluate overly generous delegations of adjudicatory power to arbitrators, such reevaluations rarely occur in the context of corporate disputes. Such disputes, indeed, are best regulated through the application of freedom of contract. Corporate disputes are highly complex and dynamic. They change constantly and vary based on an array commercial relationships common in everyday business life. The number and type of problems that can lead to corporate disputes is constantly increasing. For national laws to foresee and address such problems in advance is extremely challenging.

Arbitration's dynamism, and its ability to adapt rapidly and provide expert-oriented solutions may allow it to meet the expectations of corporate practitioners. Corporate disputes can also benefit from the presence of expert arbitrators and the flexibility inherent to the arbitration process. International disputes, likewise, require greater flexibility than those that occur in a strictly domestic context. The scope of state intervention in the international arena is generally narrower than in domestic disputes. The strength of the state authority should therefore depend on the position of the dispute.

The statutory boundaries of Turkish law indicate that, in Turkey, the traditional limitations on arbitrability are general and equal for both domestic and international disputes. To begin with, the law is silent regarding the arbitration of disputes in the realm of corporate law. This has created significant disagreement among legal scholars. The courts have adopted a similarly ambivalent position on the issue, and consensus regarding the arbitrability of corporate disputes has not been reached in Turkish legal practice. Corporate disputes thus lack consistent settlement practices in the doctrinal, adjudicatory, and legislative dimensions of Turkish law. Critics highlight the fact that respect for the will of corporate parties regarding the submission of disputes to arbitration remains equivocal. Critics dispute the arbitrability of corporate disputes on several additional grounds: the exclusivity of judicial jurisdictional rules, violations of public policy, procedural impediments, and protection of shareholder rights. Civil law systems cannot tolerate such ambiguity because it leads to confusion among legal practitioners. Instability in dispute settlement can also harm foreign investment potential. Inconsistency in legal regulations, court rulings, and doctrinal commentary could have an irreversible long-term effect on Turkey as an emerging market.

This book examines the arbitrability of corporate disputes by considering Turkish legislation, doctrinal commentary and case law. It analyzes the main problematic areas, aiming to determine the problems' underlying causes and to suggest ways to overcome them. To accomplish this, the book first establishes the general framework of arbitrability in Turkish law. This framework serves as a foundation for subsequent chapters, which focus on corporate disputes and require a basic knowledge of arbitrability. The book then conducts a complete analysis of general arbitrability rules and corporate law regulations to identify the factors that affect the arbitrability of corporate disputes.

A. An Overview of Chapters: Defining the Topic and its Limitations

This section will briefly introduce the main parts of the book. Part I (Chapters I and II) outlines arbitrability in Turkey in general. Chapter I elucidates the fundamental principles and general criteria that apply to arbitrability in Turkish law. Chapter II examines the three grounds for the inarbitrability: imperative rules, exclusive judicial jurisdiction rules, and public policy.

Part II (Chapters III–V) discusses the arbitrability of corporate disputes specifically. It contains the core chapters, which explain the significance of arbitration as a dispute resolution mechanism in corporate disputes. A brief statutory review of the topic precedes a description of the framework and methodology of corporate disputes. This section highlights the book's ultimate focus: disputes stemming from corporations' internal relations or intra-corporate disputes. Chapters III and IV explain the crucial importance of intra-corporate disputes, including those between shareholders, and those between shareholders and legal entities or organs of the corporation. These sections are critical because no statutes in Turkish law explicitly regulate the arbitrability of disputes arising from the internal affairs of corporations. This lack of regulation creates a great deal of ambiguity. The chapters highlight the need for a detailed analysis of the issue.

The scope of possible intra-corporate disputes is wide enough to include remuneration of the board members, the involvement of shareholders in resolution-making processes and takeovers, the rights of minority shareholders in the squeeze-out or selection of board members, takeover procedures that conflict with intra-corporate rules, dismissal of appointed board members, breach of corporate governance principles, and mismanagement. Other examples of arbitrable intra-corporate disputes include those arising from a corporation's articles of association, shareholder agreements about corporate policy or finance or share purchases, possible deadlocks, usage of shareholder rights with regard to voting or pre-emption, or other corporate governance factors. Annulment of general assembly resolutions is a particularly useful example because it exemplifies all potential issues surrounding the arbitration of intra-corporate disputes. In particular, it typifies all the basic objections in Turkish law to the arbitrability of intra-corporate disputes. This makes this book's discussion of the arbitrability of annulment of general assembly resolutions emblematic.

Chapter IV focuses on the arbitrability of disputes stemming from annulment of general assembly resolutions from a practical perspective, allowing for the application of rules specified by legislation and court decisions. The chapter begins by highlighting the absence of a specific statutory regulation. It then considers statutory, judicial, and doctrinal developments, and identifies related regulations in Turkish law via an extensive statutory review. The chapter then briefly describes and assesses related judicial decisions rendered before national courts on the basis of an extensive consideration of case law. Finally, it assesses the opinions of significant doctrinal commentators.

Following Chapter IV's comprehensive examination of the topic, the book appraises arguments related to:

- Compatibility with the criteria of the will of the parties;
- Judicial jurisdiction and potential exclusivity of the rule and how these factors are influenced by public policy;
- Significance of decisions for third parties and or shareholders not party to the action;
- Vested right character and attendant outcomes;

- The effects of the imperative provisions principle in the Turkish Commercial Code on Arbitration;
- Procedural advantages and requirements stipulated by the law regarding court adjudication: consolidation of cases and other multiparty dispute mechanisms.

Chapter V presents counterarguments to claims of inarbitrability regarding annulment of general assembly resolutions in corporate law. Each counterargument addresses an argument made in Chapter IV on statutory and adjudicatory grounds. This chapter, therefore, serves a nexus of theoretical and practical information, generating a series of proposals to resolve multiparty disputes through arbitration in the Turkish legal system.

B. This Book's Significance, Expected Contributions, and Methodology

The current lack of foreign language sources addressing Turkish arbitral practice in comparative jurisprudence led this book to focus on the Turkish legal system. It refers to other jurisdictions when necessary to complete theoretical explanations with comparative illustrations that provide a practical perspective. Ultimately, this book aims to widen the scope of coverage of Turkish legal studies in the realm of international legal scholarship.

Some sources relate to either Turkish arbitration or corporate law. No interdisciplinary sources, however, combine these two areas of law in English. The issues arising from the arbitration of corporate disputes have from time to time been pointed out in limited number of Turkish studies. However, none of these studies were sufficiently comprehensive to trigger meaningful change. Some major Codes in Turkish law have, moreover, undergone radical changes in recent years. The Turkish Commercial Code, the Turkish Contract Code, and the Turkish Code of Civil Procedure have, for instance, completely changed since 2011. Initial major and subsequent minor changes have left a considerable number of sources in Turkish Law outdated. This makes it even more important to use the most up-to-date regulations to reach accurate conclusions regarding civil law jurisdictions. This book applies the most recent versions of all related regulations in addition to including previous versions of the regulations in footnotes to improve general comprehension.

Whether jurisdictional exclusivity makes corporate disputes inarbitrable remains unclear; the role of the courts and statutory law in this context is similarly unclear. Evaluating the pitfalls of arbitrating corporate disputes in Turkish law is therefore critical. The issue will presumably have broad repercussions among doctrinal commentators, leading to general reappraisal among scholars and legislators and ultimately new legislation. This study presents a detailed analysis of both literature and case law to reach this goal. Effective legislation and stabilization of this problem via consistent court rulings and doctrinal commentary requires further research demonstrating its critical importance.

This book follows a solution-oriented approach as opposed to simply diagnosing legislative inadequacy. Highlighting the necessity for clarification in this area and triggering regulation is one of this book's aims. To fulfil this solution-oriented aim, the study includes a detailed analysis of possible risks and pitfalls for parties submitting their disputes to arbitration under current Turkish law. This risk analysis precedes a set of proposals to alleviate these inconveniences. It also includes arguments supporting the arbitrability of disputes arising from intra-corporate matters. The book serves as a guide for corporate practitioners arbitrating disputes in Turkey. It examines the majority of factors practitioners must consider to avoid undesirable complications in the arbitration of corporate disputes. This gives the work its practical dimension and is one of the primary reasons the project was undertaken in the first place.

Turkey recently took an innovative step towards the establishment of an arbitration center when the center's institutional rules and regulations took effect on October 26, 2016.[1] [2] This arbitration institution is named Istanbul Arbitration Centre (ISTAC). The center aims to take advantage of Turkey's geographical position as bridge between Europe, Asia, the Middle East and Africa, targeting the broad markets between those continents. Its up-to-date rules aim to meet the needs of contemporary international commercial practitioners. After the center's active and enthusiastic start, it has already received applications for arbitration. The center's long-term success, however, will depend on legal predictability, limited court or state intervention, and the systematic and sustainable revisions to Turkish arbitration law. The content of this book should also contribute to the center's activities.

1 The dates in this paper will be formatted in the American style: October 26, 2016 in the texts; or 10/26/2016 (Month/Day/Year) in court documents.

2 *Available at*: https://istac.org.tr/en/

This book's methodological techniques are, lastly, as follows: Historical research served as the primary means of determining the questions requiring analysis. For data collection, the book explored relevant statutes of Turkish corporate and arbitration law chronologically. It also thoroughly examined case law to determine whether case rulings clarify ambiguities. The book then scrutinized doctrinal opinions to elucidate scholarly positions as a part of literature review. It then synthesized all relevant information into counterarguments that form the basis of its conclusions. From time to time, the book utilized the quantitative method in data collection. It applied secondary data analysis to the evaluation of previous surveys of major arbitral institutions. Finally, the book employed statistics derived from structured surveys of numerous respondents to develop its counterarguments.

Part I. Arbitrability in Turkish Law

I. Introduction to Part I: Fundamental Principles and Literature Review

A. General Principles of Turkish Law: 'Party Autonomy'

The principle of party autonomy gives individuals the right to utilize the legal system to regulate their personal relationships.[3] It enables them to attend to their legal affairs autonomously.[4] The most significant tool bolstering party autonomy is the legal act in law—specifically, the contract. Parties form legal contracts that bind them with specific obligations and entitle them to certain rights.[5] The principle of party autonomy protects parties from the external intervention of third parties including States while regulating their private legal relationships.[6]

The principle of party autonomy also contains other concepts, such as 'freedom of contract'.[7] The term 'freedom of contract' is sometimes used synonymously with party autonomy, but it is actually one of the distinct elements[8] that arise from party autonomy.[9] The freedom of contract rule enables parties to designate the scope of contracts.[10] The freedom of contract rule is also the primary principle governing the practice and regulatory provisions of arbitration.[11]

---

3 Fikret Eren, Borclar Hukuku Genel Hukumler [The Law of Contracts General Provisions] 18 (Beta Yayıncılık, 2010) [Beta Publishing, 2010].

4 Stefan Grundmann, *Information, Party Autonomy and Economic Agents in European Contract Law*, 39 Common Mkt. L. Rev. 269 (2002).

5 Derya Ates, *Irade Ozerkligi Kapsamında MK. m 23/II Hukmu ve Karar Ozgurlugu [Article 23/II of Civil Code Within the Scope of Party Autonomy and Freedom of Decision]* Ankara Barosu Dergisi, Yıl: 65, Sayı: 2, Bahar 2007 [Ankara Bar Journal, Year: 65, Issue 2, Spring 2007] p. 136.

6 Fikret Eren, p. 18.

7 Zhaohua MENG, *Party Autonomy, Private Autonomy, and Freedom of Contract*, 10:6 Canadian Soc. Sci. 215 (2014), http://www.cscanada.net/index.php/css/article/view/5155.

8 The other two principles are obligatory effect and relative effect of the contract.

9 Derya Ates, *Sozlesme Ozgurlugu Yonunden Durustluk Kuralları [The Principle of Good Faith in Terms of Freedom of Contract]*, Turkiye Barolar Birligi Dergisi, Sayı 72, 2007 [Turkish Bar Association Journal, Issue 72, 2007] p. 75.

10 Ahmet M. Kılıcoglu, Borclar Hukuku Genel Hukumler [The Law of Contracts General Provisions] 53 (Turhan Kitabevi, Ankara, 2007) [Turhan Publishing, Ankara 2007].

11 Thomas E. Carbonneau & William Elliott Butler, International Litigation and Arbitration 573 (W. 2013).

Most jurisdictions have recognized it.[12] The rule enables parties to form their own regulations for arbitration—potentially more effective and fairly structured than strict procedural requirements.[13] This flexibility makes arbitration responsive to the needs of the parties, contributing to its effectiveness and appeal in a commercial context. [14]

In the Turkish Law of Contracts, likewise, the principle of party autonomy is a fundamental principle and constitutes the ideological basis for liberal legal philosophy and freedom of contract.[15] It is also closely linked to other important principles of Turkish law, including objective good faith, liability *ex delicto*, consideration, personality, reciprocity, etc. Several codes in Turkish law demonstrate the importance of the freedom of contract principle.[16] Article 48 of the Constitution of the Republic of Turkey states, '*Everyone has the freedom to work and conclude contracts in the field of his choice*'.[17] According to first article of Turkish Code of Contract,[18] '*A contract is concluded when both parties mutually declare their concurring assents*.' According to article 26[19] of the same Code, '*The terms of a contract may be freely determined by the parties within the limits of the law*.' These regulations demonstrate the unequivocal authority of the principle of freedom of contract in Turkish civil law.

External factors that influence State laws may also warrant examination. Many States, including Turkey, have adopted The United Nations Commission on International Trade Law (UNCITRAL) Model Law on International Commercial Arbitration.[20] The main principles of UNCITRAL apply in the Turkish legal system. The UNCITRAL Model Law takes a liberal approach to arbitration, giving the most weight to consensus of the parties and underscoring the "*...central significance of party autonomy in the process of international*

---

12 *Ibid.*

13 *Ibid.*

14 Karl-Heinz Bockstiegel, *Role of Party Autonomy in International Arbitration*, J. Disp. Resol. 25 & 30 n.3 (Summer 1997).

15 Fikret Eren, p. 18

16 Tugrul Ansay & Don Wallace, Introduction to Turkish Law 156 (Kluwer Law Int'l 2011).

17 Constitution of the Republic of Turkey which was enacted on 11/07/1982 with the code number of 2709.

18 Turkish Code of Contract numbered 6098 which was published in Official Gazette on 02/04/2011 with the number of 27836. Turkish Code of Contract numbered 818 was in force until this Code was enacted.

19 This was article 19 in this previous Code numbered 818.

20 Thomas E. Carbonneau, *The Exercise of Contract Freedom in the Making of Arbitration Agreements*, 36 Vand. J. Transnat'l L. 1198.

commercial arbitration."[21] The fact that the Turkish International Arbitration Code was formed by the adoption of UNCITRAL Model Law[22] suggests that the same key freedom of contract principle governs it.

Although the principle of party autonomy grants parties the right to submit any dispute to arbitration, national jurisdictions are likely to limit the types of disputes that can be resolved through arbitration.[23] Turkish law has some restrictions of this principle in the context of arbitration, too. The first explicit restriction is in Article 408 of Turkish Code of Civil Procedure, which regulates domestic arbitration. It states:

> *Disputes arising from in rem rights on immovable property or disputes that are not subject to the will of the parties are inarbitrable.*

The second such restriction is in Article 1 (4) of Turkish International Arbitration Code, which regulates international arbitration processes in Turkey. It states:

> *This Code shall not apply to disputes that concern in rem rights on immovable property located in Turkey and disputes that are not subject to the will of the parties.*

The existence of restrictions, however, does not diminish the principle's primacy in Turkish laws that regulate arbitration.[24] The general rules that address domestic and international arbitration in Turkey suggest that parties are free to agree on subjects that are not explicitly restricted.[25] Party autonomy is, therefore, the general rule; these restrictions are enumerated exceptions that cannot be expanded in Turkish law.[26] This principle is, indeed, a fundamental requirement

---

21 *Ibid.*

22 Nevhis Deren Yıldırım, Uncitral Model Kanunu ve Milletlerarası Tahkim Kanunu Cercevesinde Milletlerarası Tahkimin Esaslı Sorunları [Essential Concerns of International Arbitration within the Framework of UNCITRAL Model Law and International Arbitration Code] 13 (Alkım, Istanbul 2004) [Alkım Publishing, Istanbul 2004].

23 Loukas A. Mistelis & Stavros L. Brekoulakis, Arbitrability: International and Comparative Perspectives 10 (Kluwer Law Int'l 2009).

24 Cemal Sanlı, Milletlerarası, Ticari Tahkimde Esasa Uygulanacak Hukuk [The Law Applicable to the Substance in International Commercial Arbitration] ff.105 (Banka ve Ticaret Hukuku Arastırma Enstitusu, Ankara 1986) [Banking and Commercial Law Research Institute, Ankara 1986].

25 Burak Huysal, Milletlerarası Ticari Tahkimde Tahkime Elverislilik [Arbitrability in International Commercial Arbitration] 113 (Vedat Kitapcılık, Istanbul 2010) [Vedat Publishing, Istanbul 2010].

26 Fikret Eren, pp. 18–19.

of international commercial arbitration and inherently in the interest of business executives.[27]

B. The Concept of Arbitrability

The principle of party autonomy first arose in the nineteenth century[28] in reference to the choice of law in a contract.[29] Its content and application have since expanded, particularly as international commercial arbitration has become a more common and preferred means of dispute resolution.[30] National arbitration regulations mostly cover the pre-arbitral process, post-arbitral process, and the degree of court intervention, but party autonomy governs the entire process.[31]

The party autonomy rule grants parties the right to resort to arbitration for the resolution of any dispute, but certain national laws regulate and define the issues that can legally be arbitrated.[32] This is termed as "objective arbitrability" or "arbitrability *ratione materiae*" in the literature.[33] The UNCITRAL Model Law

---

27 Karl-Heinz Bockstiegel, n.3.

28 Albert Venn Dicey, Lawrence Collins & John Humphrey Carlile Morris, 2 Dicey, Morris and Collins on the Conflict of Laws ¶ 32–004 (14th ed. Sweet&Maxwell 2010).

29 Seyda Dursun, *A Critical Examination of the Role of Party Autonomy in International Commercial Arbitration and an Assessment of Its Role and Extent*, Yalova Universitesi Hukuk Fakultesi Dergisi (2012/1) [1 Yalova University Faculty of Law Journal (2012)] p. 161.

30 *Ibid.*

31 Christian Bühring-Uhle, Lars Kirchhoff & Gabriele Scherer, Arbitration and Mediation in International Business pp. 70 (Kluwer Law Int'l 2006).

32 Loukas A. Mistelis & Stavros L. Brekoulakis, p 3.

33 Emmanuel Gaillard, Berthold Goldman & John Savage, Fouchard, Gaillard, Goldman on International Commercial Arbitration 312 (Kluwer Law Int'l 1999).

The first type of arbitrability is "objective arbitrability". The second type of arbitrability is "subjective arbitrability" (or *ratione personae*).

"*Subjective arbitrability, or arbitrability ratione personae, concerns in particular the entitlement of states and public entities to submit their disputes to arbitration.*" (Fouchard Gaillard on ICA, p. 312 (para.534)).
It also bears emphasizing that that other jurisdictions may categorize objective (in) arbitrability in Turkish Law as 'subject matter (in)arbitrability'. American sources, for instance, refer subject matter inarbitrability (instead of objective inarbitrability) for "prohibition of recourse to arbitration as a matter of law".

Thomas E. Carbonneau, Cases and Materials on Arbitration Law and Practice 27 (5th ed. W. Academic 2009).

does not define 'objective arbitrability' but the code does aim to expand the usage of arbitration.[34] Article 1/5 simply states: "*This Law shall not affect any other law of this State by virtue of which certain disputes may not be submitted to arbitration or may be submitted to arbitration only according to provisions other than those of this Law.*" This article gives States the right to regulate arbitrability in their own national jurisdictions and prevents the Model Law from affecting these national regulations.[35]

States thus have the authority to limit arbitrability;[36] in practice, lawmakers impose restrictions based on moral, social, medical, political, and economic factors. These restrictions become binding for trial courts due to *stare decisis*.[37] States may restrict arbitrability for reasons including the conservation of public policy and safety, public morality, protection of weaker parties, intervening rules of national law, jurisdictional conflicts with a public judicial authority that is vested with an exclusive jurisdictional power,[38] or the prevention of manipulation.[39] Rationales can also be based on general State policies such as import or export prohibitions, quota applications, or restrictions due to monetary policy or foreign exchange regulations.[40]

"*It is a universal principle of contract law that parties are free to enter into any contract as long as it does not violate public policy. There is a point, however, at which even private commercial conduct implicates the public interest. When a commercial dispute affects public policy, most arbitration laws provide that it is inarbitrable because of its subject-matter. To some extent, subject-matter inarbitrability is a subset of the public policy exception to arbitration.*"

34 Nevhis Deren Yıldırım, Uncitral Model Law, p. 27.

35 *Ibid*

36 Mustafa Erkan, Milletlerarası Tahkimde Yetki Sorunları [The Issue of Jurisdiction in International Arbitration], 75 (Yetkin Basımevi, Ankara 2013) [Yetkin Publishing, Ankara 2013].

37 *e.g.* Turkish Supreme Court 15th Civil Circuit decision dated 09/23/2002 numbered 2002/4321.

38 Mustafa Erkan, p. 75.

39 Unal Tekinalp, *Hakem Sozlesmesinin Hukuki Mahiyeti Uzerine Dusunceler* [*Thoughts on Legal Nature of Arbitration Agreement*], *in* IV. Ticaret ve Banka Hukuku Haftası, Bildiriler & Tartısmalar [IV.th Commercial and Banking Law Week, Notices & Discussions] 28 (Banka ve Ticaret Hukuku Arastırma Enstitusu, 1966) [Banking and Commercial Law Research Institute, Ankara 1986].

40 Mehmet Koseoglu, *Milletlerarası Ozel Hukuk ve Usul Hukuku Hakkında Kanun madde 31: Sozlesme ile Sıkı Iliskili 3. Bir Devletin Dogrudan Uygulanan Kurallarına Etki Tanınması* [*The Code on Private International Law and Civil Procedure article 31: Validating the Mandatory Rules of a Third State which is in Close Relationship with*

States may intervene in two ways. They may present a broad list of reasons canceling a particular arbitral award or scatter restrictions on arbitrability throughout several national codes. The latter approach closely relates to objective arbitrability. Some States, Turkey among them, adopt both methods of intervention.[41] States may also declare arbitration agreements null and void due to the violation of the public interest; doctrinal commentators point out that, in practice, this result is very extreme and rare.[42]

Establishing an arbitration agreement based on the right of freedom of contract is legitimate, but the subject matter of the arbitration agreement must fall within the limitations established for arbitral procedures by national law. The possibility that State intervention may render arbitral awards, which cost parties considerable time and money, practically non-enforceable and void undermines the aim of the entire process. Parties must, therefore, carefully consider the national rules governing the limits of objective arbitrability for international commercial arbitration. The applicability of these rules varies in each national jurisdiction.[43] The next section explains how Turkish law regulates this issue.

C. Arbitrability and Sources of Turkish Law

Two main codes regulate arbitration in Turkey. The Turkish International Arbitration Code regulates *international* commercial arbitration. The Turkish Code of Civil Procedure regulates *domestic* arbitration procedures. Certain regulations in the latter parallel those in the Turkish International Arbitration Code. These parallels can help elucidate legal and practical gaps.

---

the Contract], MHB Yıl 28, sayı 1–2 (2008) [International Private Law Bullettin, Year 28, Issue 1–2 (2008)] pp. 149–150.

41 Nevhis Deren Yıldırım, Uncitral Model Law, p. 27,
Mehmet Sarı, *Tahkime Elverislilik* [*Arbitrability*], Terazi Aylık Hukuk Dergisi, Yıl: 4, Sayı: 32, (Nisan 2009) [Terazi Monthly Law Journal, Year:4, Issue: 32, (April 2009)] p. 147.

42 Nevhis Deren Yıldırım, Uncitral Model Law, p. 27.

43 Mehmet Tas, Turk Hukukunda Anonim Sirket Genel Kurul Kararlarının Iptali Davalarının Milletlerarası Ticari Tahkimde Gorulmesi [Settlement of the Lawsuit of Annulment of General Meeting Resolution of Companies Before International Commercial Arbitration in Turkish Law] (2007) (Yayınlanmamıs Yuksek Lisans Tezi, Istanbul Universitesi, Sosyal Bilimler Enstitusu) [Unpublished LLM Thesis, Istanbul University, Institute of Social Sciences] p. 20.

Both Codes are based on objective arbitrability.[44] The next section examines objective arbitrability in Turkish International Arbitration Code, and then analyzes subsidiary regulations in the Turkish Code of Civil Procedure and other private codes that restrict arbitration. The restrictions may vary according to international or national character of the cases in question.

---

44 Burcu Zengin, *Sirketler Hukukunda Tahkime Elverislilikle Ilgili Temel Meseleler* [*Fundamental Issues Concerning the Arbitrability in Company Law*] Terazi Aylık Hukuk Dergisi, Cilt:9, Sayı:95, (Temmuz 2014) [Terazi Monthly Law Journal, Volume:9, Issue: 95, (July 2014)] p. 103.

II. Objective Arbitrability under Turkish International Arbitration Law

A dispute's objective arbitrability determines whether it can be submitted to arbitration. Turkish law categorizes disputes as inarbitrable for main three reasons: [45] First, an imperative rule in a code may impede arbitration. Second, a judicial jurisdictional rule may exclusively authorize a national court to resolve a dispute, which some legal authorities interpret as indication of inarbitrability. This can either be stated explicitly or a 'court order' requirement in a law may result in such perception. Finally, a State's public policy concerns may render a dispute inarbitrable. The next sections analyze each of these reasons.

A. The Impact of Imperative Rules on Arbitrability

1. The General Statutory Formula for Arbitrability of a Dispute

Turkish law does not individually regulate the arbitrability of disputes impacted by imperative rules.[46] The Turkish International Arbitration Code[47] defines how much freedom parties have to make arbitration agreements. The relevant article states that for a dispute to be arbitrable, it must be "*subject to the will of the parties*".[48] To be settled by arbitrators, disputes must arise from legal

---

45 Jean-François Poudret & Sébastien Besson, Comparative Law of International Arbitration 281 & § 326 (Sweet & Maxwell 2007).

46 Burak Huysal, p. 110.

47 Article 1 para.4 of Turkish International Arbitration Code numbered 4686

"*This Code shall not apply to the disputes that concern in rem rights on immovable property located in Turkey and disputes that are not governed by the parties' mutual agreement.*"

48 The regulation stipulates for a dispute "to be subject to the will of the parties" to be within the ambit of this Code. The Code includes this regulation under the heading of "*the purpose and scope*". Some legal authorities interpret that this code does not apply to the disputes that are not subject to the will of the parties rather than to interpret that these disputes are not arbitrable.
(Ziya Akıncı, Milletlerarası Tahkim [International Arbitration] 77 (Vedat Kitapcılık, 3. Baski 2013) [Vedat Publishing, 3rd ed. 2013].)

relationships or acts that the parties can agree upon freely.[49] The Code, however, contains no concrete list of matters that are not subject to the will of the parties. This causes practical problems, necessitating interpretation for some specific types of disputes.[50] As the governing regulations, the general rules of arbitrability warrant explanation.

a) *Standards and Approaches for Establishing Whether a Dispute is Subject to the Will of the Parties*

Different States regulate the limits of arbitration differently. Codes may express limitations in a general formula in the code, in separate lists enumerating non-arbitrable or arbitrable matters, or they may contain no explicit provisions regarding limitations.[51] These varied approaches all stem from the general principle of the independence of *the power of disposition of the parties* on the right in question.[52] This principle determines a matter's arbitrability.

Swiss law accepts that all disputes of a pecuniary nature are arbitrable—a position that has influenced German law.[53] This acceptance reflects the mutuality principle in Swiss law—identifying matters at the free disposition of the parties as arbitrable.[54] Some States—Turkey among them—accept several other

The Code, however, aims at disallowing to arbitrate such type of the disputes rather than applying another code to this dispute. The strongest proof of this idea is the criterion for arbitrability in domestic law in general which is governed by Turkish Code of Civil Procedure. Article 408 of this Code states that: "*...disputes that are not subject to the will of the parties' are not arbitrable.*" It underlines that disputes that are not governed by will of the parties are inarbitrable precisely.
(Mehmet Sari, p. 163.)

49 Ergin Nomer, Nuray Eksi & Gunseli Oztekin Gelgel, Milletlerarası Tahkim Hukuku [International Arbitration Law] 40 (Cilt 1, Beta Yayıncılık, 4. Baski 2013) [Vol.1, Beta Publishing, 4th ed. 2013].

50 Such as corporate disputes subject to this book.

51 Rasih Yegengil, Tahkim: (L'arbitrage) [Arbitration: (L'arbitrage)] 152 (Istanbul, 1974).

52 *Ibid.*

53 Nevhis Deren Yıldırım, *Tahkim ve Objektif Acıdan Tahkime Elverislilik* [*Arbitration and Objective Arbitrability*] *in* Prof. Dr. Yavuz Alagonya icin Armagan [Dedication for Prof. Dr. Yavuz Alagonya] 59, 47 (Alkım Yayınevi, Istanbul 2007) [Alkım Publishing, Istanbul 2007].

54 It is pointed out pertaining to Swiss Law as:

"*Art. 177 PILS determines objective arbitrability (ratione materiae), i.e. what claims can be the object of an arbitration. The term "objective arbitrability" is very wide in meaning, and covers all claims of economic interest, irrespective of the fact that substantive law*

factors, including the availability of settlement as indicating a matter's dispositive nature. The German legislative system took an identical approach[55] until the previous German Code of Civil Procedure[56] became defunct in 1998. Germany changed its approach in recognition of the equality of arbitration proceedings with trial proceedings.[57] German legislators[58] accepted the arbitrability of pecuniary matters in general and determined that eligibility for settlement should serve as the criterion of arbitrability for non-pecuniary matters.[59]

Turkey remains one of the States that uses a general formula to determine whether a matter is arbitrable, rather than having a specific list of arbitrable matters. The Turkish Code of Civil Procedure stipulates that disputes not subject to the will of the parties are inarbitrable.[60] This reflects the mutual principle of the parties' right of disposition in Turkish law[61] because the right of disposition is one of the leading imperative principles[62] in the Turkish civil judiciary

---

governing contractual relationships might provide for a more restrictive definition of objective arbitrability108. Under Art. 5 of the Concordat, only claims which the parties are free to dispose of are arbitrable. In this sense, the Concordat has a different and more restrictive approach to PILS, regarding objective arbitrability."

Antonio Monti, *Arbitration and Corporation in* Three Essays on International Commercial Arbitration, Ed. Antonio Monti, Francesco Trezzini & Francesco Wicki (2002) (*available at* www.montiswisslaw.com) pp. 60.

55 Nevhis Deren Yıldırım, Tahkim ve Objektif Acıdan Tahkime Elverislilik, p. 55.

56 Article 1025/1 (book 10)

57 Nevhis Deren Yıldırım, Uncitral Model Law, p. 28.

58 German Code of Civil Procedure articles 1030/1, 1030/2.

59 Nevhis Deren Yıldırım, Uncitral Model Law, p. 28.

60 Article 408.
Also, article 1 para.4 of Turkish International Arbitration Code.

61 Rasih Yegengil p. 152

62 It is the first principle that the second division of Turkish Code of Civil Procedure states under "*Principles Governing the Judiciary Proceedings*" title.
Article 24 of Turkish Code of Civil Procedure:
"1) *The judge cannot examine or rule a case ex officio without any request of either party.*
2) *Unless provided in the law explicitly, no one shall be compelled to file the case in favor of him or to demand the right.*
3) *Parties' right of disposition on a matter in dispute, which has a dispositive nature, remains post litem motam.*"

system.[63] Private law gives parties the power of disposition over their own rights. This begins in the pre-dispute interval and continues through the submission of the dispute to jurisdiction and court hearings.[64] This means that the will of the parties governs the commencement of the jurisdiction, delineation of the subject matter, and settlement of the matter in dispute.[65]

The principle of disposition of the parties has additional components and consequences.[66] For instance, the rule prohibiting judges from examining or ruling on cases *sua sponte,* without a request from either party, or the rule prohibiting the compulsory filing of cases or demands of rights. The right of disposition of the parties on the matter in dispute remains *post litem motam* in accordance with the same provision.[67] Parties are, therefore, free to *reconcile, mediate, settle, or waive lawsuits* regarding the matter in dispute that follow the filing of the case.[68] The existence of these components of the main principle[69] may indirectly constitute the criterion for arbitrability because it *indicates* that the parties can freely resolve the dispute between them.[70] The parties thus have the authority of disposition, which allows them make such an agreement without a court decision. To sum up:

- if parties can freely agree to resolve a dispute between them especially by settlement, and
- if the agreement between them is valid without needing a court order,

a strong indication exists that they have the right of disposition in the case and can enter into an arbitration agreement (or arbitral clause) regarding the dispute.[71] Arbitrable matters under this rule include actions for collection of debts

63 Hakan Pekcanıtez, Oguz Atalay & Muhammet Ozekes, Medeni Usul Hukuku [Civil Procedure Law] 355 (Yetkin Yayınları, 14. baski, 2013) [Yetkin Publishing, 14th. ed. 2013].

64 Hakan Pekcanitez, Oguz Atalay &Muhammet Ozekes, p. 355.

65 Sanal Gorgun & Mehmet Kodakoglu, Medeni Usul Hukuku [Civil Procedure Law] 154 (Yetkin Yayınları, 2. baski, 2012) [Yetkin Publishing, 2nd. ed. 2012].

66 Article 24 of Turkish Code of Civil Procedure.

67 *See supra* note 64.

68 Hakan Pekcanıtez, Oguz Atalay & Muhammet Ozekes, p. 356.

69 And particularly the right of settlement.

70 Baki Kuru, Hukuk Muhakemeleri Usulu [Civil Procedure] 5946 (6. baskı, Cilt VI, Istanbul 2001) [6th ed., Vol. IV, Istanbul,2001].

71 *Ibid.*

arising from sales contracts,[72] actions for mental anguish,[73] and actions involving movable properties.[74]

2. The Specific Case of Inarbitrability: Immovable Property

Explicit regulations regarding objective arbitrability are scattered throughout various codes in Turkish law. Provisions designating disputes arising from *in rem* rights on immovable property as inarbitrable are the first example of this approach.[75] The Turkish International Arbitration Code stipulates "*being located in Turkey*" as a condition for an immovable property to be excluded from the content of the Code.[76] This restriction means disputes arising from the ownership of immovable property located

---

72 Turkish Supreme Court 11th Civil Circuit decision dated 12/28/1978, numbered 5258/5916:

"*The case is about the collection of 6.072.258 liras. The dispute arises from sales contract and is not a matter that is not subject to will of the parties. The arbitral clause in the contract, therefore, is valid in pursuant to articles 516,517,518 of Turkish Code of Civil Procedure* (articles 408 and 412 in the current revised version of Turkish Code of Civil Procedure)".

Also, Supreme Court Assembly of Civil Chambers' rule dated 06/20/1973 numbered T/147–529:

"*The dispute is about a sales contract which is not a matter that is not subject to will of the parties. The contract between the parties or the subject matter has no aspect violating public policy. Such dispute shall be heard and settled before the arbitrator to be decided by the parties.*"

73 Turkish Supreme Court Commercial Circuit (previously 11th Circuit) dated 03/22/1973 and numbered 601/1210:

"*...Principally, one can agree upon damages of mental anguish similar to liquidated damages as a result of contractual liability. In an action for mental anguish, defendant's consent binds the judge. In this respect, the subject of mental anguish shall be within the content of arbitral clause...*"

74 There are regulations about arbitrability of *in-rem* rights on immovable properties as below-mentioned. *Agumenatum a contrario al* interpretation of the law, one can say that there is no impediment to arbitrate disputes regarding moveable property. Baki Kuru, Vol.VI, pp. 5946–5948.

75 Article 408 of Turkish Code of Civil Procedure and article 1 para.4 of Turkish International Arbitration Code.

76 The exact text is: "*This Code shall not apply to the disputes that concern in rem rights on immovable property located in Turkey ...*"

Nevhis Deren, Tahkim ve Objektif Acıdan Tahkime Elverislilik, p. 57. The Code of Civil Procedure does not stipulate to be located in Turkey. The criterion for

in Turkey or restricted real estate rights such as possessory liens, incumbrance on immovable property, and servitudes cannot be resolved by arbitration.[77] Several Turkish Supreme Court decisions state the inarbitrability of matters concerning immovable property.[78] These decisions emphasize that "*only a national court may grant decisions concerning an immovable property in Turkey and the Turkish Deed Registration Offices is the only body empowered to consider Turkish Court decisions on such matters.*"[79]

Agumenatum a contrario al interpretation of the law suggests disputes not about *in rem* rights remain arbitrable even if they focus on immovable property located in Turkey.[80] In other words, arbitrable disputes include those arising from rights other than '*in rem* rights' on immovable property.[81] Disputes about renting immovable properties or about penalty clauses in preliminary sales contracts, for instance, are arbitrable.[82] Likewise, disputes involving the construction of immovable properties that arise from construction contracts are theoretically arbitrable.[83] Because i*n rem* rights are inarbitrable, the law, therefore, implies that rights other than straight-up *in rem* rights are arbitrable. The Turkish Supreme Court, however, has remained

---

international arbitration stipulated by Turkish International Arbitration Code is, therefore, narrower than the criterion for domestic arbitration stipulated by Turkish Code of Civil Procedure with regard to immovable properties.

77 Mehmet Sari, p. 163.

78 Ziya Akıncı, Arbitration Law of Turkey: Practice and Procedure 195 (Juris Net, 2011) & n.57.
(Turkish Supreme Court 14th Civil Circuit decision dated 10/07/2003, numbered 6387/6813, Turkish Supreme Court 15th Civil Circuit decision dated 03/18/1986, numbered 3919/1044, Turkish Supreme Court 15th Civil Circuit decision dated 09/23/2002, numbered 4321/4067, Turkish Supreme Court Assembly of Civil Chambers dated 07/03/1974 numbered 5/1450/810, Turkish Supreme Court 5th Civil Circuit decision dated 05/22/1972, numbered 3513/5195, Turkish Supreme Court Assembly of Civil Chambers dated 04/29/1972 numbered 5/247-269...).

79 *Ibid.*

80 Ziya Akıncı, Milletlerarası Tahkim, p. 78.

81 Ziya Akıncı, Arbitration Law of Turkey, p. 195.
Disputes arising from immovable properties located outside of Turkey are, likewise, arbitrable in accordance with this provision.
However, arbitral awards rendered in Turkey concerning *in rem* rights on immovable properties located in a foreign country may not be effective. (Nomer, Eksi& Gelgel, p. 39.)

82 Ziya Akıncı, Milletlerarası Tahkim, pp. 79–80. Turkish Supreme Court 15th Civil Circuit decision dated 03/23/2010 numbered 2010/1581.

83 *Ibid.*

ambivalent regarding this issue: at times, the Court has ruled the associated rights are inarbitrable as well. The Turkish Supreme Court, for instance, has ruled that only national courts can resolve actions for the nullity and registration of immovable property deeds stemming from construction agreements.[84]

Other Supreme Court decisions, likewise, restrict the arbitration of disputes regarding rights other than *in rem* rights on immovable property. Some Supreme Court decisions, for example, hold that disputes arising from rental agreements concerning immovable properties are inarbitrable despite the theoretical arbitrability of such disputes.[85] The Court based these decisions on the public policy regarding the protection of weaker parties—renters in such cases.[86] Code 6570 Concerning the Renting of Immovable Properties[87] governs rental agreements and regulates the rights and obligations of parties (renter and the landlord). This Code aims to protect the weaker party as a matter of public policy. The Supreme Court, therefore, ruled that disputes arising from rental agreements (although they are private law contracts) concerning immovable properties must be resolved before national courts.[88]

---

84 Turkish Supreme Court 15th Civil Circuit decision dated 06/18/2007 numbered 2007/2680:

"*The lawsuit is about registration and cancellation of title arising from contract of construction and the collection of penalty clause. The Plaintiff has appealed the decision sustaining the claim of registration and cancellation of title and dismissing the claim for collection of penalty clause given by arbitrators. The jurisdiction of the court involves in public policy; therefore, it bears consideration even if the parties do not plea. The lawsuits of registration and cancellation of title, indeed, involves in public policy. Arbitrators, thus, cannot hear such cases. Hence, article 13 of Turkish Code of Civil Procedure states that the lawsuit about in-rem rights on immovables will be heard by the court of the place of the immovable. Even though an old Supreme Court decision saying that cases about in-rem rights on immovables can be heard before arbitral tribunal exists in the court file, general practice has a tendency that cases about registration and cancellation of title can be resolved by courts.*"

Ziya Akıncı, Milletlerarası Tahkim, p. 80 & n. 141.

85 Ziya Akıncı, Arbitration Law of Turkey, p. 196 & n. 59 (Turkish Supreme Court 6th Civil Circuit Decision dated 3/11/1964 numbered 375/5196, Turkish Supreme Court 6th Civil Circuit Decision dated 07/10/1970).

86 Ziya Akıncı, Arbitration Law of Turkey, p. 196.

87 The enforcement code numbered 6101 has annulled The Code numbered 6570 Concerning Renting the Immovable Properties as of the date of 07/01/2012. Turkish Code of Obligations numbered 6098 shall govern all renting relationships after this date of enforcement.

88 Ziya Akıncı, Arbitration Law of Turkey, p. 196.

The Supreme Court ruled in 2004 that declaratory actions for rental values,[89] actions concerning evacuation of rented immovable property bound by Code 6570,[90] and disputes arising from the Turkish Code of Property Ownership[91] are inarbitrable. [92] The decision[93] states:

> *...Concluding an arbitration agreement is possible only for disputes that are subject to will of the parties. This means that parties can make arbitration agreements or arbitral clauses to resolve disputes if they are free to make agreements to settle the disputes and these agreements are valid without a court order. Considering the established practices of the Supreme Court, declaratory actions for rental values cannot be heard before arbitral tribunals. Because determining rental values involves public policy, parties can only assess rental values within clearly defined standards and limitations. The will of the parties is therefore limited in this respect. Renters are not obliged to pay the rent that landlords request. Arbitral tribunals cannot resolve such disputes about rent because Turkish Code of Civil Procedure Article 518 invalidates arbitral clauses about the settlement of disputes about rental value assessments that relate to public policy concerns.*[94]

Legal scholars have criticized the contradictory tendencies of the Turkish Supreme. Some argue that disputes arising from matters that are subject to the will of parties are dispositive in nature and, therefore, are unequivocally arbitrable.[95] The Turkish Supreme Court itself has rendered some decisions that contradict previous judicial precedent in this respect. The 15th Civil Circuit of the Turkish Supreme Court, for example, ruled in 1979 that:[96]

> Parties can freely *reinstate shares of immovable property and comply with required revision proceedings in the land register. Such transactions are subject to the parties' will. Related disputes do not involve public policy and can be legally resolved by arbitrators.*

---

89 The action to establish the rental value.

90 Now Turkish Code of Obligations numbered 6098. (*See supra* note 87.)

91 Turkish Code of Property Ownership numbered 634, which was published in Official Gazette numbered 12038 on 07/02/1965.

92 Mehmet Tas, p. 29.

93 Turkish Supreme Court 3rd Civil Circuit Decision dated 12/02/2004 numbered 2004/13018.

94 Article 408 in the new Code. See the chapter 'Sources of Turkish Law' for the explanation of the new code.

95 Baki Kuru, Vol.VI, p. 5947.

96 Mehmet Tas, p. 29 & n.40 (Turkish Supreme Court 15th Civil Circuit decision dated 5/15/1979 numbered 1195/1130)

A 1994 13th Civil Circuit decision stated that:

> *disputes arising from immovable properties are private law contracts and these transactions are only subject to the parties' will. The disputes arising from such contracts are arbitrable.*[97]

According to this decision, it is legitimate to arbitrate whenever the law explicitly or implicitly allows and the parties freely choose to do so.[98] The Court indicated that arbitration clauses are valid because contracts for sales of immovable property drawn up among the parties have no bearing on public policy.[99]

These decisions coupled with similar Supreme Court decisions[100] demonstrate the lack of a general rule prohibiting arbitration of disputes arising from 'any right' regarding immovable property. Taking into consideration other criteria and domestic legal regulations, the arbitrability of such disputes must be evaluated on a case-by-case basis.[101] The general legal precedent established by the Turkish Supreme Court concerning immovable property rental agreements confirms this approach and rule. Public policy establishes protections for renters as weaker parties, making disputes arising from immovable property rental agreements inarbitrable. Disputes, however, frequently arise from rental agreements for immovable properties held for trading, which were made for commercial purposes between two corporate entities. For instance, banks, petroleum companies, and chain retail companies open branches and sustain their business operations in rental properties. [102] Identifying an international bank in such a situation as the weaker party in need of protection is not rational.[103] Implementing such protection would violate the general principles of law.[104]

For this reason, protections for weaker parties in Code 6570 are frequently suspended for immovable properties used for commercial purposes.[105] Article 18/2 of

---

97 Ziya Akıncı, Arbitration Law of Turkey, p. 195 & n.58. (Turkish Supreme Court 13th Civil Circuit decision dated 6/16/1994 numbered 4390/5895).

98 Mehmet Tas, p. 29 & n.40.

99 *Ibid.*

100 *Ibid*, (Turkish Supreme Court 4th Civil Circuit has a decision dated 04/10/1967 numbered 2760/3075 states that one can arbitrate the disputes concerning to Law of Property Ownership which is considered as governed by mandatory rules due to the rationale that "*the Law of Property Ownership has no provision impeding in arbitration of the disputes between flat owners*").

101 Nevhis Deren Yıldırım, Uncitral Model Law, p. 30.

102 Burak Huysal, p. 136.

103 *Ibid.*

104 *Ibid.*

105 *Ibid.*

the new Turkish Commercial Code[106] obliges *merchants to be prudent in business activities;* a businessman who incorporates an arbitration clause in a rental contract cannot be said to be unaware of the financial or legal consequences. [107] Using Code 6570 to disregard the parties' choice to submit a dispute[108] about a residential building to arbitration would be a misapplication of the law. No provision in the Turkish Code of Civil Procedure restricts the resolution of disputes arising from determination of rental value by settlement between the parties when the criteria proving the cases' dispositive nature are present.[109]

3. Other Disputes that are Inarbitrable based on the General Formula

Article 1/4 of the Turkish International Arbitration Code[110] is the first imperative rule governing arbitrability in Turkish international commercial arbitration law. It establishes which disputes are subject to the will of the parties and eligible for arbitration.[111] The second imperative rule is drawn from the same Code and concerns *in rem* rights on immovable properties located in Turkey. The Code itself precisely states both rules.[112]

---

106 Article 20 of the previous Turkish Commercial Code numbered 6762 (which was accepted 06/29/1956) has stated this principle. The new Turkish Commercial Code, which was enacted on 01/13/2011, has also the same regulation in article 18. This article says:

"*Each merchant has to act like a prudent businessman with all the activities concerning his business*".

107 Burak Huysal, p. 136.

In Turkish Supreme Court Assembly of Civil Chambers' rule dated 10/15/2003 numbered 2003/13-599, The Court has denied the application of the renter, who is a merchant, for revision of the rental due to the economic depression based on the obligation of the merchant to act prudent.

108 Arising from a rental contract worth million dollars about large factories or hotel buildings.

109 Baki Kuru, Vol.VI, p. 5947.

110 Which is in parallel with the Turkish Code of Civil Procedure.

111 Baki Kuru, Vol.VI, p. 5946.

Mehmet Tas, p. 29.

Arbitrability is based on whether parties have the authority of disposition on the subject matter of the dispute. Disputes are thus arbitrable if the parties can freely agree to resolve a dispute between them especially by settlement and such agreement is valid without needing a court order.

112 Requisite of dispositive nature and in rem rights on immovables.

Additional restrictions on arbitrability due to imperative rules can be inferred from the Code's general formulation. Disputes that fall within the scope of criminal and administrative law are restricted in this manner.[113] The requirement that disputes be subject to the will of the parties means that criminal law disputes cannot be arbitrated.[114] Likewise, disputes that arise from matters covered by administrative jurisdiction cannot be resolved via arbitration.[115]

The Turkish Constitution makes one exception regarding the arbitration of administrative matters.[116] This exception relates to the arbitration of disputes arising from concession bargaining and agreements about public service.[117] Concession agreements about public service are the administrative contract equivalent of build-operate-transfer models. Foreign corporate entities involved in disputes arising from such administrative matters prefer to avoid administrative courts because opposing parties are State entities and politics may influence court decisions.[118] Such corporate entities also prefer arbitration because they lack confidence in the ability of administrative law judges to resolve their private law disputes. These preferences gave rise to the current regulations after a long period of indeterminacy about the arbitrability of disputes arising from concession agreements in Turkey.[119]

During the 1994 revision[120] of the Turkish Constitution, the modification of Articles 125 and 155 made it possible to arbitrate these types of disputes. The addition to Article 125 provided that disputes arising from concession bargaining and agreements about public service could be resolved by way of domestic or international arbitration. Article 155/2 was altered to specify that only disputes involving foreign elements were arbitrable.

These revisions also included the enactment of a new code governing the general principles and policies with which parties must comply during the arbitration of disputes arising from concession bargaining and agreements regarding

---

113 Feyiz Erdogan, Uluslararası Hukuk ve Tahkim [International Law and Arbitration] 123 (Seckin Yayıncılık, 2004) [Seckin Publishing, 2004].

114 Baki Kuru, Vol.VI, p. 5918.

115 Ziya Akıncı, Milletlerarası Tahkim, p. 80.

116 Baki Kuru, Vol.VI, p. 5945 & n. 19.

117 Ziya Akıncı, Milletlerarası Tahkim, p. 17.

118 *Id* at 18.

119 *Id* at 19.

120 The Code Concerning to Revisions of Some Articles of the Turkish Constitution numbered 4446 and dated 08/13/1999 has made the revision. It was published in Official Gazette on 08/14/1999 (23786).

public service.[121] Article 2(a) of this Code stipulates that, in accordance with the Constitution, disputes involving concession agreements with foreign elements can be submitted to ad-hoc or institutional arbitration. Some commentators may argue that disputes concerning the content of administrative law are investment disputes between State parties, but this unclear exception involves a private law factor. This chapter addresses this issue to highlight the exception.

Other private laws also specifically address the issue of arbitrability. The Turkish Code of Obligations has a relevant provision regarding 'sales on installments'.[122] Article 262, entitled 'Court of Competent Jurisdiction and Arbitration', states that "*Buyers who are Turkish residents cannot renounce the jurisdiction of the court where they live or conclude arbitration agreements for disputes arising from the contract of sale on installments*." The limitation on arbitration in Article 262 only governs the contract of sale on installments that are made by buyers who reside in Turkey.[123] The provision aims to protect Turkish residents.[124] The article explicitly states that such disputes are inarbitrable, making this limitation on arbitrability yet another example of how such restrictions arise from an imperative rule of a private law code.

B. Exclusive Judicial Jurisdictional Rules and Their Impact on the Arbitrability of a Dispute

National laws that have an impact on arbitration may be either 'substantive rules' or 'procedural rules'.[125] The former indicates a situation in which e a dispute can be found inarbitrable on the grounds that its subject matter is designated inarbitrable by the national substantive law of the country. The previously explained restriction on *in rem* rights on immovable property governed by the Turkish International Arbitration Code and the Turkish Code of Civil Procedure exemplifies such a situation. Restrictions arising from substantive law may also result from public policy concerns. The latter, however, are most often regulated by "jurisdictional" rules in which States establish exclusive judicial authority in favor of specific courts.[126] This

121 The Code Concerning the General Principles to Comply with during the Arbitration of Disputes Arising from Concession Bargaining and Agreements about Public Service numbered 4501 dated 01/21/2000.

122 Turkish Code of Obligations which was enacted on 11/01/2011 and published on Official Gazette on 02/04/2011 with the number of 27836.

123 Ergin Nomer, Nuray Eksi & Gunseli Oztekin Gelgel, p. 17.

124 Mustafa Erkan, p. 77.

125 Burak Huysal, p. 97.

126 *Ibid.*

is another example of how State regulations can prevent parties from submitting a dispute to arbitration. Two controversial issues in Turkish legal doctrine have generated debates about inarbitrability based on jurisdictional regulations:

- First, certain jurisdictional rules in the related codes contain explicit statements of 'exclusive judicial jurisdiction'.
- Second, they also contain 'court order' requirements.

The section below discusses both issues to determine whether relevant disputes can be settled via arbitration or only litigated before courts.

1. The Discussion on Inarbitrability Due to Explicit Regulations Requiring 'Exclusive Judicial Jurisdiction'

Domestic procedural codes[127] in Turkish law regulate the jurisdiction of courts. The Turkish Constitution[128] stipulates that these statutes regulate court jurisdictions[129] and a case cannot be heard before a court other than when it is authorized by law.[130] Thus, a person cannot be forced to defend itself before a court other than the one legally authorized to hear the matter; moreover, jurisdictional rules cannot be established through by-laws.[131] This is the constitutional basis for debates about arbitrability regarding codified domestic jurisdictional rules—especially exclusive judicial jurisdiction provisions.

The general division of jurisdictional rules in Turkish law provides the necessary framework. The Turkish Code of Civil Procedure determines court jurisdiction without prejudice to the jurisdictional provisions in other Codes.[132] The Turkish Code of Civil Procedure, moreover, contains two types of jurisdictional rules: *mandatory* or *non-mandatory*.[133] Non-mandatory rules can be either *general* or *specific rules*; these rules give plaintiffs the right to file lawsuits either

127 Turkish Code of Civil Procedure in general and other Codes depending on the specific areas of law.

128 Baki Kuru, Hukuk Muhakemeleri Usulu [Civil Procedure] 381 (6.baski, Cilt I, Istanbul 2001) [6th ed., Vol. I, Istanbul, 2001].

129 Article 142 of Turkish Constitution.

130 Baki Kuru, Ramazan Arslan& Ejder Yılmaz Medeni Usul Hukuku [Civil Procedure Law] 130 (Yetkin Yayınevi, 24. Baski, 2013) [Yetkin Publishing, 24th ed. 2013].

131 Baki Kuru, Vol.I, p. 381.

132 Sanal Gorgun & Mehmet Kodakoglu, p. 78. (Turkish Code of Civil Procedure Article 5)

133 Yavuz Alagonya, Kamil Yıldırım & Nevhis Deren Yıldırım, Medeni Usul Hukuku Esasları [Fundamentals of Civil Procedure Law 83 (Beta Yayınları, 7. baski, Istanbul 2009) [Beta Publishing, 7th ed. Istanbul 2009]

before a general court or before a specific court if such is stipulated in the code.[134] When multiple courts have concurrent jurisdiction over a case, the plaintiff has the right to file the lawsuit in either court.[135] In some instances, however, court jurisdiction is deemed a matter of public policy. This is why mandatory rules can exclusively authorize a single court.[136] Turkish legal scholars call these rules '*mandatory rules based on public policy*' or '*exclusive judicial jurisdictional rules*'.[137] Rules regarding court jurisdiction are not considered matters of public policy in general.[138] The general and specific rules mentioned above, for instance, are not given this designation.[139] Some jurisdictional rules, however, do relate to public policy exclusively. These are enumerated below. All jurisdictional rules that are not enumerated are non-exclusive and not related to public policy.[140]

The rule for arbitrability, meanwhile, does not list specific cases. It identifies inarbitrable issues as "*matters that are not at the free disposition of the parties*".[141] A judicial jurisdictional rule's exclusivity is determined, in such cases, according to *ratio legis* of the rule and the categorical content of the expression in the rule.[142] The exclusive judicial jurisdictional rules are: [143]

- The rule for *bankruptcy* cases:[144] A bankruptcy case can only be heard before the commercial court located in the area in which the branch office is situated.

---

134 Hakan Pekcanitez, Oguz Atalay & Muhammet Ozekes, p. 163.

135 Yavuz Alagonya, Kamil Yıldırım & Nevhis Deren Yıldırım, p. 83 (Turkish Supreme Court Assembly of Civil Chambers dated 05/17/1995 numbered 259/531).

136 Hakan Pekcanitez, Oguz Atalay & Muhammet Ozekes, p. 163.

137 Baki Kuru, Ramazan Arslan & Ejder Yılmaz, p. 150.

138 Baki Kuru, Vol.I, p. 548.

139 *Ibid.*

140 *Ibid.*

141 *See* Turkish Code of Civil Procedure article 18:

> "*An agreement of jurisdiction cannot be concluded on the matters that are not subject to the will of the parties and in the event of exclusive jurisdiction.*"

142 Baki Kuru, Ramazan Arslan & Ejder Yılmaz, p. 150.

143 *Ibid.*

144 Turkish Code of Execution and Bankruptcy numbered 2004 which was enacted on 06/19/1932.

Article 154/3:

> "*If the debtor and debtee have appointed an authorized executive office with a written agreement, the executive office of that place is also considered authorized for the*

- The rule for cases within *private legal entities*: Cases brought against associates by a private legal entity (such as a corporation, a cooperative company, an association, or a foundation) regarding the entity's business and cases brought by associates against other associates will be adjudicated exclusively by the court in the location of the private legal entity's headquarters.[145]
- The rule concerning *inheritance* cases: the court located where the testator has most recently resided has exclusive judicial jurisdiction for most inheritance cases.[146]
- The rule for the cases about *in rem rights of an immovable property:*[147] the court in the location of the immovable property has exclusive judicial authority to adjudicate. [148]
- For the cases about *life insurance* for or against the policy owner, insured, or beneficiary: the court where these individuals reside has exclusive judicial authority to rule.[149]
- The judicial jurisdictional rule in Article 22 of The Code of *Commercial Enterprise Pledge* is exclusive.[150] According to this rule, the commercial court

---

bankruptcy proceedings. However, parties cannot conclude a jurisdiction agreement for bankruptcy cases and can file bankruptcy cases only before the commercial court of the place of headquarter of the debtor."

145 Turkish Code of Civil Procedure, Article 14.

146 *E.g.* Article 11/1 of Turkish Code of Civil Procedure:

"*Jurisdiction for the Cases Arising from Legacy*

1) *For the following cases, the court located where the testator has most recently resided has the exclusive authority:*
    a) *The cases concerning the distribution of the estate, voidness of the contract of distribution, abatement and cancellation of the legacy, recovery due to legacy and the cases arising from the management of the estate among the legatees.*
    b) *All cases that will be filed against the legatees until the final distribution of the estate."*

147 Example of cases about in rem rights on immovable properties are action of replevin (Turkish Civil Code article 683), land registration case (Turkish Civil Code article 713), invalidity or adjustment of wrongful entry (Turkish Civil Code article 1025), cases on servitudes, action for partition and action for pre-emption.

148 Article 12 of Turkish Code of Civil Procedure. *See infra* note 175.

149 Article 15/2 of Turkish Code of Civil Procedure.

150 Code of Commercial Enterprise Pledge numbered 1447 which was approved on 07/21/1971.

in the location of the trade register has jurisdictional authority for any dispute arising from the Code of Commercial Enterprise Pledge and this authority is exclusive.[151]

As exclusive judicial jurisdictional rules based on public policy, the cases listed above must be filed before the court that is exclusively authorized by the Code.[152] Pleas of exclusive judicial jurisdiction are not preliminary objections.[153] This means that parties can submit these disputes at any time and the court must always examine its jurisdiction (or the other court's having exclusive judicial jurisdiction) *sua sponte*.[154] Exclusivity of judicial jurisdiction is, therefore, an actionable matter in Turkish law[155] and it must be taken into consideration because it can invalidate awards obtained at any level of the judicial process.

All jurisdictional rules beyond those listed above are *non-mandatory* and thus not related to public policy. The general jurisdiction rule in Article 6 of the Turkish Code of Civil Procedure[156] is an example of such a rule. It entitles the court in the district of which the plaintiff (real person or legal entity) resides at the time the case opens with the authority to hear the matter.[157] Other non-mandatory rules include specific jurisdictional rules like the rule concerning the jurisdiction of the court for disputes arising from contracts.[158] This rule stipulates that lawsuits concerning disputes that arise from contracts can also

---

Article 22: "Authorized Court"

"Resolution of the disputes arising from the implementation of this Code is within the jurisdiction of the Commercial Court in the location of trade register."

151 Baki Kuru, Ramazan Arslan & Ejder Yılmaz, p. 151.

152 *Ibid.*

153 Turkish Code of Civil Procedure article 116 enumerates the instances that constitute pre-liminary objection. The plea to the jurisdiction in the absence of an exclusive authority is on the top of this list.

154 Baki Kuru, Ramazan Arslan & Ejder Yılmaz, p. 151.

155 Turkish Code of Civil Procedure article 114 lists causes of action. The article includes whether a court has jurisdiction in the event that the jurisdiction as one of these causes. Article 115 of the same code, moreover, indicates that the court shall seek the causes of action at any level of the judicial proceeding *ex officio*. The parties, also, may always claim the absence of a cause of action.

156 Sanal Gorgun & Mehmet Kodakoglu, p. 79.

157 *Ibid.*

158 Timucin Musul, Hukuk Usulu Muhakemeleri Kanunu ve Ilgili Mevzuat [The Code of Civil Procedure and the Related Regulations] 83 (Alfa Yayınları, 3. baski, Istanbul 2012) [Alfa Publishing, 3rd ed., Istanbul 2012).

be heard by courts in the location in which the contract will be performed.[159] Several other general or specific rules are similarly non-mandatory in nature.[160] These rules give the plaintiff the right to elect any of the designated courts and provide parties with the option to enter into a jurisdictional agreement.[161] In contrast to exclusive judicial jurisdiction cases, jurisdiction is not a cause of action in these matters. These rules are not, therefore, among the jurisdictional rules that arguably impede arbitration. Exclusive judicial jurisdictional rules, however, are crucial part of the subject areas that are meaningful to arbitrability. Indeed, some legal scholars assert that mandatory rules *exclusively* authorizing a specific court to hear a case exist to prevent arbitral tribunals from hearing the relevant cases.[162] This line of reasoning can be used to suggest that similar rules in the Turkish Commercial Code impede the arbitration of corporate disputes.[163]

States typically establish specific jurisdictional rules in the context of commercial arbitration to make a particular dispute inarbitrable and subject it to the jurisdiction of the national courts.[164] Most States, therefore, include such jurisdictional rules as a criterion of inarbitrability in their legislation and reserve specific case types only for their national jurisdiction.[165] The categories of exclusive jurisdictional rules, their content, and their practical consequences regarding

159 Turkish Code of Civil Procedure, Article 10.

160 *E.g.* Article 10, which is a regulation about the jurisdiction in the cases arising from a contract. It, also, authorizes the court in the location of performance of the contract. Article 14, which is a regulation about the jurisdiction in the cases about branches and legal entities. It, also, authorizes the court in the location of the branch.

161 Baki Kuru, Ramazan Arslan & Ejder Yılmaz, p. 152.

162 Mehmet Helvacı, *Anonim Ortaklik Genel Kurul Kararlarinin Iptali Davalarinin Tahkim Yargilamasına Uygunlugu Uzerine Dusunceler* [*Thoughts on Arbitrability of Lawsuit of Annulment of General Meeting Resolution of Companies*] *in* II. Uluslararası Ozel Hukuk Sempozyumu "Tahkim" [II. International Private Law Symposium "Arbitration"] 200 (Ankara 2009).

163 Chapters III–V elaborately explain the arguments and counter-arguments about this issue based on corporate law regulations. The general explanations made in this section constitutes a basis for those specific explanations.

164 Burak Huysal, p. 250. & n.837. (*Citing* Karl-Heinz Böckstiegel, *Public Policy and Arbitrability*, ICCA Congress Series No.3, 182 (New York 1986)).

165 *Id* at 250& n.840.
See Jean-François Poudret & Sébastien Besson, pp. 293–295 for the Belgium, German and Swiss Law examples.
Alan Uzelac, *(In)Arbitrability and Exclusive Jurisdiction: Parallels that Matter, in* International Arbitration and International Commercial Law 454 (Kluwer Law Int'l 2011).

arbitrability, however, may vary. The meaning of 'exclusive jurisdiction' also differs from State-to-State depending on regulations and interpretations, making the notion vague and ill-defined.[166] These rules may generate different consequences at different "*levels*" as follows:

> … *[F]irst, at the level of national courts' jurisdiction, where it raises the questions regarding jurisdiction of courts of different type, level and territorial competence; second, at the level of distributing jurisdiction for particular cases among the public courts of different national jurisdictions; the third and the last level distinguishes court jurisdiction from out-of-court dispute resolution methods, including arbitration…*[167]

Switzerland's legal regulations illustrate this point. Swiss law defines the extent of jurisdictional exclusivity in the context of domestic arbitration as: 'the exclusive jurisdiction of a State authority laid down by a mandatory legal provision'.[168] This law established that the jurisdictional rules with territorial aims (*ratione loci*) will not impede arbitration and that only jurisdictional rules concerning the subject matter of a dispute (*ratione materiae*) can result in inarbitrability.[169] *Poudret* and *Besson* state that Private International Law Statutes on the exclusive jurisdiction of courts do not affect arbitration.[170] Indeed, commentators contend that the mandatory character of these jurisdictional rules does not apply in the context of arbitration and restrictions on jurisdictional agreements in specific areas do not affect arbitrability.[171] They also emphasize that the arbitration of domestic disputes may differ from the arbitration of international disputes in this regard.[172] Clearly, these rules and their impact on arbitrability lack standardized categorization from a comparative law perspective.

The arbitrability of disputes governed by the exclusive rules based on public policy in Turkish law also remains controversial. Some legal scholars have

---

166 Alan Uzelac, *(In)Arbitrability and Exclusive Jurisdiction: Parallels that Matter* p. 464.
167 *Id* at 453.

> "*To exclude jurisdiction may mean: excluding the default jurisdiction (e.g. jurisdiction according to domicile); excluding any foreign jurisdiction; excluding jurisdiction of courts of particular type; excluding courts which are territorially not competent; excluding any prorogation agreement or some of them; excluding arbitration (domestic or foreign); excluding any other option but the jurisdiction of a single body…*" (p. 464)

168 Jean-François Poudret & Sébastien Besson, p. 294.
169 *Ibid.*
170 *Ibid.*
171 *Id* at 295.
172 *Id* at 294, 295.

suggested that Turkish law uses the term 'exclusive jurisdiction' in the context of International Private Law to indicate that a national Turkish court must hear the case exclusively.[173] Other scholars assert that the term 'exclusive jurisdiction based on public policy' indicates that a case must be heard before the court stated in the Code exclusively 'in domestic law'.[174] Some legal scholars, for instance, point out the exclusive jurisdictional rule in Article 12 of Turkish Code of Civil Procedure[175] is an example of a barrier to arbitrability in the context of *in rem* rights on immovable properties.[176] Yet, others assert, however, that not all exclusive judicial jurisdictional rules in Turkish law should exclude disputes from international commercial arbitration.[177] The distinction made in domestic procedural law does not correspond to the actual jurisdiction of the arbitral tribunal and the existence of arbitrability in general.[178]

Some rules do indicate that specific types of courts are exclusively authorized to hear the related cases. There is no category of rules in Turkish law, however, prohibiting other authorities, such as arbitrators, to hear those cases. Claims that rules granting courts exclusive authority prohibit the possibility of arbitration are, therefore, based on a subjective, perhaps excessive interpretation.[179] The assumption that exclusive judicial jurisdictional rules eliminate the possibility of alternate dispute resolution mechanisms is likely inaccurate. The general aims of the various disciplines of law should also be considered. Civil procedure law

---

173 Burak Huysal, p. 250.
174 Baki Kuru, Vol.I, p. 549.
175 Article 12:

"*Jurisdiction in the Cases Arising From in Rem Rights on Immovables*

1) *The court in the location of the immovable has the exclusive authority for the cases related to in rem rights on immovables or cases that may cause a change in the ownership of in rem rights and cases related to possession or right of detention of the immovable.*
2) *The court in the location of the immovable subject to an easement shall hear the cases related to easements.*
3) *If these cases are related to more than one immovable, the case can be filed before the court in the location of one of the immovables also for others.*"

176 Nevhis Deren Yıldırım, Uncitral Model Law, p. 30. (Burak Huysal, p. 258 & n.874).
177 *Ibid.*
178 Burak Huysal, p. 257
179 *Id* at 250.

aims to enforce the rights stipulated by substantive law.[180] Not all jurisdictional rules regarding civil procedure regulations pose are antagonistic to the recourse to arbitration.[181] Only jurisdictional rules concerning the subject matter of the dispute (*ratione materiae*)[182] as opposed to those with procedural aims, can affect arbitrability. Restrictions on arbitrability in principle only apply to arbitration of content governed by either Turkish International Arbitration Law or the Turkish Code of Civil Procedure when these provisions are based on substantive law, unless lawmakers explicitly provide otherwise.[183]

a) *The Fact that the Criteria of Arbitrability shall be Determinative*

Accurately assessing the legal effect[184] of exclusive judicial jurisdiction[185] provisions requires consideration of the criterion of arbitrability adopted in State procedural laws. Some jurisdictional laws have only one general restrictive definition about the subject matter of disputes—that be subject to the will of the parties.[186] Other jurisdictional rules add limitations to this general definition.[187] [188] Still others include no general definition limiting objective arbitrability, but enumerate which matters are inarbitrable and jurisdictions that include no provisions at all on arbitrability.[189] Restrictions on arbitrability because of exclusive judicial jurisdiction are typically clearer in countries with a single, general restrictive definition. Turkey takes this approach. Limitations on arbitrability depend on whether the matter in dispute is subject to the will of the parties. This should be the primary criterion for determining

---

180 Burak Huysal, p. 258 & n. 873. (*Citing* Hakan Pekcanıtez, Oguz Atalay & Muhammet Ozekes, Medeni Usul Hukuku [Civil Procedure Law] 48 (Yetkin Yayınları, 14. baski, 2013) [Yetkin Publishing, 14th. ed. 2013]).

181 Burak Huysal, p. 258.

182 Jean-François Poudret & Sébastien Besson, p. 294.

183 Burak Huysal, p. 258.

184 Whether or not it targets to exclude arbitration.

185 Burak Huysal, p. 251.

186 *E.g.* Germany (German Code of Civil Procedure Article 1030/1), Austria (Austrian Code of Civil Procedure Article 582/1), Sweeden (Swedish Arbitration Act, Article 1) Finland, Greece, and Turkey

187 Italian Code of Civil Procedure, Article 806.

188 Rasih Yegengil, p. 152.

189 *E.g.* Denmark: Civil Procedure Code has no related provision although practitioners used to accept commercial disputes as arbitrable only.
Rasih Yegengil, p. 152.

arbitrability.[190] Requiring parties to litigate disputes on the basis of exclusive judicial jurisdictional rules is a flawed approach for the reasons stated below.

Some legal scholars in Turkey argue that arbitral clauses remain valid when the applicable jurisdictional rule in the Turkish Code of Civil Procedure addresses the jurisdiction and authority of the court provided the matter is at the free disposition of the parties.[191] The rule may, for example, address the distinction between a civil court of peace and civil court of general jurisdiction.[192] This would not have an impact on arbitrability. Scholars have used the provision in Turkish Code of Civil Procedure that governs cases about *in rem* rights on immovable property[193] to illustrate this point.[194] The provision exclusively authorizes the court in the location of the immovable property.[195] Scholars specify, however, that exclusively authorizing a court in a particular location does not explicitly eliminate arbitration.[196] Public policy-based jurisdiction in this instance relates to the authority of the court only with respect to *location*.[197] The public policy portion of this rule stipulating that the court in the location of the immovable property hear the case[198] applies only when the matter is submitted to the judicial litigation and should not restrict arbitrability.[199] Parties are also able to reach a settlement over such disputes and this is an indication of their dispositive rights over this issue.[200] Those disputes are, therefore, subject to the will of parties, and arbitration agreements are valid in such cases according to

190 Such as parties' having the authority of disposition on the subject matter of the dispute or parties' right to settle. *See supra* note 60 *et seq*.
191 Rasih Yegengil, p. 174.
192 Civil Court of Peace and Civil Court of General Jurisdiction are the two courts of first instance in Turkish civil procedure.
193 Or a right arising from immovable.
194 Rasih Yegengil, p. 174.
195 Turkish Code of Civil Procedure article 12 (counted as an exclusive jurisdiction rule based on public policy above). *See supra* note 175.
(This section ignores the arguments based on Article 1 (4) of Turkish International Arbitration Code, which specifically regulates arbitrability of *in rem* rights on immovable properties, to concentrate only on the relationship between the exclusive judicial jurisdictional rules and arbitrability.)
196 Rasih Yegengil, p. 175.
Baki Kuru, Vol.VI, p. 5947.
197 Rasih Yegengil, p. 175.
198 Turkish Code of Civil Procedure article 12. *See supra* note 175.
199 Baki Kuru, Vol.VI, p. 5947.
200 *Ibid*.

legal commentators.[201] The Supreme Court has also rendered decisions in which it adopted this approach.[202] Broad interpretations of jurisdictional provisions that yield results of inarbitrability do not comply with the general idea of civil procedure and international law. It is possible to assume that all exclusive judicial jurisdictional rules in domestic law involve public policy and to classify a matter as inarbitrable on this basis. This view, however, disregards the arbitrability criterion of whether the matter is at the free disposition of the parties. Every dispute should be examined for the presence of this criterion because, as in this example, it determines arbitrability.

Arbitral clauses are included in contracts so that arbitral tribunals, rather than the courts, resolve disputes arising from the contracts.[203] This reflects the principle of freedom of contract. The freedom of parties to make such choices is not unlimited.[204] States set the boundaries of arbitrability.[205] States set 'red lines' for reasons, including public policy or jurisdictional rules where the parties' freedom of contract ends and the exclusive authority of the courts begins.[206]

---

201 Baki Kuru and the other authors mentioned in Baki Kuru, Vol.VI, p. 5947 & n. 27.

202 Turkish Supreme Court 15th Civil Circuit decision dated 05/31/1979 numbered 1195/1330:

"*Turkish Code of Civil Procedure articles 516 and 536 (407–444 in the new current Code) govern the regulations about arbitration. The courts, as a general rule, have the authority to resolve any kind of dispute that is within the jurisdiction of civil or criminal judiciary and borne between the parties. It is, however, possible for the parties to a dispute, which does not involve public policy, to agree on submitting their dispute, to private persons rather than courts. Resolution of a dispute by arbitrators is a private judicial remedy in our Procedural Code. The option of arbitration is possible in the events that it is allowed explicitly and implicitly by the laws. Whether such dispute can be resolved by an arbitral tribunal is subject to the will of the parties. In this respect, provisions of the construction contract dated 08/07/1972 about restitution of an immovable property share and having the required adjustment proceedings in the land registry are from the acts that parties are able to implement freely. These kinds of acts shall be deemed as subject to the will of the parties. Settling the dispute by way of arbitration here is shall not be regarded as a violation of law. It does not involve public policy.*" (Baki Kuru, Vol.VI, p. 5948).

Similar decision of Supreme Court 13th Civil Circuit decision dated 06/16/1994 numbered 4390/5895.

203 Ziya Akıncı, Milletlerarası Tahkim, p. 91.

204 Alan Uzelac, *(In)Arbitrability, p.* 454.

205 Mustafa Erkan, p. 74.

206 Thomas E. Carbonneau & Francois Janson, *Cartesian Logic and Frontier Politics: French and American Concepts of Arbitrability*, 2 Tul. J. Int'l & Comp. L. 194 (1994).

The success of international arbitration, however, depends substantially upon the limited intervention of domestic courts.[207] A distinction between national and international commercial practice must, therefore, be drawn.[208] Domestic courts should intervene in international arbitration cases only to prevent flagrant abuses and support contemporary arbitral regulations.[209] The European Convention on International Commercial Arbitration,[210] to which Turkey is a party, keeps the intervention of domestic courts to the minimum in arbitration.[211] National courts can only intervene in arbitration to support arbitral tribunals, meaning their intervention must be positive and limited to issues related to civil procedure.[212] Contrary to the traditional approach, the modern approach favors the notion that exclusive jurisdiction provisions do not make disputes inarbitrable.[213] German law, which has a significant influence on Turkish international arbitration regulations, also supports this notion. In German law, subject areas that lawmakers specify as within the courts' 'judicial monopoly' are inarbitrable; the fact that a court is given exclusive authority, however, is not sufficient to make an inarbitrable subject matter.[214] The jurisdictional rule, indeed,

(The State "*determines the point at which the exercise of contractual freedom ends and the public mission of adjudication begins.*")
Mustafa Erkan p. 75. (Sibel Ozel, Milletlerarası Ticari Tahkimde Kanunlar Ihtilafı Meseleleri [The Issues of Conflict of Laws in International Commercial Arbitration], 38 (Istanbul, 2008)).

207 Cemal Sanlı, Uluslararası Ticari Akitlerin Hazırlanması ve Uyusmazlıkların Cozum Yolları [Preparation of International Commercial Agreements and Ways for Resolution of Disputes] 241 (Beta Yayınevi, 3. basım, Istanbul 2005) [Beta Publishing, 3rd ed. Istanbul 2005].

208 Burak Huysal p. 252.

209 Cemal Sanlı, Uluslararası Ticari Akitler, p. 243.

210 Signed on the date of April 21,1961 in Geneva. It is ratified by Turkey with the Code numbered 3730 on May 8,1991 and was published in Official Gazette numbered 21000 and enacted.

211 Feyiz Erdogan, p. 100.

212 Cemal Sanlı, Uluslararası Ticari Akitler, p. 242.

213 Burcin Yıldırım, Anonim Ortaklıklarda Sirket Ici Uyusmazlıkların Milletlerarası Tahkim Yoluyla Cozumlenmesi [Resolution of Intra-Corporate Disputes of Companies by International Commercial Law] (2012) (Yayınlanmamıs Yuksek Lisans Tezi, Galatasaray Universitesi, Sosyal Bilimler Enstitusu) [Unpublished LLM Thesis, Galatasaray University, Institute of Social Sciences] p. 36& n.110. (*Citing* Olivier Caprasse, Les Societes et l'Arbitrage 23 (Bruxelles 2002)).

214 Burak Huysal, p. 253. (*Citing* Klaus Peter Berger, *The New German Arbitration Law in International Perspective*, 26 FORUM International 7 (July,2000)).

can serve several additional purposes at different levels.[215] To exclude a case from arbitration, lawmakers must designate that the dispute area is entitled to special legal protection through exclusive national court adjudication.[216]

2. Legal Consequences of a 'Court Order' Requirement in a Statute

Turkish law contains another controversial issue related to limiting effect of courts' jurisdiction on arbitration. The articles of several codes include another expression of '*(by) court order*'. Some doctrinal authorities interpret this as granting the court exclusive judicial jurisdiction. Article 219 of the Turkish Commercial Code numbered 6102, which has also been subjected to the court decisions, is a useful example. The article states:

> *In the event that the articles of partnership give management duty to a partner, his management right and duty cannot be restricted by other partners and he cannot be discharged from the duty either. However, the right and duty of management can be restricted or revoked 'by court order' for just cause upon the request of one of the partners...*[217]

The debate here emerges from whether the 'court order' requirement impedes the settlement of such disputes by arbitration.[218] The Turkish Supreme Court has rendered a decision regarding this article.[219] In this case, the plaintiff claimed that the dispute must be resolved by arbitrators as required in article 14 of the articles of partnership. The trial court dismissed the case for lack of jurisdiction based on article 14 of the articles of partnership and determined that the case should be submitted to a duly authorized arbitrator because the claim was made within the legal time limit.[220] The defendant's attorney appealed this decision and the Supreme Court, indeed, reversed the decision based on Article 161[221] of the Turkish Commercial Code stating that "*the right and duty of management can be restricted or revoked 'by court order' for just cause at the request of one of the partners*" and stated that the trial court must resolve this dispute. [222]

---

215 *See supra* note 167.

216 Burak Huysal, p. 253.

217 The article continues as "*Improvidence in performing the duty, gross negligence or cases such as incapacity in management are considered just cause.*"

218 Burcin Yıldırım, p. 33.

219 Turkish Supreme Court 11th Civil Circuit decision dated 02/04/1980 numbered 1980/448.

220 Mehmet Helvacı, p. 190.

221 It was article 161 in the previous Turkish Commercial Code numbered 6762. It is article 219 in the new Turkish Commercial Code numbered 6102.

222 Mehmet Helvacı, p. 190.

The ruling differs from exclusive judicial jurisdictional rules in procedural codes because Article 161 related to the dismissal of the managing partner and (technically) contained no explicit imperative statement on jurisdiction attribution (even though, in substance, the court's decision suggests that it does).[223] The rationale of the decision, however, is not evident.[224] A conflicting Supreme Court decision asserts that the arbitral clause (in the articles of partnership) for disputes between partners of a general partnership is binding.[225] This finding proves more persuasive in current circumstances.

Another decision about *in rem* rights on immovable property regarding the "court order" requirement warrants consideration. The Supreme Court ruled[226] that:

> *The case requests the transfer of the ownership of an immovable property pursuant to a preliminary contract of sale. Although article –M- of the general sales specification includes the provision that 'the possible disputes between the promisor company of the sale and the promisee of the sale shall be resolved by way of arbitration', Turkish Civil Code[227] article 706 and 1017 and Land Register Code[228] article 26 and 27 and the Code numbered 5519 stipulate that transfers in the land registry are possible by the declarations of the promisor and promisee in the presence of a deed officer or by 'court order'. The abovementioned articles relate to public policy and arbitration agreement is invalid regarding these matters. Therefore, the appeal claims made by the defendant's attorney in this respect are not admissible. Besides, the ownership of the immovable property, which is the subject of the dispute, has been transferred to defendant promisee during the litigation.*

Additional Supreme Court decisions concern the land registry and immovable property. In one of these decisions,[229] the Court ruled similarly that:

---

223 *Id* at 191.

224 Burcin Yıldırım, p. 32; Mehmet Helvacı, p. 190.

225 Turkish Supreme Court Commercial Circuit (previous name of 11th Circuit) dated 11/03/1969 and decided with the number 5118. Burcin Yıldırım, p. 35 & n.107. (*Citing* Ismail Doganay, Turk Ticaret Kanunu Serhi [Commentary on Turkish Commercial Code] 734 vol.1 (Istanbul 2004)).

226 Turkish Supreme Court 14th Civil Circuit decision dated 10/07/2003 numbered 2003/6387.

227 Turkish Civil Code numbered 4721 which was published in Official Gazette with the number of 24607 and enacted on 12/08/2001.

228 Land Register Law numbered 2644 published in Official Gazette on 12/29/1934 with the number of 2892.

229 Turkish Supreme Court 15th Civil Circuit decision dated 09/23/2002 numbered 2002/4321.

> *'The terms of a contract may freely be determined by the parties within the limits of the law.' pursuant to Turkish Code of Contract Article 19;*[230] *however, the freedom of contract of the parties is not unlimited. Hence, lawmakers impose restriction on the subject of contracts on moral, social, and economical grounds, and on public policy in practice. The present case requested the cancellation of the construction contract between the parties in return for an apartment as well as the cancellation and registration of the title, which was transferred to contractor. In this case, because the dispute between the parties relates to in rem rights on immovable property, and also because transfer of ownership in the land registry can only be made by consensus or 'court order', arbitration of such a matter, which is against the rule legally stipulated as a matter of public policy, is not permitted. Thus, the arbitral clause for the dispute between the parties is not enforceable. The court's ruling of lack jurisdiction should be reversed. The court should hear the case.*

This decision demonstrates that the Turkish Supreme Court assesses the 'court order' requirement as analogous to the exclusive authorization of national courts, despite the absence of an explicit statement of such imperativeness in the law.

In short, the Supreme Court tends to consider the requirement of a 'court order' as an impediment to arbitration.[231] However, the rationale for using the expression 'court order' must be examined before reaching this conclusion.[232] Regarding land registration cases, some legal scholars assert that a judge's decision should transfer the ownership of the property to the plaintiff in contrast with the decision to grant or compel performance. This means the judge is entitled to render a '*constitutive*' decision.[233] The following brief definition will clarify the meaning of the 'constitutive' character of a court order. Turkish civil law classifies lawsuits according to nature of the request in three ways:

- A lawsuit can be based on an action for performance;[234]
- A lawsuit can be based on an action for declaratory judgment,[235] and
- A lawsuit can be a constitutive lawsuit.[236]

---

230 It is article 26 in the current Turkish Code of Contract.

231 Burcin Yıldırım, p. 33.

232 *Ibid.*

233 Burcin Yıldırım, p. 34 & n.105. (*Citing* Sulhi Salahattin Tekinay, Esya Hukuku [Law of Property] 716 (Vol., Istanbul, 1978)).

234 The plaintiff files such a case in order to compel the defendant to perform (or non-perform) or submit something.

235 The plaintiff files such a case in order for existence, absence or content of a legal relationship to be determined.

236 Ufuk Aydın, Medeni Usul Hukuku [Civil Procedure Code] 66 (TC Anadolu Universitesi Yayını no.1706) [Republic of Turkey Anadolu University Publishing, number 1706].

A constitutive lawsuit is filed when the defendant cannot unilaterally create, cancel, or alter a legal situation; or when the parties cannot agree upon the resolution of that issue; or when a 'court order' is required.[237] A constitutive lawsuit can only be filed when the code includes an explicit statement authorizing such an action.[238]

Article 161 of the previous Turkish Commercial Code,[239] which was subject to the aforementioned Turkish Supreme Court decision, authorized the court to restrict or revoke a partner's right of general partnership concerning management based on the articles of partnership. As in the land registration cases, the 'court order' requirement in the related articles aimed to entitle the court to render a decision that had a constitutive effect.[240] The requirement, indeed, entitled the judge to change the legal situation of the plaintiff against his will. When parties agreed to arbitrate, however, they authorized the arbitrators to resolve their disputes. This means that plaintiffs, against whom arbitral cases were filed, pre-consented to changes in their legal situation by the arbitral tribunal, unlike in comparable situations before courts.[241] Consequently, each provision of law[242] that contains the 'court order' requirement must be appraised on a case-by-case basis. Courts are entitled to render 'constitutive' decisions.[243] So, any conclusions that disputes are inarbitrable due to the exclusive judicial jurisdiction of the court should be made reluctantly for the reasons outlined for exclusive judicial jurisdictional rule.

C. The Issue of Public Policy and Relationship with Arbitrability in Turkish Law

Turkish corporate law contains no specific regulations regarding public policy arbitrability.[244] The next chapter on corporate arbitration will, therefore, refer to general explanations of arbitrability and particularly regulations related to public policy (outlined in this chapter) as needed. This section explains the

237 Ufuk Aydın, p. 67.

238 *Ibid.*

239 It is article 219 in the current Turkish Commercial Code.

240 Burcin Yıldırım, p. 34.

241 *Ibid.*

242 Except the debate about inarbitrability of disputes arising from *in rem* rights on immovable properties. *See supra* note 76 *et seq.*

243 *Ibid.*

244 Mehmet Tas, p. 33.

notion of public policy as a basis for future technical discussions. The book has mentioned the term 'public policy' ('*ordre public*' in civil law countries[245]) as grounds for inarbitrability. The term's specific meaning, however, requires further clarification.

Defining the meaning and limits of public policy is crucial for several additional reasons including the fact that it is subject to major international conventions and regulations. Turkey is a party to the New York Convention on the Recognition and Enforcement of Foreign Arbitral Awards.[246] The Convention acknowledges public policy as a widely-recognized exception.[247] The relevant article[248] states that:

> *...Recognition and enforcement of an arbitral award may also be refused if the competent authority in the country where recognition and enforcement is sought finds that: ...The recognition or enforcement of the award would be contrary to the public policy of that country.*[249]

Parties may refer to this article to argue that recognition and enforcement of an arbitral award should be refused.[250] Several additional conventions and treaties include similar public policy exceptions. Article 1/e of the Geneva Convention on the Execution of Foreign Arbitral Awards of 1927, for instance, states "*...To obtain such recognition or enforcement, it shall, further, be necessary: ... That the recognition or enforcement of the award is not contrary to the public policy or to the principles of the law of the country in which it is intended to apply.*"[251] The Brussels

---

245 Jacob Grierson & Annet van Hooft, Arbitrating Under the 2012 ICC Rules n.12 (Kluwer Law Int'l 2012).

246 Turkey has ratified the Convention on 5/8/1991 with the code numbered 3731 and enacted on 5/21/1991 by publishing in Official Gazette numbered 20877.

247 Cemal Sanlı, Esasa Uygulanacak Hukuk, p. 408.

248 Article V §2b.

249 Anton G. Maurer, Public Policy Exception Under the New York Convention 11 (Juris Publishing, Inc. 2013).

250 Kemal Dayınlarlı, Milli- Milletlerarası Kamu Duzeni; Tahkime Etkileri ve Sonucları [Domestic and International Public Policy; Effects on Arbitration and Consequences] 148 (Dayınlarlı Hukuk Yayınları, 2. Baski 2011) [Dayınlarlı Legal Publishing, 2nd ed. 2011].

251 *See* Register of Texts of CONVENTIONS AND OTHER INSTRUMENTS CONCERNING INTERNATIONAL TRADE LAW, Vol. II (United Nations, New York 1973) p. 13 for full text of the convention.

I Regulation[252] likewise allows the refusal of recognition and enforcement of judgments that violate the "*state's fundamental international public policy*." [253]

A significant volume of case law has emerged around this regulation,[254] making public policy the most common ground for the unenforceability of arbitral awards.[255] Defining this term under the relevant national law is, therefore, even more crucial. The article's application depends on one's interpretation of 'public policy' and the arbitral policy of the requested jurisdiction.[256] This section, therefore, examines perspectives and tendencies in Turkish legal doctrine and jurisdiction regarding the limits and definition of public policy. It will also point out how the public policy exception applies under Turkish law and explains the possible consequences of its application.

1. Regulations under Turkish Law

The Turkish Supreme Court has frequently evaluated the relationship between arbitrability and public policy [257] It has ruled that disputes involving the application of provisions adopted in the public's interest cannot be arbitrated.[258] In a decision dated 11/07/1991 and numbered 1991/4163, the 15th Civil Circuit of Turkish Supreme Court stated:

> *... the legislator has brought an order regarding the appeal of arbitral awards. As indicated in article 533 / 1*[[259]] *of Turkish Code of Civil Procedure, arbitral awards may be reversed only on the grounds listed in this article where the particular circumstances match those stipulated in the article's four provisions.* [[260]] *Arbitral awards, therefore, can be reversed*

---

252 Council Regulation (EC) No. 44/2001, of December 2000 on jurisdiction and the recognition and enforcement of judgments in civil and commercial matters (Official Journal L 12 of 16.01.2001).

253 Christian Bühring-Uhle, Lars Kirchhoff & Gabriele Scherer, p. 25.

254 Cemal Sanlı, Esasa Uygulanacak Hukuk, p. 408.

255 *Id* at 407.

256 Feyiz Erdogan, p. 136.

257 Mehmet Helvacı, p. 185.

258 *Id* at 186.

259 The related article in the current Turkish Code of Civil Procedure numbered 6100 and enacted on 1/12/2011 is article 439.

260 The text of the article:

"Article 533: *The awards of arbitrators may be reversed only on the following grounds:*

1. For rendering decision after the expiration of arbitration's time period,
2. For rendering decision on something that is not requested,

on the grounds included in these provisions. To put it in a different way, it is impossible to reverse the decisions of arbitrators except for the reasons stated in the article. However, an arbitral award can be reversed in the event of breach of public policy for reasons other than those listed in article 533... [[261]]

The new Turkish Code of Civil Procedure numbered 6100[262] adopted in 2011 clearly addresses the relationship between public policy and arbitrability in addition to the four instances mentioned in the previous code and the court decision above. The arbitration regulations in the new code differ from those of the previous code because the new code was developed in accordance with the Turkish International Arbitration Code numbered 4686.[263] [264] The new Civil Procedure Code, indicates that awards may be set aside if:

a) the subject-matter of the dispute cannot be settled by arbitration under Turkish law, or
b) the award conflicts with public policy.[265]

The International Arbitration Code contains a similar regulation.[266]

It is worth emphasizing that the current Turkish Codes stipulate that the objective (subject-matter-based) arbitrability of disputes and breaches of public policy are different grounds for the setting aside or the non-enforcement of

---

3. For rendering decision on a matter beyond the authority of arbitrator,
4. *For not rendering decision on each of the claims of both parties.*"

261 Kemal Dayınlarlı, p. 49 n.100.

262 Which governs domestic arbitration.

263 International Arbitration Code regulates the procedure and substance of international arbitration while the Turkish Code of Civil Procedure regulates the procedure and substance of domestic arbitration.

264 Ejder Yılmaz, *Hukuk Muhakemeleri Kanunun Getirdikleri* [*Amendments by new Turkish Code of Civil Procedure*] Ankara Barosu Dergisi, 2011/2 [Ankara Bar Journal, 2011/2] p. 252.

265 Article 439.

266 Article 15:

"*...Awards may be set aside on the following grounds:*

...

2) *If the court finds that;*

a) *a subject-matter of the dispute is not capable of settlement by arbitration under the Turkish Law,*
b) *the award is in conflict with public policy...*"

arbitral awards.[267] This differentiation suggests that public policy is a basis for setting aside an arbitral award and leads to its unenforceability. Public policy is not, however, initially an impediment to arbitration because it is not directly associated with objective inarbitrability. Equating issues of public policy with inarbitrability is, therefore, not analytically sound.[268] Nevertheless, there are Supreme Court decisions stating that public policy issues must be considered along with other causes of inarbitrability.[269] Unfortunately, this case law may reinforce the tendency to equate the two.[270]

The Supreme Court has thus given critical weight to public policy. It is, therefore, important for parties engaged in arbitral proceedings in Turkey to understand public policy and remain within its bounds. The impact of setting aside an arbitral award is enormous and thereby makes the issue of public policy crucial

---

267 *See* Turkish International Arbitration Code article 15/2 (a) and article 15/2 (b). *See also* Turkish Civil Procedure Code article 439/2 (g) and article 439/2 (ğ).

268 By way of applying to a court for setting aside an arbitral award, cancellation of an award or unenforcement of an award etc.

269 The statement 'not being at the disposition of the parties' which causes inarbitrability of a dispute according to Turkish Law was interpreted as 'public policy'. Turkish Supreme Court has stated in a decision on the unification of conflicting judgement dated 10/23/1972 numbered 2/12 that:

"...*As a result of freedom of contract principle, articles 19 and 20 of Turkish Code of Contract and article 516 of Turkish Code of Civil Procedure, it is possible for real or legal persons to prefer arbitration and conclude arbitration agreement for the disputes do not involve public policy...*".

270 Mehmet Sarı, p. 151 & n.21.
The 3rd Civil Circuit of Turkish Supreme Court has decided in an analogous manner on 12/02/2004 with the number of 2004/13018 more recently that:

"...*Concluding an arbitration agreement is possible only for the disputes that are subject to will of the parties. This means that parties can make arbitration agreement or arbitral clause for resolution of a dispute if they are free to make an agreement to settle this dispute and this agreement is valid without any needing a court order. Considering the Supreme Court's established practices, arbitral tribunals cannot hear the declaratory actions for rental value. Because the matter of the determination of rental value involves public policy, the parties can assess the rental value only by definite standards and limitations. The will of the parties is, therefore, not unlimited. The renter, thus, is not obliged to pay the rental that the landlord asks for. In that case, arbitral tribunals cannot hear a dispute on rent because the arbitral clause about the settlement of disputes on rental value assessment, which involves public policy, will be invalid according to Turkish Code of Civil Procedure article 518.*"

for the evaluation of the state of arbitration under Turkish law. This chapter examines public policy in more detail to establish a foundation for assessing risk avoidance in the relationship between corporate law and arbitration.

a) Definition and Specifications of Public Policy in Turkish Law

> *Whether or not a particular type of dispute is 'arbitrable' under a given law is in essence a matter of public policy for that law to determine. Public policy varies from one country to the next, and indeed changes from time to time. The most can be done here is to indicate the categories of dispute that may fall outside the domain of arbitration.*[271]

Domestic law in Turkey includes no definitive provision regarding public policy. [272] Furthermore, no consensus has been reached regarding the definition, content, and elements of the concept of public policy; it is based on numerous variables including social, moral, economic, and political considerations.[273] With reference to the common elements of previous judicial and scholarly definitions, it consists of the "fundamental principles that the domestic rule of law is based on the Turkish sense of morality and decency and rules protecting the essential interests of Turkish society."[274] Comprehensively defining public policy is difficult; Turkish legal scholars Professor *Celikel* and Professor *Erdem* define the public policy as:

> *Public policy rules are the regulations facilitate the better execution of public services, safety, and security of the country and compliance with peace and moral rules in individual relationships.*[275]

Supreme Court Assembly of Civil Chambers' decision, dated 06/21/2000 and numbered 2000/2–1051, further clarifies the definition:

> *...Neither statute nor legal doctrine has provided an inalterable definition of public policy. However, and particularly in terms of Turkish International Private Law, the issues*

---

271 Constantine Partasides et al., Redfern and Hunter on International Arbitration para 2.116 (5th ed. Oxford Univ. Press 2009).

272 Turgut Kalpsuz, Turkiye'de Milletlerarası Tahkim [International Arbitration in Turkey] 146 (2. Baskı, Yetkin Yayınevi, Ankara 2010) [2nd ed. Yetkin Publishing, Ankara 2010).

273 Yılmaz Altug & Mustafa Yasan, *Milletlerarası Ozel Hukukta Kamu Duzeni* [*Public Policy in International Private Law*] *in* Prof. Dr. Ergun Onen'e Armagan [Dedication for Prof. Dr. Ergun Onen] 139 (Alkım Yayınevi, Istanbul 2003) [Alkım Publishing, Istanbul 2003].

274 Turgut Kalpsuz, p. 146.

275 Aysel Celikel & Bahadır Erdem, Milletlerarası Ozel Hukuk [International Private Law] 149 (11. Basi, Beta Yayınları) [11th ed., Beta Publishing].

> *identified in Supreme Court decisions as against public policy include reckless conduct and uncivil manners, and actions incompatible with the fundamental rules of Turkish law and the general policies that Turkish laws are based on.*[276]

The Turkish Constitutional Court has also declared that:

> *...public policy aims to secure peace and order in the country, to protect the State and State Organization; in other words, it embodies the rules that constitute the base of the regime of the community at every stage.*[277]

b) Characteristics and the Legal Nature of Public Policy

The key concepts of public policy are ambiguous and open to variegated interpretations. Public policy is a relative concept that varies by location and by historical time.[278] The criteria of public policy differ based on a State's political and social conditions; public policy's effect on legal acts, therefore, differs from state to state.[279] Public policy is a dynamic notion influenced by various domestic factors, which means it can change over time even in the same State.[280] Issues not initially considered breaches of public policy may, therefore, later come to be considered breaches.[281] Article 2 of the Law on Enforcement and Implementation of Turkish Civil Code[282] itself acknowledges the differences between the notions of public policy in the previous and current codes.[283] It states that rules violating

---

276 Kemal Dayınlarlı, p. 8.
Turkish Supreme Court 13th Civil Circuit decision dated 6/16/1994 numbered E2012/8426 and K10349 states another definition:

> "*...the entire set of rules and institutions, which protects the fundamental interests of the society and designates the fundamental structure of the society from political, social, economic, ethical and legal perspectives within a specific time period.*"

(Available at: http://www.cerrahoglu.av.tr/doc/ILO_Arbitration_Updates/22.pdf)

277 Official Gazette dated 04/17/1964 and numbered 11685. Kemal Dayınlarlı p. 9.

278 Cemal Ruhi & Yavuz Kaplan, *Yabancı Mahkeme ve Hakem Kararların Tenfizi Acısından Kamu Duzeni (Ordre Public)* [*Public Policy in Terms of Enforcement of Foreign Judicial and Arbitral Decisions (Ordre Public)*] *in* Prof. Dr. Ergin Nomer'e Armagan; Milletlerarası Hukuk ve Milletlerarası Ozel Hukuk Bulteni [Dedication for Prof. Dr. Ergin Nomer; International Law and International Private Law Bulletin] 644 (Yıl: 22, Sayi: 2, 2002) [Year:22, Issue:2, 2002].

279 Rasih Yegengil, p. 157.

280 *Ibid.*

281 Ziya Akıncı, Milletlerarası Tahkim, p. 272.

282 Numbered 4722 and dated 21/3/2001.

283 The new Civil Code numbered 4721, which is currently effective, was adopted on 2001.

public policy and general public morality under the previous code will no longer apply after the implementation of the new code.[284] The dynamic character of public policy can give rise to practical questions. In disputes regarding arbitral awards or enforcement, judges may face conflicts between previous and current regulations. Regarding the enforcement of foreign awards or the resolution of disputes involving foreign elements, judges should base their decisions on current public policy.[285]

The *exceptional* nature of the notion of public policy, lastly, is its most important characteristic. The section below examines debates about this characteristic because it is theoretically affected by the distinction between domestic and international public policy.

2. Application of Public Policy in Turkish Law: Domestic and International Law Contrasted

Most scholars[286] adopt the division between domestic and international public policy first asserted by *Charles Brocher* (a professor at the University of Geneva Law School) in 1872.[287] *Brocher* argued that domestic public policy consists of imperative rules that cannot be disposed through the will of the parties.[288] The distinction between domestic and international public policy must also be made.[289] Presenting "*Ordre Public Transnational (ou réellement international) et Arbitrage International*" to the Fifth International Arbitration Congress, Professor *Pierre Lalive* argued that public policy is clearly domestic in essence.[290] He added,

284 Rasih Yegengil, p. 158.

285 Isılar Umut Mutlu, Yabancı Hakem Kararlarının Tanınmasında ve Tenfizinde Kamu Duzeni Etkisi [The Effect of Public Policy in Recognition and Enforcement of Foreign Arbitral Awards] (2003) (Yayınlanmamıs Yuksek Lisans Tezi, Ankara Universitesi, Sosyal Bilimler Enstitusu, Devletler Ozel Hukuku Ana Bilim Dali) [Unpublished LLM Thesis, Ankara University, Institute of Social Sciences, Department of International Private Law] p. 20.

286 Authors mentioned by Cemal Sanlı, Esasa Uygulanacak Hukuk, p. 383 & n. 830.

287 Yılmaz Altug & Mustafa Yasan, p. 141.
Kemal Dayınlarlı, p. 17.

288 Kemal Dayınlarlı, p. 17.

289 *Id* at18.

290 Kemal Dayınlarlı, p. 194 & n.186–187. Furthermore, the same opinion has taken place in the order of Paris Court of Appeals dated October 3, 1984 "*Security of commercial and financial relationships constitute a public policy; this is a universal public policy and includes mutual issues with various public policies which protect the interests of*

however, that this does not impede its "supranational (*supra-nationaux*)" nature in practice or its application to an international task as needed.[291]

The distinction between domestic and international public policy is controversial in Turkish legal doctrine. Professor Dr. *Kemal Dayınlarlı* points out that some Turkish doctrinal scholars find the distinction superfluous because it confuses legal practices. [292] The commentators argue that, while each State has its own public policy, there is no real international public policy, and—therefore—domestic conceptions of public policy apply in international relationships.[293] Professor *Dayınlarlı* highlights Professor *Osman Fazıl Berki's explanation:*[294]

> *When public policy is in question in international law, this actually signals a confrontation with that a mandatory rule of domestic law. Such rules override the international private law provisions that are normally applicable. Public policy overriding such a provision is the same as public policy overriding a dispositive transaction based on the will of two Turkish people. Dividing public policy that arises from the same rule of law only confuses the concept of public policy, which is already complicated.* [295]

Some scholars, however, promote the distinction.[296] They point out the various factors that require consideration when it comes to the application of public policy exceptions to international versus domestic disputes.[297] These authors generally argue that not every domestic public policy rule can apply to matters of international arbitration.[298] They maintain that international applications should occur on more limited and narrower basis than applications of the domestic

---

shareholders of corporations." The public policy is particular to a special legal condition for 'objective' purposes and is differentiated from domestic public policy here.

291 *Ibid.*

292 Kemal Dayınlarlı, p. 18.

293 *Ibid.*

294 Kemal Dayınlarlı, p. 19.

295 *See* Cemal Sanlı, Esasa Uygulanacak Hukuk, p. 389 for a similar approach. The author states that public policy considered as 'international', which interferes with the application of foreign law exceptionally, is originally domestic in nature. The judge, indeed, intervene in application of a foreign law based on public policy also for domestic social, political, religious and moral considerations. In other words, the reason for such intervention is because applying the regulation would harm the forum State's value judgement and social pattern severely. Therefore, one can say that considering this type of public policy 'international' is misleading. It is hard to assert that those two public policies arise from different principles. The difference can only be their scope.

296 Kemal Dayınlarlı, pp. 18 and other authors mentioned in the footnote n. 44.

297 *Ibid.*

298 Cemal Ruhi & Yavuz Kaplan, p. 645.

concepts.[299] The division between domestic and international[300] public policy is a workable and effective distinction that is widely supported by legal doctrine.[301] The countervailing view is eccentric and primarily of theoretical value. '*Domestic*' public policy refers to the mandatory rules that may contravene the will of the

---

299 List of some of the authors supporting this point:

- Feyiz Erdogan, p. 134,
- Burak Huysal, p. 119,
- Kemal Dayınlarlı, p. 86,
- Aysel Celikel & Bahadır Erdem, p. 148,
- Turgut Kalpsuz, p. 147,
- Nomer Eksi Gelgel, p. 3,
- Cemal Sanlı, Esasa Uygulanacak Hukuk, 388,
- Mehmet Tas, pp. 20–21.

300 There is also a third division of "community public policy" adopted by some authors such as Cemal Sanlı (Esasa Uygulanacak Hukuk, pp. 384.) This term refers to the supra-national communities like European Union (the laws of European Economic Community and COMECON). This chapter will not explain the third type as a separate heading but will mention the European Union regulations and their effects on Turkish law as needed.

301 For similar explanations from Swiss Law, *see* Francesco Trezzini, *The Challenge of Arbitral Awards for Breach of Public Policy according to Art. 190 para. 2 lit. e) of the Swiss Private International Law in* Three Essays on International Commercial Arbitration, Ed. Antonio Monti, Francesco Trezzini & Francesco Wicki (2002) (*available at* http://www.montiswisslaw.com) § 11.

"*The distinction between domestic and international public policy is, in fact, very well known. Over many years there have been numerous legal writings (both Swiss and foreign) and many examples in case law. For instance, Art. 19 para. 1 of the Swiss Code of Obligations (CO) uses the word "public policy" to qualify specific principles at a domestic level, which are to be distinguished from public policy in an international context (i.e. International public policy). There are in fact two different concepts. What is to be considered pertaining to public policy in domestic relations does not necessarily pertain to public policy in international relationships. This distinction is justified by the different purposes of law in specifically domestic or international relationships. In fact, international private law, by reason of its specifically international contents and its intrinsic function to harmonize the different national legislations, is perfectly adapted to conceive solutions which may be unfamiliar to Swiss law (with the exception, of course, of the "lois d'application immédiate" ex Art. 18 PIL).*

In synthesis this means that a domestic mandatory rule does not necessarily violate international public policy."

parties in accordance with the national law; '*international*' public policy refers to the rules that impede the application of a foreign law because they conflict with the *lex fori* in a dispute involving foreign elements.[302] The following discussion assesses the content of both domestic and international public policy.

a) *Domestic Public Policy under Turkish Law* (Ordre Public National)[303]

Internationally, public policy specifically relates to choice of law.[304] Domestically, it relates to the substance of a particular subject area in Turkish law. As *Feyiz Erdogan* put it: "*...domestic public policy includes imperative rules and principles that cannot be disposed through the will of the parties.*"[305] Public policy is the crucial factor in establishing imperative rules of law.[306] Imperative rules are not listed or limited, making it necessary to clarify the content of the domestic public policy rules. The issues that require the intervention of public policy in Turkish law include:

1) *Conflicts with fundamental principles of Turkish laws,*
2) *Conflicts with the Turkish sense of decency and morality,*
3) *Conflicts with fundamental rights and freedoms established in the Turkish Constitution,*[307]
4) *Conflicts with international (public) law.*[308]

---

302 Cemal Sanlı, Esasa Uygulanacak Hukuk, pp. 388–389.

303 For further explanation on the changing balance of *ordre public, ius cogens* character of norms and State immunity, which has been more limited after First World War as adopted by UN Convention on Immunity of States and some national codes in international law, *See*:
Fusun Arsava, Yabancı Mahkeme Kararlarının Icrası ve Devletlerin Yargı Bagısıklıgı [Enforcement of Foreign Court Decisions and Judicial Immunity of States], Turkiye Adalet Akademisi Dergisi Cilt:1 Yıl:3 Sayı:8, (Ocak 2012) [Turkey Justice Academy Journal, Vol:1 Year:3 Issue:8, (January 2012)], p. 2.

304 Particularly conflict of laws.

305 Feyiz Erdogan, p. 126; Cemal Sanlı, Esasa Uygulanacak Hukuk, p. 383 & n.831.

306 Aysel Celikel & Bahadır Erdem, p. 148.

307 Ziya Akıncı, Milletlararasi Tahkim p. 270.

308 Kemal Dayınlarlı, p. 20. (The first three provisions are mentioned by both Professor Akıncı and Dayınlarlı while the fourth provision is mentioned by Dayınlarlı only.)
In the Turkish Supreme Court 13th Civil Circuit's decision dated 6/16/1994 numbered E2012/8426 and K10349:

"*...the intervention of public policy is essential when there is violation of imperative provisions of law, which aim to protect the public interest and public policy, morality*

Rules stemming from both public and private law govern these issues.[309] Article 26 of the Turkish Code of Contracts,[310] for instance, stipulates that "*The terms of a contract may be freely determined by the parties* ***within the limits of the law.***" Agreements that violate the conditions stipulated in Article 27[311] of the same Code[312] will, consequently, be null and void.[313] The article states: "*Agreements that are contrary to the mandatory rules of law, morality, public policy, personal rights, or address subjects that cannot be regulated by private contract are null and void.*"[314] Arbitration agreements that violate Article 27 of the Code of Contracts will therefore be considered null and void.[315] Article 27 suggests that public policy directly relates to the *arbitrability* of such a dispute, which would prohibit resolution of the dispute by way of arbitration.[316] This explicit public policy regulation applies to all legal issues including corporate matters.

Turkish law regulates provides that the arbitrability of a subject matter and whether an arbitral award violates public policy are two separate grounds for setting aside an arbitral award.[317] This stems from the fact that public policy has

---

and fundamental rights and freedoms. For instance, customs codes and tax legislations are related to public policy. Public policy would intervene in a final arbitral award which resolves a debt owed contrary to tax legislation because such award does not comply with the basic principles considered essential in Turkish law."

309 Kemal Dayınlarlı, p. 19,
Turgut Kalpsuz, p. 146,
Ziya Akıncı, Milletlerarası Tahkim p. 270.

310 Numbered 6098.

311 Under the heading of 'absolute nullity'

312 Namely Turkish Code of Contracts.

313 Ziya Akıncı, Milletlerarası Tahkim p. 271.

314 Article 27 follows as:

"*The nullity of the terms of the agreement partly does not affect the validity of the rest of the terms. However, the contract is deemed as null and void completely if it is understood that the contract could not have been concluded without the terms considered void.*"

315 Ziya Akıncı, Milletlerarası Tahkim, p. 271.

316 Indeed, matters that are not at the free disposition of the parties mostly involve public policy. (Suha Tanrıver, *Yabancı Hakem Kararlarının Turkiye'de Tenfizi Baglamında Kamu Duzeninin Etkisi* [*Effect of Public Policy in The Context of Enforcement of Foreign Arbitral Awards in Turkey*] *in* Hukuk - Ekonomi Perspektifinden Uluslararası Tahkim ve Kamu Hizmeti [International Arbitration and Public Service from the Perspectives of Law-Economy] 83 (Liberte Yayınevi, 2001) [Liberte Publishing, 2001].)

317 Turkish International Arbitration Code article 15/2 (a) and article 15/2 (b). *See also* Turkish Civil Procedure Code article 439/2 (g) and article 439/2 (ğ).

applications beyond imperative rules and not every imperative rule is involved in public policy.[318] As Professor *Akıncı* explains: "*...Not every infringement of imperative provisions of Turkish law constitutes a violation of public policy. What is required is an infringement of public policy.*"[319] Some imperative rules protect personal interests while others protect public interests.[320] Only the latter are true public policy rules.[321] The Turkish Supreme Court affirms this by pointing out that arbitral awards that violate *public law rules*—which are subject to penal sanctions—violate Turkish public policy.[322] The rules governing arbitrability relate to public policy while not all public policy rules relate to arbitrability.[323] These facts explicitly clarify the relationship between the concepts of arbitrability and public policy.

This relationship suggests that just because a rule relates to public policy does not mean that the rule's application will make a dispute inarbitrable. This has led some commentators to argue that "*in light of the criteria*[324] *of arbitrability,*[325] *matters that are at the free disposition of the parties may be resolved by way of arbitration even if the matter in dispute is involved in public policy.*" Thus, arbitral tribunals take public policy concerns into consideration during the proceedings and decision-making in the same manner as the courts.[326] This comparison implies an equivalency between arbitral and judicial adjudication. When an arbitral award violates public policy rules, parties have recourse to official judicial authorities to challenge the arbitral ruling. The assumption that arbitral tribunals do not have jurisdictional authority on the matters involving public

---

318 Turgut Kalpsuz, p. 146,
Burcin Yıldırım, p. 29,
Ziya Akıncı, Milletlerarası Tahkim p. 270.

319 Ziya Akıncı, Arbitration Law of Turkey, p. 196–197.
The author also states that "Violation of every mandatory rule does not necessarily mean violation of public policy." (Ziya Akıncı, Arbitration Law of Turkey, p. 154.)

320 Burcin Yıldırım, p. 29.

321 *Ibid.* (Mauro Rubino - Sammartano, International Arbitration Law and Practice 110 (Kluwer Law Int'l 2001)).

322 Turkish Supreme Court 13th Civil Circuit Decision dated 02/05/1998 numbered E.997/9703 and K.998/978. (Turgut Kalpsuz, Turkiye'de Milletlerarası Tahkim, p. 147.)

323 Burak Huysal, p. 165.

324 *See supra* Chapter II (A) 1. (a) for the criteria of being subject to will of the parties and dispositive nature of disputes.

325 Mehmet Tas, pp. 28–29.

326 *Id* at 29.

policy regulations is, therefore, inaccurate.[327] Cases with a commercial and international character require even greater sensitivity because of the global interest in commerce and dysfunctionality of the trans-border enforcement of court judgments. Public policy as grounds for inarbitrability applies less frequently to disputes in such cases.[328]

Another regulation regarding the outcome of public policy violations[329] requires that arbitral awards be set aside as indicated by both the International Arbitration Act and the Civil Procedure Code.[330] Parties have recourse to a court

---

327 *Ibid.*

328 For reasons that the next section about the international division specifies.

329 The first regulation was article 26–27 of Turkish Code of Contracts as abovementioned. *See supra* note 310 *et seq.*

330 **International Arbitration Act**

"*Article 15:*
…*Awards may be set aside in the following circumstances:*
…

2) If the court finds that;

a) a subject–matter of the dispute is not capable of settlement by arbitration under the Turkish Law,
b) *the award is in conflict with public policy…*"

Civil Procedure Code

"*Article 439: The award may be set aside if*

a) the subject-matter of the dispute is not capable of settlement by arbitration under the Turkish Law,
b) *it is in conflict with public policy.*"

This regulation is in parallel with German Regulations. *See* Karl-Heinz Böckstiegel, Stefan Michael Kröll et al., Arbitration in Germany: The Model Law in Practice §139 (Kluwer Law Intl 2007).

"*The grounds to be taken into account by the courts ex officio are the lack of arbitrability of the dispute and the violation of public policy. In connection with the latter, the courts are limited to verifying whether the result is compatible with the fundamental principles of the German legal system. Even severe misapplications of the law will only constitute a violation of public policy where they lead to completely arbitrary decisions, which are so contrary to the fundamental principles of law that they would seriously damage confidence in dispute resolution by arbitration. Procedural public policy may be violated where a party's right to be heard has not been respected.*"

against an arbitral award only by seeking to set aside the award[331] under the relevant code. This possibility proves important because such an action could void an entire arbitral award in both the domestic and international context. Applications for recourse will also receive priority and expeditious handling by the court.[332] Judges who find conflicts with public policy can set the awards aside *ex officio*.[333] Authorized judges[334] can, likewise, evaluate whether an award conforms to Turkish public policy[335] if a party applies for the enforcement of a foreign arbitral award regulated by the Code on Private International Law and the Civil Procedure Code.[336] Regulations on enforcement also bind the recognition of foreign arbitral awards.[337] The national courts can therefore, *ex officio*,

---

331 International Arbitration Act article 15/A.
332 International Arbitration Act article 15/A.
333 Ziya Akıncı, Milletlerarası Tahkim, p. 269.
334 Article 60:

"*Enforcement of Foreign Arbitral Awards*

(1) Foreign arbitral awards that are final and enforceable or binding for the parties can be enforced.
(2) Enforcement of the foreign arbitral award can be requested by petition from the court of first instance agreed by the parties in writing.

If there is no such agreement between the parties, the court in the location of domicile of the person who the enforcement is requested against;
If not available, the court in the location of residence;
If not available, the court in the location of the goods which can be subject to enforcement is considered authorized."

335 The exact text of the regulation is as follows:
Article 62:

"*Grounds of Refusal*

(1) *The Court may refuse to enforce a foreign arbitral award*

...

(b) *if the arbitral award is in conflict with the public morality and public policy,*
(c) *if the dispute subject to the arbitral award is inarbitrable in accordance with Turkish Law,*

..."

336 Numbered 5718 and enacted on 11/27/2007 with publishing on Official Gazette dated 12/12/2007 and numbered 26728.
337 The Code on Private International Law and Civil Procedure article 63.

refuse the enforcement or recognition of foreign arbitral awards if they violate public policy.[338] "[A]*lthough public policy is not commonly used as grounds for setting aside an award in practice*",[339] the critical effect of setting aside an award highlight the importance of considering public policy in arbitral proceedings.

(1) Issues Considered as Non-arbitrable Due to Public Policy

Legal scholars generally accept that some issues are inarbitrable under Turkish law. The nature of arbitrability and the relationship between arbitrability and public policy make arbitration an inappropriate process for resolving disputes in some legal areas. These areas include criminal procedure,[340] *ex parte* proceedings,[341] disputes in relation to charitable foundations and associations,[342] and disputes concerning administrative law[343] (except disputes arising from concession bargaining and agreements about public service, as previously stated,[344] and the legal actions of administration that are subject to private law).[345] Disputes regarding dispositive transactions involving goods the sale or purchase of which is prohibited are deemed null and void in Turkish law for public security purposes.[346] Such transactions are not subject to will of the parties and arbitral agreements about such goods are invalid.[347]

Disputes about consumer law[348] or disputes arising from individual labor agreements[349] also cannot be resolved through arbitration. Both are matters of

338 Feyiz Erdogan, p. 123.
339 Ziya Akıncı, Arbitration Law of Turkey, p. 154.
340 Feyiz Erdogan p. 123.
Ziya Akıncı, Milletlerarası Tahkim, p. 80.
Suha Tanrıverdi, p. 86.
341 Nevhis Deren Yıldırım, Tahkim ve Objektif Acıdan Tahkime Elverislilik, p. 55 & n.41.
Feyiz Erdogan, p. 123.
Baki Kuru, vol.VI, p. 5951.
342 Mustafa Erkan, pp. 77.
343 Ziya Akıncı, Milletlerarası Tahkim, p. 80.
Suha Tanriverdi, p. 86.
344 *See supra* note 116 *et seq*. for further explanations.
345 Mustafa Erkan, pp. 77.
346 Rasih Yegengil, pp. 169.
347 *Id* at 170.
348 Mustafa Erkan, p. 77.
349 Yavuz Alagonya, Medeni Usul Hukukumuzda Tahkimin Niteligi ve Denetlenmesi [Nature and Inspection of Arbitration in Our Civil Procedure Law] 84 (Fakulteler Matbaası, Istanbul 1973) [Faculties Press, Istanbul 1973].

private law, but the existence of a weaker interest in need of protection makes them inarbitrable.[350] The protection of the employee and the consumer receives priority as a matter of public policy.[351] [352] Recognition of weaker parties in Consumer Code[353] disputes stems from the fact that sellers or providers can put contract provisions in contracts unilaterally in the absence of negotiation with consumers. Such rules may violate the contractual rights and duties of consumers, breaching the utmost good faith rule.[354] Adhesive contracts are unfair to consumers and, as a result, are not legally binding. Arbitral clauses

---

Mustafa Erkan, p. 77.
Nevhis Deren, Tahkim ve Objektif Acıdan Tahkime Elverislilik, p. 54.
Feyiz Erdogan, p. 123.
Ziya Akıncı, Milletlerarası Tahkim, p. 82.

350 Ali Yesilırmak, Turkiye'de Ticari Hayatın ve Yatırım Ortamının Iyilestirilmesi Icin Uyusmazlıkların Etkin Cozumunde Dogrudan Gorusme, Arabuluculuk, Hakem-Bilirkisilik ve Tahkim: Sorunlar ve Cozum Onerileri [Reconciliation, Mediation, Arbitral Referree and Arbitration for the Effective Resolution of Disputes in Order for Optimization of Commercial Life and Investment Environment: Problems and Solution Suggestions] 85 (On Iki Levha Yayıncılık, 1. Baskı, Istanbul 2011) [On Iki Levha Publishing, 1st Ed. Istanbul 2011].

351 Explicit and direct legal regulations to be adopted can always enable arbitration of those disputes in a way protecting the rights of consumers and employees.

352 Ali Yesilırmak, p. 85.
Ziya Akıncı, Milletlerarası Tahkim, p. 82.

353 Turkish Code of Consumer Protection numbered 6502 published in the Official Gazette dated 11.28.2013 and numbered 28835. (This Code was numbered 4077 and dated 23.02.1995 until it was changed and new code numbered 6502 enacted. Therefore, the old-dated Supreme Court decisions mentions the Code numbered 4077.)

354 Turkish Supreme Court 13th Civil Circuit Decision dated 09/25/2006 numbered E.2006/7789 and K.2006/12275:

"...*In accordance with article 6 of the Code numbered 4077* (currently the Code numbered 6052), *contract provisions against the consumer causing instability in parties' rights and duties breach the utmost good faith principle. If the seller or provider unilaterally puts such provisions in the contract, those provisions would be unfair terms and not be binding for the consumer because they lack negotiation with the consumer. According to abovementioned article, one shall deem a contract provision not negotiated with the consumer if the contract provision is previously prepared and the consumer does not have an effect on that standard agreement. In the present case, it is clear that the package tour contract is a standardized contract consists of standard terms drawn up by the defendant. The defendant could not prove with an evidence that arbitral clause has been mutually agreed following a negotiation with the consumer plaintiff. Therefore, agreement eliminating the authorization of*

in such contracts are likewise not binding.[355] The aim is to protect consumers as weaker parties and lawmakers believe the courts can provide this protection more effectively than arbitrators.[356]

The Supreme Court has ruled that the Consumer Code aims to maintain the health, security, and economic interests of consumers; these aims are matters of public policy, which is why consumer courts have the jurisdiction over such disputes and any arbitral clauses in the consumer contracts are invalid.[357] The Supreme Court has also ruled that labor law disputes are not subject to the will of

---

Consumer Courts for resolution of disputes arising from the contract between the plaintiff consumer and defendant has no binding effect on plaintiff…"

355 Ziya Akıncı, Milletlerarası Tahkim, p. 90.

356 *Id* at 88.

357 *Id* at p. 89 & n.163. Turkish Supreme Court 13th Civil Circuit Decision dated 09/25/2008 numbered E.2008/3492 and K.2008/11120:

"…the purview of article 1 of the Turkish Code of Consumer Protection numbered 4077 (currently numbered 6502) states that "The purview of this Code is to take the measures maintaining health and security and economic interests of consumers in accordance with public interest; informing; educatory; compensative for damages; maintaining protection from environmental risks and incenting the attempts of consumers to protect themselves and regularizing the issues about incenting voluntary policy-making organizations in this respect". Article 2 defines the content as "This code contains any type of consumer transaction of which one party is consumer in product and service market with the purposes mentioned in Article 1". Article 3 includes definitions with regard to the application of the Code. Article 22, then, states that Arbitration Committee for Consumer Problems will be established in addition to the conditions for referring to the Committee compulsorily or voluntarily. Article 23 underlines that consumer courts shall hear any type of dispute arising from application of this Code. Reviewing the purview and provisions of the Code numbered 4077, the lawmaker has clearly drafted it in compliance with social and financial developments of contemporary law aiming at protecting the consumers who are weaker and in need of wider protection than the seller, supplier etc.

Article 172 of Turkish Constitution, indeed, foresees that "The State shall take the measures informing and educating the consumers and incent the self-protective attempts of consumers". The State undertakes protection of health and security and economic interests of consumers and informing are firstly based on the Constitution. The Code aims at protecting public policy, providing social order, justice and harmony between consumers and sellers / suppliers etc. The Code targets maintaining public policy as well as protecting the consumer, and it is beyond doubt that this is a special Code directly related to public policy. One shall infer, therefore, that the law-maker has tacitly barred private arbitration from establishing an arbitration committee as the Arbitration Committee for Consumer Problems in accordance

the parties (employee and employer) and can only be resolved before labor courts. Arbitral clauses adopted in contracts by the parties (employee and employer) with regard to the resolution of disputes arising from a service (labor) contract that is subject to Labor Code[358] are void in Turkish law.[359] In related decisions, the Turkish Supreme Court acknowledges that the nature of labor contracts makes it possible for one party to use economic and social advantage to create situations in which the stronger party can benefit from its leverage.[360] Cases against employees cannot, therefore, be submitted to arbitration, especially in the context of labor contracts. Employers and employees do not have an equal power of negotiation. Depriving employees, who are economically weaker, of their natural judge—the labor court—is not rational. [361] Professor *Kuru* criticizes this approach, however, arguing that it inaccurately interprets statutory law, even if it is fair as a matter of natural law. He contends that the parties have free disposition over disputed matters by way of settlement in labor cases.[362] Labor cases are, therefore, subject to will of the parties, which is why arbitral agreements in labor cases should be deemed valid.

The Turkish Constitutional Court barred[363] arbitration of disputes arising from the Legal Practitioners Act in Turkey. [364] It claimed that arbitration of such

with Article 22 of this Code. The Code explicitly designates the authorized court, and thus, consumer courts or consumer arbitration committees shall certainly settle the disputes arising from application of this Code depending on the amount. Private arbitrators, therefore, cannot resolve any type of dispute on application of this Code considering the statement in Article 23 entitling the consumer courts. In the present case, the dispute arising from the package tour holiday contract between the parties falls within the ambit of Code numbered 4077 articles of 1,2, 3/c-f and 23. Arbitral clause in the contract, thus, is invalid because consumer courts are authorized for resolution of the dispute. Arbitrators are not entitled to resolve the dispute. The award rendered by the arbitral tribunal is, therefore, on the contrary of the proceedings and the statute shall be reversed in accordance with Turkish Code of Civil Procedure Article 533/3 as it is beyond the arbitral tribunal's jurisdiction."

358 Numbered 4857 and enacted on 05/22/2003 with publishing on Official Gazette dated 06/10/2003 and numbered 25134.

359 Baki Kuru, Vol.VI, p. 5951 & n.41.

360 Turkish Supreme Court 9th Civil Circuit Decision dated 01/20/2009 numbered E.2008/44630 and K.2009/537 (Ziya Akıncı Milletlerarası Tahkim, p. 82 & n.154).

361 Ziya Akıncı, Milletlerarası Tahkim, pp. 82–83.

362 Baki Kuru, Vol.VI, p. 5951.

363 Constitutional Court decision numbered E2003/98, K2004/31 and dated 03.03.2004 published in the Official Gazette dated 07/10/2004. (10/07//2004/25518).

364 Ali Yesilırmak, p. 85 & n.268.

disputes, which relate to public policy, violates the Turkish Constitution.[365] The relevant statutory provision in the Legal Practitioners Act, numbered 1136, which was cancelled by the Constitutional Court, is as follows:

> Article 167: *Resolution of Disputes through Arbitration:* [366]
> *Any disputes arising from attorney agreements and attorney fees shall be resolved by the Arbitral Tribunal of the Bar where the legal aid is provided…*[367]

The Constitutional Court prohibited the arbitration of the disputes between attorneys and clients through the Arbitral Tribunal of the Bar because most tribunal members are attorneys; parties can also appeal this tribunal's decisions based on Articles 533 (2) (3) (4) of the Turkish Code of Civil Procedure.[368] Finally, the court found that the repealed Article 167 violated Articles 9 and 36 of the Turkish Constitution. Article 9 provides that "*Judicial power shall be used by independent courts on behalf of the Turkish nation.*" Article 36, meanwhile, stipulates: "*Everyone has the right to claim, defend, and receive due process as claimants or defendants before judicial authorities using legitimate methods. No court shall refuse to hear a case within its jurisdiction.*"[369]

---

365 *Ibid.*

366 The title of the article was "*Cases Concerning Attorney' Fees to be Filed by Attorneys*" prior to amendment made by article 80 of the Code numbered 4667 and dated 05/02/2001.

367 Article 167 follows as:

> "…*Arbitral tribunal shall consist of the senior civil court of first instance judge in the judicial location of the bar and two attorneys eligible for Board of Directors to be designated by the Board of Directors of the Bar. The judge of the civil court of first instance presides at the Tribunal. The elected tribunal members serve for three years. The members whose terms expires can be re-elected.*
>
> *Half of the arbitrator's fee shall be paid with the case. One copy of the decision given by the arbitral tribunal and finalized shall be sent to the bar of the attorney.*
>
> *Regulations of Turkish Code of Civil Procedure numbered 1086 concerning arbitration except articles 527, 529, 532, 533/1 and 536 shall be applied to arbitral proceedings. Other issues about arbitral proceedings shall be regulated in Bar Arbitration Bylaw to be issued by Union of Turkish Bar Associations.*"

368 Constitutional Court decision numbered E2003/98, K2004/31 and dated 03.03.2004 published in the Official Gazette dated 07/10/2004. (10/07//2004/25518).

369 *Ibid.*

The Supreme Court's approach paralleled that of the Constitutional Court prior to the cancellation of the provision concerning arbitration. The Supreme Court previously held that arbitral clauses in attorney's fee agreements were invalid because some provisions of the Legal Practitioners Act concerning attorney's fees involve public policy[370] The Court found that these provisions exceeded freedom of contract in Turkish law and it highlighted that it (the Supreme Court) cannot review conflicting arbitral awards.[371] Recent decisions indicate that the Court's view has changed. The Court now holds that arbitral clauses in attorney agreements (and concluding an arbitration agreement regarding attorney's fee) are valid.[372]

The most controversial issues related to arbitrability and public policy in Turkish legal doctrine and court decisions have to do with immovable property.[373] Some doctrinal commentators argue that disputes arising from immovable property are inarbitrable because contracts to transfer immovable property

---

370 Turkish Supreme Court 13th Civil Circuit Decision dated 09/26/1974 and numbered 2385/2161 (Yargıtay Kararları Dergisi [Journal of Supreme Court Decisions] 1976/1 pp. 75–76).

"*...freedom of contract principle prevails in Turkish law within some exceptions such as of Turkish Code of Contract articles 19 and 20. Lawmaker has stipulated restrictive provisions on agreements of attorney's fee based on public policy and certainly forbidden the acts conflicting with these provisions. The articles 129,130, 131 of former Legal Practitioners Act numbered 3499 and articles 164, 168, 169 of current Legal Practitioners Act numbered 3499 have, thus, similar mandatory regulations. Those regulations states that the contracts about pursuing the lawsuit and any kind of consultancy fee will be in writing; no evidence will be cited except written agreement in the cases arising from the fee; minimum attorneyship fee tariff will be applied in the events that a written fee agreement does not exist, in so far as such amount will not exceed %25 of the subject of the case or decision; the fact that an attorney will not have a share in the subject matter as if he is a party and such agreements will be null and void. These provisions involve public policy and judicial review of conflicting arbitral awards by Supreme Court is not possible. Disputes about attorney's fee, therefore, cannot be resolved by arbitrators. This and other Supreme Court circuits have had the tendency in this direction since before now. The fact that the arbitrators have decided on a dispute arising from agreement of attorney's fee on the contrary of these provisions requires reversal...*"

371 Baki Kuru, Vol. V, pp. 5369, 5370.

372 Baki Kuru, Vol. V, p. 5370.

373 *See supra* note 78 for further explanation.

have to be done officially.[374] The majority of commentators, however, disagree.[375] They argue that disputes regarding immovable property are arbitrable because such disputes can be settled by the parties.[376] In a 1979 decision, likewise, the Turkish Supreme Court ruled in favor of defendants who followed the adjustment proceedings required by the land registry in accordance with the construction contract dated 08/07/1972 to restore their immovable property shares.[377] It stated that "*Parties can perform such act in law freely. These kinds of acts shall be deemed as subject to the will of the parties. The settling of such disputes by way of arbitration does not contravene the law. It does not relate to public policy.*" The Turkish Supreme Court has, however, issued several decisions regarding the inarbitrability of matters related to *in rem* rights on immovable property.[378]

Personal law, family law,[379] [380] and inheritance law provisions are also involved in public policy; legal scholars, therefore, regard disputes arising from these areas of law as inarbitrable.[381] Compensation claims resulting from the infringement of personal rights are monetary and, therefore, at the free disposition of claimants.[382] Compensation claims made after the compensation is due are subject to the same rules as general debt claims.[383] No contrary regulation exists and monetary claims are eligible for settlement and waiver; claims regarding compensation arising from the infringement of personal rights are, therefore,

374 Ilhan E. Postacıoglu, Medeni Usul Hukuku Dersleri [Lectures on Civil Procedure Law] 646 (6. Basi, Istanbul, 1975) [6th ed. Istanbul 1975].

375 Nevhis Deren Yıldırım, Objektif Acıdan Tahkime Elverislilik, p. 54.

376 *Ibid.*

377 Baki Kuru, Vol.VI, p. 5948. Turkish Supreme Court 15th Civil Circuit decision dated 05/31/1979 numbered 1195/1330 (*See supra* note 202 for the further text of the case).

378 Nevhis Deren Yıldırım, Tahkim ve Objektif Acıdan Tahkime Elverislilik, p. 55 & n.40.

379 And divorce law (Ali Yesilırmak, p. 85).

380 Including law on paternity. (Nevhis Deren Yıldırım, Tahkim ve Objektif Acıdan Tahkime Elverislilik, p. 55)

381 Rasih Yegengil, p. 171.
Mustafa Erkan, p. 77.
Ali Yesilırmak, p. 85.
Nevhis Deren Yıldırım, Tahkim ve Objektif Acıdan Tahkime Elverislilik, p. 55.
Feyiz Erdogan, p. 123.
Baki Kuru, Vol. VI, p. 5951.

382 Rasih Yegengil, p. 171.

383 Actions of debt such as arising from sales agreement can be subject to arbitration agreement in Turkish Law. Supreme Court Assembly of Civil Chambers' rule dated 06/20/1973 numbered T/147–529

arbitrable.[384] Inheritance law provisions related to legal heirship are directly involved in public policy. Disputes about the certainty of relationships, descent or matrimony in the ratios designated by law, on the one hand, cannot be resolved through arbitration.[385] On the other hand, individuals can dispose of their rights before they die and those who inherit the rights are free to dispose of them after the original right-holders die.[386]

Turkish law also deems bankruptcy cases to be inarbitrable.[387] The law aims to protect other creditors.[388] As expressed in case law: "…*Arbitral clauses are valid for disputes that do not involve public policy. Bankruptcy cases relate to public policy and do not satisfy this condition.*…"[389] Finally, the law states that disputes about intellectual property rights, competition law, bribery, and taxation as well as allegations of corruption and bribery resulting from contracts cannot be resolved through arbitration because they relate to domestic public policy.[390] [391]

"…*the subject of the agreement and the dispute is about sales contract which is not a matter that is not subject to will of the parties… there is no side of the contract between the parties or of the subject matter against public policy, the dispute arising this shall be heard and settled before the arbitrator* …"

See supra note 73 for further explanations of related Supreme court decisions. (Baki Kuru, Vol.VI, p. 5946)
Rasih Yegengil, p. 171.

384 Rasih Yegengil, p. 171.

385 *Id* at 172.

386 *Ibid.*

387 Ali Yesilırmak, p. 85.
Nevhis Deren Yıldırım, Tahkim ve Objektif Acıdan Tahkime Elverislilik, p. 55.
Feyiz Erdogan, p. 123.
Baki Kuru, Vol.VI, p. 5951 & n.39.
Ziya Akıncı, Milletlerarası Tahkim, p. 81.

388 Feyiz Erdogan, p. 123.

389 İİD 13.2.1969, 1332/1729: İBD 1970(1-2 s.101) [Supreme Court Enforcement and Bankruptcy Office, General Assembly on the Unification of Judgement Decision] (Baki Kuru, Vol.VI, p. 5951 & n.39).

390 Mustafa Erkan, p. 77.

391 In addition, there are some other issues that fall within the content of public policy beyond doubt in most jurisdictions. Slave trade, slavery, piracy, terrorism, genocide, use of force, arrest or kill unjustly, religious; race or sex discrimination are the examples of those issues. As they are not at the core of the topic, the book will not give detailed information about each of those issues. One shall note, however, that

b) *International Public Policy under Turkish Law (*Ordre Public International*)*

The notion of public policy has a different meaning in the context of private international law disputes than in domestic law.[392] Cases are related to imperative rules and are involved in public policy in domestic law. They may not, however, be involved in public policy in the context of private international law.[393] [394] The range of international public policy is narrower than domestic public policy[395] because domestic public policy has a limited role in international arbitration.[396] Domestic public policy includes the *direct application of imperative rules even if they contradict the will of the parties.* International public policy, however, relates to *applicable laws: namely, restrictions on the application of such laws in private law relationships with an international character.*[397] The term 'international' in the context of public policy refers to intervention in the application of foreign laws to the cases with an international character.[398]

Legal scholars have two theories about the legal characteristics and functions of public policy in private international law.[399] *Pasquale Mancini*, who represented the Italian School, developed the first theory, and French scholar *Antoinne Pillet*

---

any contract or decision among corporations about those issues shall also be invalid due to public policy.
(Cemal Sanlı, Uluslararası Ticari Akitler, p. 390).

392 Suha Tanrıver, *Yabancı Hakem Kararlarının Turkiye'de Tenfizi Baglamında Kamu Duzeninin Etkisi* [*Effect of Public Policy in The Context of Enforcement of Foreign Arbitral Awards in Turkey*], MHB Yıl 17–18, (1997–98) [International Private Law Bulletin, Year 17–18 (1997–98)] p. 477.

393 Ziya Akıncı, Milletlerarası Tahkim, p. 271.

394 *I.e.* Turkish law domestically foresees regulations about the issue of legal age. A contrary regulation about legal age in a foreign law, however, does not violate Turkish public policy. (Kemal Dayınlarlı, p. 23)

395 Sulbha Rai, How Do or Should Arbitrators Deal with Domestic Public Policy or Regulatory Issues? Does It Affect Arbitrability? (2009) (Unpublished LLM Thesis, King's College, London) p. 8 (Available at: http://ssrn.com/abstract=1433799).

396 Domestic public policy, indeed, undertakes a duty in parallel with order and safety rules at many points. (Kemal Dayınlarlı, Kamu Duzeni p. 86).

397 Camal Sanlı, Esasa Uygulanacak Hukuk, p. 384.

398 Yılmaz Altug & Mustafa Yasan, p. 142.

399 Aysel Celikel & Bahadır Erdem, p. 150.
Kemal Dayınlarlı, pp. 10.

subsequently supported it.[400] [401] The first theory recognizes that public policy rules apply to the cases as conflict of laws rules.[402] The theory stipulates that public policy rules should apply directly regardless of the authorized law.[403] The theory maintains, in other words, that, regardless of the application of authorized foreign law, domestic rules should apply as a conflict of laws rule as long as they relate to public policy.[404] Scholars who support this theory argue that public policy rules apply in general not as an exception[405] because they function as conflict of laws rules. [406] Many scholars oppose the categorization of public policy rules as conflict of laws rules and few hold this view today.[407] Critics of this theory suggest that it mistakes the notion of public policy for the territoriality of laws.[408] They also criticize *Pillet's* notion that, under normal conditions,

---

400 Isadora Cipriani, The Public Policy Exception to the Enforcement of Foreign Arbitral Awards in Brazil (2012) (2009) (Unpublished LLM Thesis, Bucerius Law School) p. 25 (Available at: http://www.gbv.de/dms/buls/734889984.pdf).

401 *See* also André Garnefsky, Public Policy in Soviet Private International Law (2nd ed. Springer).

402 Kemal Dayınlarlı, p. 23.

403 Aysel Celikel & Bahadır Erdem p. 150.

404 Kemal Dayınlarlı, p. 23.
Aysel Celikel& Bahadır Erdem, p. 150.

405 A. Gunduz Okcun, Devletler Hususi Hukukunun Kaynakları ve Kamu Duzeni [Sources of International Public Law and Public Policy] 18 (Ankara, 1967).
The author states that domestic law applies to the relationships involving a foreign element in principle. Public policy rules, however, shall directly apply within the State of the jurisdiction as one of the instances to which domestic law cannot apply due to the fact that absolute personality principle cannot be adopted.

406 Kemal Dayınlarlı, p. 61. "Public policy is not more than general laws. If the law is connected to public policy with regard to its social aim, it is general. On the other hand, a general law is involved in public policy. Public policy law is a regulation which requires the application of foreign law. *Pillet* categorizes public policy laws as follows:

- Public policy laws,
- Laws with regard to security of the person,
- Laws on ownership,
- Laws on public credit,
- Execution laws,
- Financial Laws,
- Moral laws,
- Laws on public order."

407 Aysel Celikel& Bahadır Erdem, p. 150.

408 Public policy, therefore, does not generate a new conflict of laws rule.

authorized law should be recognized as domestic law.[409] Scholars point out that, on the contrary, in private international law, authorized and applicable laws are normally foreign laws.[410]

The second theory recognizes that public policy rules are not directly applicable but are the *exception* to the application of foreign authorized or selected law.[411] Scholars supporting this idea have "*...denied that lex fori takes precedence over foreign law...*."[412] They suggest that authorized foreign law should, therefore, apply[413] unless such law yields results contrary to the public policy of the forum State.[414] In other words, they view public policy as an exception that interferes with the application of foreign law. The German scholar *Von Savigny* introduced this theory and the American scholar *Joseph Story* adopted it;[415] the German, English, and American legal systems also subscribe to it.[416] *Savigny* argues that two types of legal rules exist: those based on personal interests and those based on morality and the public interest.[417] He maintains that public policy considerations make the application of foreign laws that violate the latter unacceptable. [418]

French legal scholars have criticized *Pillet's* theory,[419] maintaining that public policy rules are exceptional in nature.[420] Turkey follows the French legal system

---

Kemal Dayınlarlı, p. 62. The author states the reasoning behind this idea as the question of;

"*If all territorial laws are both general and public-policy-related, is it necessary to resort to public policy notion for the authorization of territorial law, which is originally authorized; and thus, giving a place for this notion bigger than other notions in international private law just because it is a general law?*".

409 Kemal Dayınlarlı pp. 62–63.
410 *Id* at 63.
411 Aysel Celikel& Bahadır Erdem, p. 150.
412 Gerhard Kegel, 3 International Encyclopedia of Comparative Law; Chapter 3 Fundamental Approaches 7 (Kurt & eds., Brill Archive 1986).
413 Kemal Dayınlarlı, p. 24.
414 Yılmaz Altug- Mustafa Yasan, p. 145.
Aysel Celikel & Bahadır Erdem, p. 150.
415 Kemal Dayınlarlı, p. 24.
416 Aysel Celikel, & Bahadır Erdem, p. 150.
417 *Ibid.*
418 Kemal Dayınlarlı, p. 24.
419 Gunduz Okcun, p. 65.
420 Aysel Celikel& Bahadır Erdem, p. 151.

in this regard.[421] Most Turkish legal scholars recognize the exceptional nature of public policy rules.[422] It is a view that has considerable force.[423] The Turkish Supreme Court has, at different times, supported both theories. One decision,[424] which recognized the exceptional nature of public policy rules,[425] stated:

> *...to reach a conclusion, one must scrutinize and consider whether or not provisions of domestic law, which must apply to the case, violate public policy according to the Turkish Civil Code...*

Other decisions, however, have qualified public policy rules as conflict of law rules or have found that Turkish law applies because of public policy.[426] Most of

---

Kemal Dayınlarlı, p. 33: "*In the doctrine, French legal writers Bartin, Niboyet, Lerebourg-Pigeonniere, Donnedieu De Vebres have agreed on the issue that public policy constitutes an exception to the conflicts of law rules in international private law.*"

421 Gerhard Kegel, p. 8.

422 Aysel Celikel & Bahadır Erdem, p. 151 and other authors mentioned on p. 153 & n. 131.
Kemal Dayınlarlı, p. 33.
Yılmaz Altug & Mustafa Yasan, p. 145.
Cemal Ruhi & Yavuz Kaplan, p. 645.
There are other ideas on some issues in Turkish Law as Professor *Celikel* states, too. (p. 153). *I.e.*, capacity to act, mental illness, parentage, impediments to marriage such as one of the parties' being married in Turkish Code of Civil Procedure. Rules related to those issues shall apply in the cases with foreign factor. Therefore, those issues shall be considered as involved in public policy. In such case, Turkish law shall apply instead of the foreign law.

423 (Aysel Celikel & Bahadır Erdem, p. 151):
Other foreign jurisdictions adopt a similar approach in practice. German law accepts that public policy applies to exceptional cases. The provision of Introduction Law to German Civil Law (article 6) explicitly stresses the exceptional nature of public policy. ("*If application of a foreign law will give birth to results clearly on the contrary of fundamental principles of German law and especially does not comply with fundamental rights, it will not be applied.*")
English law accepts public policy as a rule which is an impediment to the application of the foreign law. The principle of domicile designates both authorized court and applicable law for the matters about status, capacity and family law which requires resorting to public policy for such matters.
American court decisions also adopt the same approach. Application of foreign provisions to the disputes arising from criminal law and financial law, administrative law and procedural law are rejected based on public policy notion.

424 Turkish Supreme Court 2th Civil Circuit decision dated 11/10/1960.

425 Aysel Celikel & Bahadır Erdem, p. 152.

426 *Id* at 151,152.

these decisions relate to issues of family law such as guardianship[427] and alimony in divorce proceedings.[428] Another Turkish Supreme Court decision raised the issue of time limits. The Court stated, "*Time limits do not involve public policy.*"[429] This opens room for the interpretation that public policy is not an exception to the application of foreign law.[430] If time limits are related to public policy, Turkish law, as opposed to foreign law, applies directly. The direct application of Turkish law violates contemporary views of public policy. Many criticized the decision in this regard; they also criticized the Court for approaching the imperative rules of domestic law in the same manner as violations of public policy.[431]

Turkish legal doctrine generally recognizes the *exceptional* character of public policy[432], despite the ambiguity in case law. Foreign laws authorized with regard to conflict of laws rules, therefore, apply in principle while public policy acts as an exception to the function of this principle.[433] Public policy rules, in other words, are not alternative conflict of laws rules; they act only as exceptional provisions.[434] The general nature of public policy rules and values may conflict with the notion of public policy's exceptional character.[435] Public policy rules apply to a wide range of issues. The application of these rules, however, remains

---

427 The reasoning of the decision was because the guardianship's being involved in public policy. Turkish Civil Code will, therefore, apply in the event of a conflict. This decision, however, disregards that the imperative rules of domestic law may not be involved in public policy in international private law. If application of a foreign law conflicting with these provisions have consequences violating Turkish public policy understanding, it may not be applied.
(*Id* at p. 151& n.127.)

428 Turkish Supreme Court 2th Civil Circuit decision dated 12/25/1952.

429 Turkish Supreme Court11th Civil Circuit decision dated 04/05/1979.

430 Aysel Celikel & Bahadır Erdem, p. 152.

431 *Ibid.*

432 Cemal Sanlı, Esasa Uygulanacak Hukuk, p. 384.
Feyiz Erdogan, p. 124.
Yılmaz Altug &Mustafa Yasan, p. 145.
Cemal Ruhi & Yavuz Kaplan, p. 645.
Gulgoren Tekinalp, Milletlerarası Ozel Hukuku [International Private Law] 35 (Istanbul 1997).

433 Osman Fazıl Berki, Devletler Hususi Hukuku, Kanun Ihtilafları [International Private Law, Conflicts of Law] 80 (Cilt 2, Ankara 1966) [Vol. 2, Ankara 1966].

434 Yılmaz Altug & Mustafa Yasan, p. 145.

435 *Ibid.*

conditional, meaning they should not be applied excessively or in a manner that overreaches their scope and underlying purpose.[436]

Other specific public policy regulations show a parallel tendency in Turkey. Legal scholars emphasize that public policy only intervenes when the application of a specific foreign law "*intolerably*" violates the fundamental philosophy and legal understanding that prevails in the *lex fori*.[437] This idea mainly stems from regulations in the related code. Article 5[438] of the Turkish Code on Private International Law and Civil Procedure[439] states:

> If a provision of an authorized foreign law, which is applied to a definite case, is *explicitly* contrary to Turkish public policy, this provision will not be applied; Turkish law will be applied when necessary.

Turkish law has adopted the theory of *renvoi* (recourse).[440] [441] Article 5 suggests that, in accordance with *renvoi*, Turkish adjudicators should apply foreign

---

436 *Ibid.*

437 Cemal Sanlı, Esasa Uygulanacak Hukuk, p. 384.

438 Entitled as "Contrariety to Public Policy".

439 Numbered 5718.

440 Huseyin Ali Sadrolesrafi, *Devletler Ozel Hukuku'nda Genel Olarak Atıf Teorisi (Renvoi)* [*A General View: Theory of Renvoi in International Private Law*], Kudret Ayiter'e Armagan; Dokuz Eylul Universitesi Hukuk Fakultesi Dergisi Cilt 3 Sayı 1–4 Ankara, 1988 [Dedication for Kudret Ayıter; Dokuz Eylul University Faculty of Law Journal Vol.3 Issue 1–4 Ankara, 1988] p. 521.

441 Turkish Code on Private International Law and Civil Procedure,

"*Article 2: Application of Foreign Law*

(1) *Adjudicator applies Turkish conflict of laws rules and the foreign law authorized in accordance with these rules ex officio. Adjudicator may request the contribution of the parties to determine the content of the authorized foreign law.*
(2) *Turkish law will be applied in the event that related provisions of foreign law cannot be determined despite all the research.*
(3) *Authorizing another law by the conflict of laws rules of the law to be applied is taken into consideration only for the disputes related to law of persons and family law and set of rules of this law is applied.*
(4) *In the events that recourse to the law to be applied is allowed, set of rules of the law chosen is applied unless contrary is agreed.*
(5) *If the State, of which the law will be applied, has two or more regional unit and these regional units have different law systems, what regional law to be applied will be determined in accordance with the law of that State. In the absence of*

laws,[442] unless they "explicitly" contradict public policy. It stipulates that, in the case of such an explicit contradiction, the adjudicator should set the foreign law aside and resolve the dispute by applying the *lex fori*. [443] Article 5's use of the term "explicit" aims to preclude its application to "any" provision that does not parallel Turkish laws related to public policy.[444] The violation must be obvious and cause intolerable results because of public policy.[445] Article 5 of the Turkish Code on Private International Law and Civil Procedure articulates both the positive and negative effects of public policy:

- Public policy's "negative effect" impedes the application of provisions of authorized foreign law when they contradict public policy;
- Its "positive effect" fills the legal gap arising from the impeded application of authorized foreign law with Turkish legal provisions. [446]

Another regulation related to public policy in the Turkish legal system involves the recognition and enforcement of awards. Article 54[447] of the Turkish Code on Private International Law and Civil Procedure[448] stipulates that the authorized court may render the decision of recognition if the order does not

---

a determinative provision in the law of that State, the regional unit law that is relating most closely to the dispute applies."

442 Cemal Ruhi & Yavuz Kaplan, p. 645.
443 *Ibid.*
Aysel Celikel & Bahadır Erdem, p. 156.
444 Cemal Ruhi &Yavuz Kaplan, p. 645.
Aysel Celikel& Bahadır Erdem, p. 156.
445 Aysel Celikel& Bahadır Erdem, p. 156.
446 Cemal Ruhi & Yavuz Kaplan, p. 645.
Aysel Celikel & Bahadır Erdem, p. 157.
447 "Article 54:

Authorized court renders the decisions of recognition on the following conditions:

...

(c) *The order's not being explicitly on the contrary of public policy.*

..."

448 Turkish Code on Private International Law and Civil Procedure numbered 5718. It was article 38 in Turkish Code on Private International Law and Civil Procedure numbered 2675 enacted on 05/10/1982 and published on Official Gazette dated 05/22/1982 and numbered 17701 which was previously effective.

explicitly violate public policy.[449] Judges should, therefore, take this condition into consideration *ex officio*.[450] These regulations clearly support the notion of public policy's exceptional character in Turkish law.

3. Final Review and Evaluation of Public Policy Notion in Turkish Law

The factors outlined above justify efforts to minimize the public policy interventions especially in international disputes allowed in Turkish law. Instances of public policy violations are variable. Regulating all possibilities in advance is impossible. Legislation that aims to limit the application of public policy and allows for subsequent adjustments to clarify the regulation would be one way to address this problem. Another way would be to give authorized judges (*i.e.*, in cases involving setting aside or recognizing arbitral awards) the right of judicial discretion. Rejecting the domestic law approach would prove more judicious. Judges should approach the evaluation of violations of public policy in a manner consistent with the characteristics of international arbitral practice.[451] This approach would give judges a decisive role in the adjudication of cases about setting aside or recognizing arbitral awards. It would entrust them with the task of being more selective and hesitant when considering public policy intervention in arbitral decisions involving foreign characteristics.[452]

Judges should have as narrow a role as possible in the application of public policy to international cases. The reality is, however, that national courts should administer justice based on the legal systems of the States they belong to.[453]

---

449 There are two different ideas about examining the foreign court orders in terms of public policy:

The first idea lays emphasis on the legal rule that the foreign court applies. It propounds that it is sufficient if the recognition judge finds the rule conflicting with the public policy of the State of recognition independently from the case.

The second idea, however, predicates upon the content and consequences of foreign order. Namely, one should consider the legal consequences that the foreign court order may cause while evaluating public policy. The judge shall evaluate the consequences rather than solely evaluating the legal rules that the foreign court has applied.

It can be said in accordance with article 54 that Turkish law adopts the latter. (Ruhi- Kaplan, p. 647)

450 Cemal Ruhi &Yavuz Kaplan, p. 646.

451 Ziya Akıncı, Milletlerarası Tahkim, p 273.

452 Feyiz Erdogan, p. 125.

453 Cemal Sanlı, Esasa Uygulanacak Hukuk, p. 392.

The national courts' dependence on State legal systems is a natural consequence of the obligation to protect and maintain the legal apparatus supporting the social, political and economic order of the forum State. Every national court, therefore, considers whether applicable law or the foreign award subject to enforcement is in compliance with some elements such as the fundamental legal principles and understanding of legal concepts in the forum State.[454] They take the public policy and politics of *lex fori* into account.[455]

Arbitral tribunals are not bound by *lex fori* even though they conduct adjudicatory activity like courts.[456] The following points support this conclusion:

- Arbitrators who work in an international context consider the legal systems of many countries, usually regarding commercial law;[457]
- The authority of arbitrators derives only from a private contract between parties;[458]
- Arbitrators do not conduct judiciary activity on behalf of the State with an official title;[459]
- Arbitrators have different nationalities themselves most of the time; [460]
- Arbitrators hear cases and render decisions wherever the parties, through various tools, choose (arbitration can, for instance, take place at sea or on a plane without settling in a State or by way of reciprocal phone, telex or letter).[461]

International commercial law arbitrators thus do not have a *lex fori* in the traditional sense.[462] Nor are arbitrators[463] obliged to consider the public policy interventions of States during the application of the law to disputes or contractual

454 *Ibid.*
455 *Ibid.*
456 Mehmet Tas, p. 21.
457 Feyiz Erdogan, p. 127.
Cemal Sanlı, Esasa Uygulanacak Hukuk, p. 392.
458 *Ibid.*
459 Feyiz Erdogan, p. 127.
Cemal Sanlı, Esasa Uygulanacak Hukuk, pp. 392–393.
460 Feyiz Erdogan, p. 127.
Cemal Sanlı, Esasa Uygulanacak Hukuk, p. 393.
461 Cemal Sanlı, Esasa Uygulanacak Hukuk, p. 393.
462 Mehmet Tas, p. 21.
Cemal Sanlı, Esasa Uygulanacak Hukuk, p. 393.
Feyiz Erdogan, p. 127.
463 Who do not have any *lex fori*.

regulations agreed to by the parties.[464] A "foreign" law violating the *lex fori* public policy must be present to warrant public policy intervention regarding applicable laws in court jurisdictions.[465] Because arbitral tribunals and arbitrators have no explicit national legal system, however, no laws with a "foreign" nature exist in the context of international commercial arbitration.[466]

The fact that arbitrators may not have a *lex fori* or be bound by public policy in the traditional sense does not mean that public policy doctrines have no role in international commercial arbitration.[467] Like courts, arbitrators are obligated to comply with the fundamental principles of law, morality, and justice of the State where the arbitration takes place.[468] Therefore, "*arbitrators have the right—and even the obligation—themselves to raise the issue of whether disputed contracts or legal provisions put before them satisfy the requirements of international public policy.*" [469] There are several reasons for this. Firstly, as Professor *Sanlı* points outs:

> *...International commercial law arbitrators are responsible, in particular, for the parties who have given them judicial authority, and, in general, for international commerce and the society that carries out the commerce. Indeed, international commercial arbitration institutions and their arbitrators function as an International Commercial Court and seem to undertake a significant responsibility to regulate the relationships between those who carry out the commerce. Arbitration will remain a preferred judicial method in private legal relationships with an international character and be developed as long as arbitration institutions and arbitrators can satisfy their responsibility. Therefore, arbitrators' responsibilities, which are to the parties that have chosen them in particular and to the international commercial community in general, require them to take various public policies into consideration as each concrete case dictates....*[470]

This general conclusion stems from the notion and rationale of international commercial arbitration. Certain additional, practical scenarios require arbitrators to apply public policy. The *raison d'être* of arbitration is obviously the awards given by arbitrators. It is important that parties volunteer to comply with these awards.[471] When parties intentionally disregard the decision, national courts have the

---

464 Cemal Sanlı, Esasa Uygulanacak Hukuk, p. 393.

465 This law can either be chosen by the parties or determined in accordance with the conflict of laws rules.

466 Cemal Sanlı, Esasa Uygulanacak Hukuk, p. 393.

467 Feyiz Erdogan, p. 127.

468 *Ibid.*

469 Devin Bray & Heather L. Bray, International Arbitration and Public Policy 41 & n.94 (Juris Publishing, Inc. 2014).

470 Cemal Sanlı, Esasa Uygulanacak Hukuk, pp. 393–394.

471 *Id* at 394.

authority to enforce. The court may decide to set aside or not enforce the decision. This would jeopardize the entire arbitral proceeding and undermine the parties' aims. International commercial law arbitrators should, therefore, take into consideration the public policies of national law systems[472] as a practical precaution.[473]

Arbitrators are responsible for the enforceability of their decisions. The most effective factor in the enforcement of a decision is its quality.[474] Arbitral tribunals must attempt to satisfy the requirements for the recognition and enforceability of their decisions. They can accomplish this by disabling possible successful claims against their decisions should a court need to rule on enforcement.[475] The party that loses a case will obey the award when it perceives that it cannot successfully appeal enforcement of the decision before a court. A high-quality decision can, in this sense, preclude court intervention.[476] These practical concerns dictate that arbitrators should consider specific public policy rules that each case requires for minimizing the risk of review and strengthening enforceability.

It is important to clarify which public policy rules relate to the case. The public policy of the State where the arbitral award will be enforced[477] or recognized[478] [479]

---

472 Which are in relation to the arbitration or the parties.

473 Cemal Sanlı, Esasa Uygulanacak Hukuk, p. 394.

474 Pierre Lalive, *Enforcing Awards in 60 Years of ICC Arbitration: A Look at the Future* (ICC Publication no.412, 1984) p. 349.

475 Isılar Umut Mutlu, p. 226.

476 Andreas Bucher, *Court Intervention in Arbitration, in* International Arbitration in the 21st Century: Towards "Judicialization" and Uniformity? (Richard B. Lillich & Charles Nelson Brower eds., Brill – Nijhoff 1994) p. 38.
Isılar Umut Mutlu, n.227.

477 The major problem while taking the public policy into consideration is being unable to know the State or States where the enforcement of the arbitral award will be requested at an early stage of arbitration. The sole remedy, here, is to consider any State that the party, who the arbitral award is given against, has his business, quarters or assets as the State of enforcement. (*See* Cemal Sanlı, Esasa Uygulanacak Hukuk, p. 396).

478 Feyiz Erdogan, p. 131.

479 On the other hand, this issue has been subject to some criticisms for the infringement of the party autonomy principle. Arbitrators has explained taking transnational public policy into consideration with a similar approach as follows:

"Since the source of an arbitrator's decision-making authority is not necessarily linked to any particular State, it seems that 'basing a decision on transnational public policy is nevertheless more consistent with the transnational source of the arbitrators' decision-making powers than the application of mandatory rules other than those of the law chosen by the

ranks in highest priority. The main conventions[480] that regulate the enforcement of arbitral awards related to international commerce stipulate that the award must comply with the public policy of the State in which enforcement is requested.[481] The public policy of the State where the arbitral award was rendered or the arbitration proceedings took place is also important.[482] Arbitrators analyze arbitral jurisdictions as a component of the general judicial order of the seat of arbitration and thus naturally give importance to the public policy of the seat of arbitration.[483] The public policy rules of the seat of arbitration have a crucial

---

parties. However, one of the main criticisms against allowing arbitrators to apply transnational public policy is that this may permit them to override the parties' own choice of law. Allowing arbitrators to override party autonomy in the name of transnational public policy may grant the arbitral tribunal a greater discretion than was envisioned by the parties when they elected to submit their dispute to arbitration:

It would mean that arbitrators have a discretion to override the applicable law, commonly chosen by the parties, and to substitute a view concerning the enforceability of the contract or the nature of the contractual obligations assumed by the parties, founded on what might be considered rather vague, loose or uncertain criteria."

(*See* Devin Bray & Heather L. Bray, International Arbitration and Public Policy pp. 38–39 for further explanations.)

(*See* Feyiz Erdogan, p. 132.)

480 For the recognition or enforcement of an arbitral award, the condition of arbitral award's compliance with the public policy and legal principles of the State, where the enforcement or recognition is requested, is first regulated in article I (e) of Geneva Convention on the Execution of Foreign Arbitral Awards 1927.

(*See supra* note 251 for further explanation.)

Likewise, it is regulated in New York Convention on the Recognition and Enforcement of Foreign Arbitral Awards article V (2) that:

"*Recognition and enforcement of an arbitral award may also be refused if the competent authority in the country where recognition and enforcement is sought finds that:*

(a) *The subject matter of the difference is not capable of settlement by arbitration under the law of that country; or*
(b) *The recognition or enforcement of the award would be contrary to the public policy of that country.*"

481 Feyiz Erdogan, p. 131.
Cemal Sanlı, Esasa Uygulanacak Hukuk, p. 396.

482 Kemal Dayınlarlı, p. 100.
Feyiz Erdogan, p. 132.

483 Feyiz Erdogan, p. 132.

impact on issues including the arbitration proceedings, the validity of the arbitral agreement or clause, the validity and binding nature of arbitral awards, and the arbitrability of the disputed matter.[484] In addition, it can be an institutional arbitration instead of an ad-hoc arbitration.

In such cases, the arbitral tribunal may need to consider the public policy rules of the State in which the arbitration occurs. Arbitrators should consider the positive and negative effects of public policy to prevent the arbitral award from being set aside.[485] [486] A sufficient connection between the State and arbitration must also exist for the State to justify judicial intervention in to the arbitral process. French law calls this the "softened effect" (*effet attenué*) of public policy.[487] [488] Whether the fact that the arbitration occurs within a State's territory constitutes a sufficient connection for intervention remains controversial.[489] States are frequently related in some way to the arbitration that occurs within their borders. Parties may, on the other hand, choose to undertake arbitral proceedings in a particular State for convenience or objectivity. The State in which the arbitration occurs cannot impose its own public policy unless it is not bound to do so for social or legal reasons.[490]

Transnational public policy, which involves more than one country and consists, in part, of the *lex mercatoria* may also include the general principles that

---

484 *Ibid.*

485 According to the definition of Federal Court, observance of positive public policy means that arbitrator cannot render arbitral decision explicitly incompatible with the fundamental principles of Swiss Law. With reference to the matters obligatory to comply with positive public policy, one can say that public policy requires applying some international mandatory rules independently of the law to be applied to the arbitration. *I.e.* sanction of an arbitral tribunal's failing to comply with Swiss public policy in an arbitral decision, of which the place of arbitration is Switzerland, is invalidity of the decision. That is why, Intercantonal Arbitration Convention "Concordat" (1969) states that parties can claim cancellation of the arbitral award due to the violation of the mandatory procedural rules.

See Antonio Monti, *Arbitration and Corporation in* Three Essays on International Commercial Arbitration, Ed. Antonio Monti, Francesco Trezzini & Francesco Wicki (2002) (*available at* http://www.montiswisslaw.com/wp-content/uploads/2017/01/International_Commercial_Arbitration.pdf) pp. 12.

486 Kemal Dayınlarlı, pp. 103, 104.

487 "*Binnenbeziehung*" condition in Swiss and German case law.

488 Kemal Dayınlarlı, p. 104.

489 Isılay Umut Mutlu, n.260.

490 Kemal Dayınlarlı, p. 106.

international public law imposes on practitioners of international commerce.[491] The prohibition of corruption, for example, is related to such a public policy.[492] The parties' obligation to engage in arbitral proceedings with the utmost good faith is another example of the application of transnational public policy.[493] [494] Finally, arbitrators may need to consider other public policies including *lex contractus* during arbitration because that law will apply to the substance of the dispute.[495] The public policy of the State in which the subject of the dispute is registered could require similar consideration.[496]

This section has examined the list of public policies to be considered during arbitral proceedings for two reasons. First, the section highlights these policies to minimize the risk of the non-enforcement or setting aside of an arbitral award due to public policy. Second, the section emphasizes that Turkish public policy will inevitably come into play in arbitration. Questions of inarbitrability and especially public policy are dynamic and influenced by various factors, and they differ from one State to another. This chapter examined doctrinal approaches, legal regulations, and general practices including court decisions to make the Turkish approach clear. It demonstrated that Turkish Supreme Court has rendered some contradicting decisions. These court decisions have even interpreted the content of public policy notion so widely that it includes ruling against arbitrability from time to time.[497] In its more recent decisions, however, the Turkish Supreme Court has rendered opinions favoring arbitration against

491 *Id* at 100.
Cemal Sanlı, Esasa Uygulanacak Hukuk, pp. 404, 405.

492 Kemal Dayınlarlı, p. 101.

493 *Ibid.*

494 This chapter does not include the doctrinal debates or theories about international public policy in detail because it is a topic as wide as constituting a basis for another dissertation. This chapter only mentions the topic among other public policies.

495 Isılay Umut Mutlu, n. 294 & 295.

496 Cemal Sanlı, Esasa Uygulanacak Hukuk p. 401.

497 Okan Demirkan & Burak Eryigit, *Developing Court Practice in Turkey Regarding Applications to Set Aside Arbitral Awards*, 26:4 Am. Rev. Int'l Arb. 596 (2015). (*Citing*: 16th Commercial Court of Istanbul decision numbered 2013/157 and dated 08/20/2013:

"*There is no conclusive definition of public policy in legislation or doctrine. One can observe particularly in terms of Turkish International Private Law, however, in the Court of Appeals' decisions that elements such as contradiction with public morality and customs, incoherence with the fundamental rules and the general policy of Turkish laws are considered as a violation of public policy. In order for public policy to come into question,*

public policy intervention. Whether disputes arising from the bankruptcy law are arbitrable or they involve public policy, to illustrate, was controversial in Turkish law. More specifically, whether a plaintiff can file a motion to dismiss the objections of a defendant; or, request a denial compensation in arbitration remains ambiguous.[498] In accordance with the rulings of the Turkish Supreme Court, Turkish courts have finally accepted that this issue does not involve public policy; and thus, arbitrators can hear such cases.[499] This is an important development in Turkish law. Other recent Court decisions, indeed, follow this tendency to limit intervention on the basis of broad public policy concerns.[500] The policy adopted regarding international disputes, therefore, differs from the one adopted for domestic disputes in Turkish law. "*In any case, the concept of public policy is interpreted more narrowly in international arbitration then in domestic arbitration.*" [501] Continuance of this tendency would result in an arbitration-friendly[502] Turkey, which makes it a hospitable forum for arbitration because it has a consistent and reliable legal practice on arbitration.

The categorical separation of regulations for international arbitration and domestic arbitration in Turkish law has a practical rationale. It aims to apply a more flexible set of rules to international arbitration—as international commercial practice requires. The need to minimize domestic law interventions in international arbitration stems from this aim.[503] It does not, however, eliminate the crucial power of public policy in arbitral proceedings. Violations of public policy jeopardize the entire arbitration process. The specific regulations and interpretations of public policy in Turkish law are very important. To resolve commercial disputes, arbitrators must consider such issues. These issues relate

---

the contradiction with a rule must violate one of the fundamental principles of the local legal order or severely damage the general sense of law."

498 Okan Demirkan & Burak Eryigit, p. 596.

499 *Id* at 596 & n.19. (2013 *Citing* 44th Commercial Court of Istanbul, 2013/268 numbered, 12/19/2013 dated.)

500 *Id* at 596–597.
(4th Civil Court of Ankara decision numbered 2013/273 dated 01/21/2014: "[*T*]*he award causing the decrease in public revenue alone cannot be considered a violation of public policy. Further merits of the award cannot be examined. The application to set the award aside, which seems to decrease public revenue…, is not approved due to the absence of a legal basis… The decrease in public revenue is not sufficient alone for such approval.*")

501 Ziya Akıncı, Arbitration Law of Turkey, p. 155.

502 Okan Demirkan & Burak Eryigit, p. 597.

503 Turgut Kalpsuz, p. 147.

to questions of compatibility with Turkish public policy and arbitrability in Turkish law. The aim should be to reduce the disadvantages or possible risks and guarantee both the validity of arbitral awards rendered in Turkey and the enforcement in Turkey of international arbitral awards rendered in other countries.

Part II Arbitrability of Intra-Corporate Disputes in Turkish Law

III. Objective Arbitrability of Intra-Corporate Disputes and Statutory Regulations

A. Application of Arbitration to Corporate Law Disputes

Arbitration's significant adjudicatory advantages make it a preferred system for the resolution of disputes, especially those involving corporate actors. Corporate actors (including corporate counsel) who participate directly in the practice of arbitration point to an array of studies demonstrating its superiority over traditional judicial litigation.[504] These studies show that, in the corporate world, arbitration is likely to be speedier, less complicated, and less expensive than judicial litigation.[505] Several commentators contend that arbitration is more efficient than litigation because it has a more limited discovery.[506] Arbitration usually reduces the cost of gathering evidence and involves fewer procedural rules.[507] The absence of an appeals system contributes to its speed and cost-effectiveness as well.[508] Another reason why parties frequently opt for arbitration is because it is confidential and private.[509] Respondents in the studies conducted on

---

504 Douglas Shontz, Fred Kipperman & Vanessa Soma, Business-to-Business Arbitration in the United States: Perceptions of Corporate Counsel (Rand Inst. for Civil Justice 2011), *available at* http://www.rand.org/content/dam/rand/pubs/technical_reports/2011/RAND_TR781.pdf.
Loukas Mistelis, *International Arbitration - Corporate Attitudes and Practices - 12: Perceptions Tested: Myths, Data and Analysis Research Report*, 15 Am. Rev. Int'l Arb. 540 (2004).

505 Thomas E. Carbonneau, *Arguments in Favor of the Triumph of Arbitration*, 10 Cardozo J. Conflict Resol. 404 (2009).
Douglas Shontz, Fred Kipperman & Vanessa Soma, p. 1 & n.3.

506 Thomas E. Carbonneau, Carbonneau on International Arbitration: Collected Essays 120 (Juris 2011).
Julie K. Bracker & Larry D. Soderquist, *Arbitration in the Corporate Context,* Colum. Bus. L. Rev. 1 (2003).

507 *Ibid.*
Paul Weitzel, *The End of Shareholder Litigation? Allowing Shareholders to Customize Enforcement Through Arbitration Provisions in Charters and Bylaws*, BYU L. Rev. 85 (2013), *available at*: http://digitalcommons.law.byu.edu/lawreview/vol2013/iss1/2

508 Michael Hwang, Corporate Governance in Emerging Markets Enforcement of Corporate Governance in Asia (The Organization for Econ. Co-operation & Dev. 2007).

509 *Id* at 88.

in-house lawyers regarded confidentiality[510] as one of arbitration's most important advantages.[511] Court proceedings are always open to the public and confidential information can easily be divulged. Unlike litigation, however, arbitration resolves disputes privately, and enables corporations to protect their confidential commercial information from rival corporations and the public.[512]

Some commentators also argue that arbitral tribunals yield fairer and more objective results than national court judges.[513] National court judges are sponsored by particular governments and reflect local cultures and languages. Arbitration enables parties to select their own arbitrators.[514] They can choose a variety of nationals as arbitrators, taking into consideration language, expertise, and law. The neutral character of arbitration may be a significant benefit for corporate practitioners, especially in cases involving foreign parties and corporations. Foreign investors may not trust national courts, especially in emerging markets and less developed jurisdictions.[515] Such corporate actors tend to prefer neutral forums and tribunals over national courts.[516] Citizens of States may hold more advantageous positions than foreign shareholders before national courts. Disputes between foreign shareholders and Turkish shareholders in the same company illustrate these advantages. Corporate practitioners typically prefer arbitration in such circumstances because of its neutrality and objectivity.[517]

Disputes in corporate law generally require special expertise and more creative solutions. Some commentators argue that the flexible nature of arbitration makes it better suited to these requirements. Its flexibility enables parties to choose arbitrators who have the necessary expertise to resolve specific types of disputes.[518] Issues arising from corporate governance, structure, accounting, and finance exemplify

---

510 "*the process to adopt when corporations do not want the dispute publicized for various strategic reasons including where the image of the corporation may be brought to disrepute*".

511 Loukas Mistelis, p. 544.

512 *Ibid.*

513 Alexis Mourre, *Arbitrage, conflits de juridictions et ADR dans la résolution des litiges entre actionnaires/Arbitration, Jurisdiction Conflicts and ADR for the Resolution of Disputes between Shareholders*, Rev. dr. aff. int./Int'l Bus. L.J. 299 (2004).

514 Loukas Mistelis, p. 544.

515 Michael Hwang, p. 87.

516 Alan Redfern et al., Law and Practice of International Commercial Arbitration (4th ed. Sweet & Maxwell 2004).

517 Michael Hwang, pp. 87, 88.

518 Thomas E. Carbonneau, *Arguments in Favor of the Triumph of Arbitration*, p. 404. Julie K. Bracker & Larry D. Soderquist, p. 2.

such disputes. The widely-recognized advantages of arbitration, therefore, include the involvement of professionals with expertise in these specific areas.[519]

Arbitration may also promote the amicable resolution of disputes[520] in contrast to adversarial proceedings before official judicial authorities. Such resolutions can be crucial for intra-corporate disputes between shareholders of the same corporation. Initiating lawsuits before national courts can cause irremediable conflicts. Such actions can affect a company's operations because if shareholders cannot agree on one thing, they may not agree on corporate policy. Lawsuits in national courts can also result in governance deadlocks, which could have disastrous consequences in a competitive market.

In summary, arbitration "*guarantees the rule of law domestically and internationally through affordable access, expedited proceedings, expertise, and bridging the gap between national legal systems.*"[521] Arbitration, thus, meets the needs of corporate actors in many respects. Its expeditiousness, simplicity, flexibility and typically lower cost only bolster its appeal. It involves greater levels of expertise and ensures the confidentiality crucial to the resolution of disputes between multinational parties. Arbitration may also integrate the tolerance for different legal practices necessary in international commercial affairs.[522] This allows it to resolve disputes more effectively in such cases because it can overcome discrepancies between legal systems.[523] These advantages make it convenient in the context of intra-corporate disputes. For those reasons, indeed, companies are not 'migrating to the courtrooms to resolve their own disputes'.[524] The increasing tendency, world-wide, is to expand the arbitrability of company law disputes.[525] The

Marco Ventoruzzo et al., Comparative Corporate Law 637 (1st ed. W. Academic Publ'g 2015).

519 Thomas E. Carbonneau, *Arguments in Favor of the Triumph of Arbitration*, p. 397. Marco Ventoruzzo, p. 637.

520 F. Hodge O'Neal, *Resolving Disputes in Closely Held Corporations: Intra-Institutional Arbitration,* 67 Harv. L. Rev. 290 (1954).

521 Thomas E. Carbonneau, *Arguments in Favor of the Triumph of Arbitration*, p. 397.

522 Thomas E. Carbonneau, Carbonneau on International Arbitration: Collected Essays 118.

523 Thomas E. Carbonneau, *Arguments in Favor of the Triumph of Arbitration*, p. 404. Not only for transborder corporations but also "*...managers of domestic corporations seek to avoid the inefficiencies and the expensive histrionics of potentially commercially inexpert judicial trials.*"

524 Thomas E. Carbonneau, *Arguments in Favor of the Triumph of Arbitration*, p. 404.

525 Michael Hwang, p. 91.

advantages described above make it very common for agreements concerning the management of the shareholders to include arbitral clauses.

B. A Review of the Statutory Regulations for Arbitrating Intra-Corporate Disputes in Turkey

A dispute submitted to arbitration must be *objectively arbitrable*.[526] Objective arbitrability is also required for corporate disputes. Different countries, however, regulate the arbitrability of corporate disputes differently. According to Organization for Economic Cooperation and Development (the OECD) reports, the resolution of matters of corporate law through arbitration is "commonplace" in several jurisdictions. [527] Turkey, however, does not make this distinction clearly. Comparative law periodically mentions this issue, but these discussions have not influenced Turkish legal commentators or legislators. The interest of legal scholars from other jurisdictions in the area of arbitrability of corporate disputes has declined. Many jurisdictions favor and encourage the arbitrability of corporate disputes. Because Turkish law does not share that regulatory view, it needs to regulate and stabilize the arbitrability of corporate disputes. The arbitrability of corporate disputes, therefore, needs further elaboration in Turkish law.

1. An Overview of Current Regulations

First and foremost, no specific regulation governs the arbitrability of corporate-related disputes in Turkey. General rules address the boundaries of arbitrability. Given the absence of a specific regulation, these general rules also limit the arbitrability of corporate disputes. The Turkish International Arbitration Act[528] contains most general rules and limitations on arbitrability in Turkey. Some provisions in the Turkish Commercial Code also indirectly relate to the arbitration of corporate disputes. Those provisions can have an impact on

526 *See supra* Chapter II for more information.

527 Louis Bouchez & Alexander Karpf, *The OECD's Work Programme on Corporate Governance and Dispute Resolution,* The Quality of Corp. L. & the Role of Corp. L. Judges 6 (2006).

528 It bears repeating that Turkish International Arbitration Act governs arbitration of international disputes. Turkish Code of Civil Procedure, moreover, governs arbitration of domestic disputes, which is generally in parallel with International Arbitration Act. Examinations may refer to Turkish Code of Civil Procedure as needed especially when Turkish International Arbitration Act lacks a specific regulation.

the arbitrability of corporate disputes. These two statutes are the basis of the present analysis of the arbitrability of corporate disputes.

To begin with, the general rules of arbitrability in Turkish law merit attention. Turkish civil law relies heavily on the main principles of party autonomy and freedom of contract to regulate arbitrability.[529] Turkish citizens have a constitutional right to submit any civil dispute to arbitration, unless a specific statutory provision prohibits it. Inarbitrability applies only to a few matters in both domestic and international arbitration. Those matters deal with immovable property and the will of parties. Regarding international disputes, the article 1 (4) of the Turkish International Arbitration Code states:

> *This Code shall not apply to the disputes regarding in rem rights on immovable properties located in Turkey, and disputes that are not subject to the will of the parties.*[530]

These regulations remain valid for the arbitrability of all corporate law disputes. Firstly, disputes arising from *in rem* rights on immovable property located in Turkey cannot be arbitrated. Secondly, any corporate law dispute is arbitrable as long as it is subject to the will of the parties. The criteria for the latter requirement need clarification. Certain principles govern judicial proceedings in Turkish law. Related provisions of the Turkish Code of Civil Procedure identify those principles. One provision establishes *the power of disposition of the parties* as a fundamental element.[531] Doctrinal commentators infer that the will of the parties reflects this element in arbitration law.[532] Corporate disputes are arbitrable if the right in question is within the power of disposition of the parties.

---

529 *See supra* Chapter II for further explanations.

530 It means that those disputes cannot be arbitrated under this Code, which governs international arbitration, in Turkey.

For domestic disputes, article 408 of the Turkish Code of Civil Procedure similarly states that:

> *"Disputes arising from in rem rights on immovable properties, or disputes that are not subject to the will of the parties are not arbitrable"*

531 Article 24 of the Turkish Code of Civil Procedure:

> "…
>
> 3) *Parties' right of disposition on a matter in dispute, which has a dispositive nature, remains post litem motam.*"

532 Rasih Yegengil, p. 152.
See supra note 52 for further explanations.

Whether a corporate law-related dispute is at the free disposition of parties is, therefore, critical to determining its arbitrability. Doctrinal commentators recognize several factors that indicate that free disposition applies to corporate law and governance disputes.[533] These factors include whether the parties are free to reconcile, mediate, settle, or waive the lawsuit regarding the matter in dispute.[534] Determining the arbitrability of corporate-related disputes requires close analysis of these factors.

As noted earlier, three additional concepts govern the boundaries of arbitrability as a general rule in Turkish law: imperative provisions, explicit exclusive judicial jurisdictional rules, and public policy. These concepts do not specifically govern matters of corporate law; however, they apply to the arbitration of any dispute. They may, therefore, be relevant in instances of corporate arbitration. Deciding on the arbitrability of corporate- related disputes also requires further study of these concepts.

C. Framework and Methodology of Corporate Disputes

OECD reports indicate that intra-corporate disputes typically arise from internal relationships between the shareholders of individual corporations.[535] Such disputes arise from a number of issues including: remuneration of the boards, conflicts arising from bankruptcy, the involvement of shareholders in resolution-making processes and takeovers, the rights of minority shareholders in squeeze out attempts or in the selection of members of the board, takeover procedures that conflict with intra-corporate rules,[536] dismissal of appointed board members, breach of corporate governance principles, mismanagement, or insider trading.[537] Other examples of arbitrable intra-corporate disputes include those arising from the corporation's articles of association, shareholder agreements about corporate policy or finance or share purchases, possible deadlocks, usage of shareholder rights with regard to voting or pre-emption, or other corporate governance matters.[538]

---

533 Explanations of general arbitrability from the previous chapter shed light on the dispositive nature of corporate disputes.

534 *See supra* note 68 for further explanations.

535 *OECD's Work Programme,* pp. 11, 14–16.

536 For instance, articles of association.

537 *OECD's Work Programme,* pp. 11, 14–16.

538 Alexis Mourre, pp. 287–288.

Parties may submit a wide range of corporate-related disputes to arbitration, but Turkish law in no way regulates this aspect of the process. This lack of regulation creates a great deal of ambiguity. The possible issues stemming from the arbitration of intra-corporate matters in Turkish law require careful analysis. This analysis considers a specific type of intra-corporate dispute: annulment of general assembly resolutions. Annulments of general assembly resolution are among the issues for which lawsuits are most frequently filed. This issue accommodates all matters regarding corporate disputes that require consideration. Most assertions made in Turkish law against the arbitrability of intra-corporate disputes apply to this issue. This makes the discussion of the arbitrability of the annulment of general assembly resolutions necessary to the analysis of the role of arbitration in this area. Explanations from now on will refer to this specific issue to provide a practical examination of the rules' applications.

IV. Example of Disputes Arising from Internal Corporate Affairs: Annulment of General Assembly Resolutions

No explicit statutes in Turkish law regulate the arbitrability of disputes arising from the internal affairs of corporations, including the annulment of general assembly resolutions. Disputes arising from the annulment of general assembly resolutions are widely considered arbitrable in comparative law.[539] In Turkish law, however, their arbitrability raises controversy.[540] The sources of law used in cases that lack statutory regulations shed light on the issue.

---

539 Sami Karahan, Sirketler Hukuku [Corporations Law] 529 & n.1 (1. Baskı Seckin Yayıncılık 2012) [1st ed. Seckin Publishing 2012].

540 *Ibid.*

Turkish law contains both primary and subsidiary sources.[541] [542] Turkish Civil Code Article 1[543] indicates that statutory regulations[544] are the primary written sources. Court decisions and doctrinal opinions serve as subsidiary sources[545] for subjects that lack explicit statutory regulations. Turkish law lacks an explicit statutory regulation regarding the arbitrability of intra-corporate disputes.[546] This section, therefore, examines the relevant case law and doctrinal opinions.

---

541 Turkish Civil Code, article 1 indicates that:

"*INTRODUCTION*

A. *Application of the Law and the Sources*
1. *The statute shall apply to all cases that it refers through its wording and spirit.*

In the absence of an applicable provision in the statute, the judge shall decide in accordance with customary law; and in the absence of this, the judge shall decide in accordance with how he would establish a rule if he was the legislator himself.

The judge makes use of scientific opinions and court decisions while deciding."

542 *See* Article 38(1) of the Statute of the International Court of Justice as an example of this application in a comparative perspective:

"*1. The Court, whose function is to decide in accordance with international law such disputes as are submitted to it, shall apply:*

a. *international conventions, whether general or particular, establishing rules expressly recognized by the contesting states;*
b. *international custom, as evidence of a general practice accepted as law;*
c. *the general principles of law recognized by civilized nations;*
d. *subject to the provisions of Article 59 judicial decisions and the teachings of the most highly qualified publicists of the various nations, as subsidiary means for the determination of rules of law.*

..."

"The Statute of the International Court of Justice is annexed to the Charter of the United Nations, of which it forms an integral part. The main object of the Statute is to organize the composition and the functioning of the Court."

(*Available at*: http://www.icj-cij.org/documents/?p1=4&p2=2)

543 *See supra* note 541.

544 And the customary law, if applicable, as a non-written source.

545 Kemal Gozler, Hukuka Giris [Introduction to Law] 142 (Ekin Basım Yayın Dagıtım 5. Baski 2008) [Ekin Publishing 5th Ed. 2008].

546 General assembly resolutions in particular.

Some of these doctrinal opinions are based on specific statutory regulations in the Turkish Commercial Code to which the present discussions will refer.

A. Judicial Perspective: Examination of Case Law

In its 3/11/1969 decision,[547] the Turkish Supreme Court Commercial Circuit stated that:

> *An arbitral clause inserted in the articles of incorporation for disputes arising from an unlimited liability in a company's internal affairs has a binding effect. Arbitrators can review cases in which shareholders claim that a company has not conducted the business fairly (pursuant to the provisions of the articles of incorporation). Each shareholder has the right to file a lawsuit for dissolution of the company separately or collectively based on one of the grounds listed in Article 187 of the Turkish Commercial Code.... The trial court has decided to hear the case and deny the motion to dismiss for lack of jurisdiction. This decision must be reversed. This situation does not impede another shareholder from submitting the case to arbitration; nor does it preclude the case from being heard before an arbitrator.* [548]

Regarding this ruling, professor *Akıncı* asserts that: '*the parties' agreement to refer all the disputes between the...company and its shareholders is binding; thus, any shareholder can refer a dispute to arbitration. In this decision, the Turkish Supreme Court ruled that disputes between parties and the...company are arbitrable*.'[549]

In a 2012 decision,[550] however, the Court reached a contrary conclusion. The plaintiff in this case, in his capacity as a shareholder of the company, asked the lower court to annul a specific shareholder resolution made at a shareholder assembly on November 5, 2011. The plaintiff-shareholder alleged that: 1) the company failed to invite him to the shareholder's assembly held on November 5, 2011; 2) the shareholder assembly was not held in the specified place; and 3) the company failed to inform him about the operations of the company.[551] The defendant-company filed a motion to dismiss, alleging that the dispute needed to be resolved through arbitration, in accordance with Article 13 of the articles of incorporation. The lower court granted the defendant-company's motion to

547 Supreme Court Commercial Circuit decision dated 3/11/1969 1969/3878 E. and numbered 5118 K.

548 Ismail Doganay, Turk Ticaret Kanunu Serhi [Commentary of Turkish Commercial Code] 734 (Beta Yayıncılık, Istanbul 2004) [Beta Publishing, Istanbul 2004].

549 Ziya Akıncı, Arbitration Law of Turkey, p. 269.

550 Turkish Supreme Court 11th Civil Circuit decision dated 12/05/2012 numbered 2011/13485E and 2012/19915 K.

551 *Ibid.*

dismiss. The plaintiff-shareholder appealed the lower court decision to dismiss the case and to have it resolved through arbitration.[552]

The Turkish Supreme Court held that arbitration clauses or agreements in the articles of incorporation are void. The court explained that arbitration is available only for disputes that are subject to the will of the parties. Those disputes can be concluded by settlements between plaintiffs and defendants without court decision. Disputes regarding the annulment of general assembly resolutions, however, cannot be settled by agreements between plaintiffs and defendants. The Court[553] remanded the case to the trial court for review in light of its decision.[554] The decision referred mainly to the work of Professor Moroglu. In the book cited in the decision, Professor Moroglu argues that disputes arising from the annulment of the general assembly resolutions cannot be resolved via arbitration.[555] Setting aside Professor Moroglu's rationale,[556] two court decisions referred to in his book shed light on judicial approach to the issue. The first decision dealt with

552 *Ibid.*

553 The court has highlighted other issues that can impede the arbitrability of intra-corporate disputes:

"...*Moreover,*

- *the provision that exclusively authorizes the court of the place of the company headquarters in accordance with sub-article 1 of article 381 of the Turkish Commercial Code, and*
- *the provision that requires consolidation of cases in accordance with sub-article 3 of the same article*

do not comply with the concept of arbitration. (See Prof. Dr. Erdogan Moroglu, Anonim Ortaklıkta Genel Kurul Kararlarının Hukumsuzlugu [Annulment of General Assembly Resolutions in Joint-stock Company], Ucuncu Baski [Third Edition], s.226,227 [p. 226,227]).

..."

The following chapter addresses those issues in the context of arguments and counter-arguments in detail.

554 *Ibid.*

555 Erdogan Moroglu, Anonim Ortaklıkta Genel Kurul Kararlarının Hukumsuzlugu (6102 Sayılı Turk Ticaret Kanunu'na Gore) [Annulment of General Assembly Resolutions in Joint-stock Company (In Accordance with Turkish Commercial Code numbered 6102)], 12 Levha Yayıncılık, 6. Baskı, Istanbul 2012 [12 Levha Publishing, 6th Ed. Istanbul 2012], s.262 [p. 262].

556 Following section will assess the bases for this conclusion in detail.

cooperatives. In 1981, the Turkish Supreme Court[557] held that Article 95[558] of the Cooperatives Code made general arbitral clauses concerning disputes between Cooperative Corporations and cooperators invalid.[559] In the second decision,[560] however, the Turkish Supreme Court Assembly of Civil Chambers[561] reached another conclusion. This landmark 1966 decision held that arbitral clauses concerning disputes between shareholders arising from their activities do not contradict related provisions of the Turkish Commercial Code.[562]

In 2010, the Turkish Supreme Court decided another case regarding the arbitrability of disputes arising from the internal affairs of corporations.[563] The plaintiff brought an action before the lower court for the dismissal of a director. The defendant filed a motion asking the lower court to dismiss the plaintiff's request, alleging that the lower court lacked jurisdiction because Article 14 of the articles of incorporation stipulated that disputes between parties must be resolved via arbitration. The lower court granted the defendant's motion to dismiss and ruled that the case should be submitted to arbitrators in accordance with Article 14 of the articles of incorporation. The plaintiff appealed the lower court's decision. The Turkish Supreme Court reversed the lower court's decision. It held that a director's rights and duties can be restricted or dismissed only by a court order at the request of one of the directors in accordance with the related article of the Turkish Commercial Code. [564] Selection of the decisions from varied years reflect the adjudicatory tendencies in Turkey over time. These

557 11th Civil Circuit decision dated 4/24/1981 numbered 471E and 894 K.

558 "D) *Disputes, Arbitration Rules*:
Article 95

Arbitral tribunals, which are foreseen in the articles of incorporation, can hear disputes arising from the matters within the cooperatives and its organs; cooperatives and cooperative unions that they are affiliated; cooperative center unions and Turkish National Cooperative Union reserving the general provisions."

559 Cooperatives Code numbered 1163, which was ratified on 4/24/1969 and published on 5/10/1969.

560 Erdogan Moroglu, Anonim Ortaklıkta Genel Kurul Kararlarının Hukumsuzlugu, p. 263 & n.497.

561 The Supreme Court Assembly of Civil Chambers decision dated 1/12/1966 and numbered 7/428E and 6K.

562 *Ibid.*

563 Mehmet Helvacı, pp. 190–191.

564 *Ibid.*

rulings indicate that court decisions have not provided a well-established judicial precedent regarding the arbitrability of disputes related to general assembly resolutions.

B. Statutory Perspective: Specific Regulations of Turkish Commercial Code

Turkey adopted a new Commercial Code numbered 6102 in 2012. This new Commercial Code replaces the previous Commercial Code numbered 6762.[565] Some provisions of this current Code relate directly to general assembly resolutions. This section reproduces the full text of the Code's most relevant provisions because many scholarly assessments referred in this section are derived directly from these provisions. The current Code states the following about the annulment of general assembly resolutions:

> G) Annulment of General Assembly Resolutions
> I- Causes for Annulment[566]
> Article 445: (1) The *persons identified in Article 446 can file annulment actions against general assembly resolutions that violate the law or articles of incorporation, particularly good faith, before the commercial court of first instance in the location of the company headquarters, within 3 months from the date of the decision.*

These provisions have triggered several doctrinal arguments against the arbitrability of cases for annulment of general assembly. The main rationale behind those arguments is the statement about a court in a specific location for such cases. This point highlights the need for analysis of judicial jurisdictional rules and arbitrability.

The following miscellaneous provisions of the Code relate to certain arguments regarding court proceedings:

> I) Miscellaneous Provisions
> I- Announcement, Security and Right to Appeal

At the time of the decision, the previous Commercial Code numbered 6762 was in effect. The related provision was article 161. In the current Commercial Code numbered 6102, the related provision is article 219.

565 Each time an article in the previous Code is mentioned, a footnote will refer to the related article in the current Code to avoid any confusion.

566 In the previous Commercial Code numbered 6762, article 381 has covered the issues in articles 445, 446 and 448 of the current code.

Article 448: (1) The *board of directors duly announces the filing of an action for annulment or nullity, the date of the hearing, and uploads the announcement to the company web-site.*[567]
(2) *In an annulment action, an oral hearing cannot commence before the time limit of three months ends. If more than one annulment action is filed, the actions shall be consolidated to be heard.*
(3) *The court can decide that the plaintiff must provide a security at the request of the company. The court determines the quality and quantity of the security.*

These provisions also serve as the basis for arguments on annulment of general assembly resolution cases. The regulations actually shed light on some of the drawbacks of legal proceedings during annulment cases. The fact that they target litigation, however, allows some commentators to argue against the arbitrability of such cases.

The Turkish Commercial Code regulation regarding the effect of decisions on annulment of general assembly resolutions is one the most frequently referred provisions:

Effect of the Decision
Article 450: (1) *A court decision pertaining to an annulment or nullity of general assembly resolution inures to the benefit of all shareholders after it is finalized. The board of directors shall immediately register a copy of this decision in the trade registry, and upload it to the company web-site.*

Court decisions regarding the annulment of general assembly resolutions affect all shareholders whether or not they are party to arbitral agreements. The *inter partes* impact of arbitral awards, by contrast, is a central principle of arbitration. Arbitral awards, as a rule, only affect the parties included in the arbitration agreement. Arguments about this provision stem from this contrast. The regulations[568] listed above are the most critical to arguments against the

567 An obligation regarding company web-site announcements was not adopted in the previous Code. This part is inserted in the current Code.
568 There are few other provisions of the Turkish Commercial Code directly regulating annulment of general assembly resolutions. They, however, do not constitute basis to arguments as often as the one stated above. Those regulations are as follows:

"Persons Who Can File an Annulment Action
Article 446: (1)

a. *Shareholders who are present at the meeting, who dissented, and whose dissent is included in the minute,*
b. *Shareholders who claim that:*

the invitation was not made in due form; the agenda was not announced properly; or persons who are not authorized to attend the general assembly -or their agents- attended the meeting and voted;
they were unjustly not allowed to attend the general assembly and vote; and
those abovementioned violations had an impact on issuing the general assembly resolution, regardless of the shareholder's presence at the meeting or having dissented,

c. *Board of directors,*
d. *Each member of the board of directors who will be subject to personal responsibility in the event of fulfillment of the resolution*

can file annulment action."

(The related provision of the previous Code stated that:

"*Shareholders who had presence at the meeting and dissent to the resolution, and had this reported in the minute; or were not allowed to vote unjustly; or claim that the invitation was not made in due form; or the agenda was not announced or disclosed properly; or claim that persons who are not authorized to attend the general assembly have contributed to the resolution.*"

The expression "*regardless of shareholder's presence at the meeting or having dissenting vote or not*" was added in the current Commercial Code. This addition clarified that any shareholder can file a claim notwithstanding the shareholder was at the meeting, or had a dissenting vote against the resolution. This point was not clear in the previous version of the Code.

Also, for sub-section (d), the previous Commercial code numbered 6762 entitled auditors as well as members of the board of directors to file the lawsuit under the same condition. The new current Code, however, omitted auditors. Now, only members of the board of directors can file the lawsuit in the event that fulfilling the resolution results in their personal responsibilities.)

"H) Nullity

Article 447: (1) *Resolutions of general assembly, which are especially*

a. *Restricting or abolishing shareholder's right to attend at the general assembly, minimum vote, sue and inalienable rights arising from law,*
b. *Restricting shareholder's right to demand information, investigate and audit beyond the limits of the law,*
c. *Infringing the fundamental structure of the joint-stock company, or are against the provisions of capital maintenance*

are void."

(To underline, the previous version of the Commercial Code numbered 6762 did not include the last article about the nullity of general assembly resolutions. It is one of the additions to the new version of the Code.)

arbitrability of annulment cases in Turkish law. They serve as background for the next section's examination of the opinions of legal scholars.

C. Doctrinal Perspective: Assessments of Legal Commentators

The stance of legal commentators regarding the arbitrability of annulment of general assembly resolution cases mirrors the stance of the courts. No consensus exists among the commentators, either. To maintain objectivity, this section examines the underlying grounds for assertions of the inarbitrability of such disputes. Related Turkish Commercial Code provisions are the main grounds. Additional factors[569] may contribute to the inarbitrability of these disputes. Those factors derive from regulations in other general codes such as the Turkish Code of Civil Procedure and the Turkish International Arbitration Act.

1. Doctrinal Arguments on the Inarbitrability of Disputes Arising from General Assembly Resolutions

The issue of the annulment of general assembly resolutions is a much-debated matter. Commentators present several conflicting views on the validity of demands for arbitration in the annulment of general assembly resolution cases.[570] Opponents of arbitrability object on several grounds. Some refer to the statutory regulations governing general arbitrability in Turkish law.[571] Others base their arguments on the statutory regulations about general assembly resolutions mentioned above.

The court supported the inarbitrability of the annulment of general assembly resolutions in a 2012 case.[572] The court corroborated its decision by referring

---

"Suspending the Execution of the Resolution

Article 449: (1) *When an action of annulment or nullity against a general assembly resolution is filed, the court may decide to suspend the execution of the resolution subject to this action, after taking the opinion of members of the board of directors.*

Liability of Persons Who File the Action for Annulment of Nullity in Bad Faith

Article 451: (1) *In the event that an action for annulment or nullity is filed against the resolution of general assembly in bad faith, plaintiffs are severally liable for any damages that the company incurs as a result of the action.*"

569 *Supra* Chapter II has detailed those factors.

570 Burcu Zengin, p. 106.

571 *Supra* Chapter II has detailed those regulations and comments.

572 *See supra* note 553 and accompanying text.

to Professor *Moroglu*'s book[573] that presented three arguments to support his assertion of the inarbitrability of the annulment of general assembly resolution cases.[574] The first argument recalls the fundamental rule of arbitrability in Turkish law.[575] For a dispute to be objectively arbitrable, the disputed matter must be subject to will of the parties.[576] This is possible only if the parties have the ability to conclude the dispute by reaching a settlement with each other without resorting to the courts.[577] *Moroglu* contends that concluding a dispute arising from the annulment of a general assembly resolution through a settlement between the plaintiff (joint stock company) and defendant (shareholders and others) is impossible.[578] The second argument refers to exclusive judicial jurisdictional rules.[579] Moroglu's argument highlights an intervening rule in Article 445[580] of the Turkish Commercial Code. This rule *exclusively* authorizes the court in the location of the company headquarters to adjudicate such disputes. Scholars who subscribe to this argument contend that the exclusive authorization of a specific court disqualifies these disputes from arbitration.[581]

Moroglu's third argument focuses on the effect of court decisions on the annulment of general assembly resolution cases. Article 450 of the Turkish Commercial Code[582] states that court annulment decisions bind all shareholders of the corporation. In these cases, the plaintiffs are typically shareholders with partial shares. The defendants are the joint-stock corporations themselves. Commentators assert that arbitral tribunals appointed by partial share owners can render decisions that bind all shareholders

---

573 Erdogan Moroglu, Anonim Ortaklıkta Genel Kurul Kararlarının Hukumsuzlugu, p. 262.
574 *Ibid.*
575 "Disputes arising from *in rem* rights on immovable property, or disputes that are not subject to the will of the parties' are inarbitrable" (Article 408 of Turkish Code of Civil Procedure).
576 Erdogan Moroglu, Anonim Ortaklıkta Genel Kurul Kararlarının Hukumsuzlugu, p. 262.
577 *Ibid.*
See supra Chapter II for further information.
578 *Ibid.*
579 *Supra* Chapter II (B) on general arbitrability in Turkish law explained these rules in detail.
580 *See supra* note 566 and accompanying text.
581 Erdogan Moroglu, Anonim Ortaklıkta Genel Kurul Kararlarının Hukumsuzlugu, p. 262.
582 *See* the full article *supra* notes 567-568.

and organs of the corporation. [583] These arguments are generally predicated upon the fact that Commercial Code regulations governing the system of the annulment of general assembly resolutions *exclude* arbitration.[584]

Other doctrinal commentators make different arguments regarding the arbitrability of the annulment of general assembly resolution cases. Professor *Helvacı* highlights the lack of a direct provision excluding arbitration for corporations in the Turkish legal system.[585] He adds, however, that this does not mean all corporation-based disputes are arbitrable.[586] He argues against the arbitrability of disputes arising from the annulment of general assembly resolutions. He contends that the arbitral clause as applied to these specific disputes contradicts imperative rules and public policy.[587] *Helvacı* acknowledges, on the one hand, that disputes arising from the annulment of general assembly resolutions are subject to will of the parties and, therefore, capable of settlement.[588] On the other hand, he argues that the special procedural rules set forth in the related section of the Commercial Code—rules that he claims are binding on parties—disallow arbitration.[589]

The rules *Helvacı* identifies as imperative are: the specification of the authorized court and the consolidation of the cases.[590] The specification of the authorized court is the judicial jurisdictional rule to which *Moroglu* refers in his second argument. Article 448(2) requires the consolidation of actions when more than one action exists. Commentators take the position that this rule prohibits arbitration because the consolidation of cases is not possible in arbitration.[591] *Helvacı* contends that these specific *imperative* procedural requirements reflect the intent of legislators. He argues that legislators have two aims: to protect shareholders and third parties not involved in the action, and to maximize the speed and transparency of the adjudication of the cases.[592]

---

583 Erdogan Moroglu, Anonim Ortaklıkta Genel Kurul Kararlarının Hukumsuzlugu, pp. 262–263.

584 *Id* at 263.

585 Mehmet Helvacı, p. 187.

586 *Ibid.*

587 Mehmet Helvacı, pp. 200–201.

588 *Id* at199–200.
This factor makes such disputes arbitrable in accordance with Turkish Code of Civil Procedure Article 408. ("*Disputes arising from in rem rights on immovable property or disputes that are not subject to the will of the parties' are inarbitrable.*")

589 Mehmet Helvacı, p. 200.

590 *Ibid.*

591 Erdogan Moroglu, Anonim Ortaklıkta Genel Kurul Kararlarının Hukumsuzlugu, p. 262.

592 Mehmet Helvacı, p. 200.

Bahtiyar presents another argument regarding the inclusion of arbitral clauses in the articles of association. He emphasizes that the Turkish Commercial Code contains no explicit provision regarding this issue.[593] He considers arbitral clauses in the articles of association valid.[594] He claims, however, that arbitrating any type of dispute even when such clauses exist in the articles of association is impossible. He mentions several requirements for validating arbitration clauses in articles of association.[595] [596] He finds the annulment of general assembly resolution cases inarbitrable.[597] [598] He makes this claim on the grounds of imperative rules rather than the will of the parties.[599] Using the same rationale, he also identifies some other types of intra-corporate dispute as inarbitrable. These include actions for the annulment of board of directors' resolutions,[600] repudiation due to

---

593 Mehmet Bahtiyar, Anonim Ortaklık Sozlesmesi [Articles of Association in Joint Stock Corporations] 208 (Beta Yayıncılık 2001) [Beta Publishing 2001].

594 In parallel with other jurisdictions in comparative law.
Id at 209.

595 *Id* at 209,210.

596 These issues include:

- *General procedural requirement* such as official form, capacity, compliance of bilateral intentions and declarations, and
- *Special requirements* such as:
  - the agreement's being in writing,
  - the subject matter of the dispute's being subject to the will of the parties, and having dispositive nature in accordance with article 408 of Turkish Code of Civil Procedure,
  - the dispute's being specific; and parties' having the capacity to arbitrate.

597 He, however, finds pecuniary matters including claims of receivables arbitrable.

598 Mehmet Bahtiyar, Anonim Ortaklık Sozlesmesi, p. 210.

599 *Id* at 211.

600 Article 12 of Capital Markets Law numbered 2499 enacted on 7/28/1981. This Code, however, has been changed with the Code numbered 6362 which was enacted on 12/6/2012. According to the current code:
"Registered Capital System

...

Article 18 (6): *Members of the board of directors or shareholders, whose rights were violated, can file an action for annulment against the resolutions taken by the board of directors in accordance with the principles under this article before the commercial court in the location of the headquarters within 30 days from the announcement of the resolution.*

..."

bankruptcy,[601] the absence of a relevant corporate department,[602] or a decrease in the numbers of the shareholders to fewer than five.[603]

---

601 "A) Termination
I-Grounds for Termination
1.General
Article 529: (1) *Joint-stock corporation is terminated in the events of:*
...
e) *the decision of its bankruptcy*
..."
and
"...
a) Obligation of invitation and announcement
Article 376:
...
(3) *In the event that there are indications raising doubts on the company's being deep in debt, the board of directors issues an interim financial statement of current assets on the bases of continuity of the company at the rate of possible sale price. If one can understand that the current assets fall short of the debts of the company from this financial statement, the board of directors declares this situation to the commercial court in the location of the headquarters and requests the bankruptcy of the corporation. Excepting that the creditors of the company debts, whose receivables equate to the amount that may meet the deficit of the company and eliminate the situation of being deep in debt have agreed in writing (before the decision of bankruptcy is given) that their place will be put in order after the places of all other creditors; and the experts who are appointed by the court has verified the legitimacy, literality and validness of this declaration or agreement. Otherwise, the application made to the court for expert examining is considered as a bankruptcy declaration.*
..."

602 "2. Special Situations
a) Absence of Organs
Article 530- (1): *In the events that legally required organs of the company does not exist or the board of directors cannot meet for a long time, the court in the location of the headquarters sets a period of time for the company's condition to be adjusted in accordance with the law after listening to the board of directors at the request of shareholders, creditors of the company or Ministry of Customs and Trade. If the condition is not adjusted within this period of time, the court decides on the company's termination.*
2) *The court can take required measures at the request of one of the parties when the case is filed.*"

603 The changes that the new Code made to the joint-stock companies have eliminated this requirement.
Mehmet Bahtiyar, Anonim Ortaklık Sozlesmesi, p. 211.

Professor *Poroy*[604] evaluates miscellaneous problems regarding actions for annulment of general assembly resolutions in his explanation of the Turkish Commercial Code. He refers to Article 452 of the Commercial Code as relevant to the arbitrability of those disputes. Article 452[605] provides that:

> *The general assembly can amend all provisions of the articles of association in compliance with the conditions stipulated in the Statute unless otherwise provided, with the reservation of vested*[606] *and inalienable rights.*

Filing an action for the annulment of a general assembly resolution could be considered a shareholder's *vested right*. The effect of the vested right to file lawsuits on the arbitrability of annulment actions is another concern for doctrinal commentators. The right may prevent the general assembly from inserting an arbitral clause in the articles of association because vested rights would be excluded. *Pulaslı* reaches the

---

604 Reha Poroy, Unal Tekinalp & Ersin Camoglu, Ortaklıklar Ve Kooperatif Hukuku: Genel Bilgiler, Adi Ortaklık, Ticaret Ortaklarına Iliskin Genel Hukumler, Kollektif, Komandit, Anonim, Halka Acık Anonim, Sermayesi Paylara Bolunmus Komandit, Limited ve Holding Ortaklıklar ile Kooperatif [The law of Corporations and Cooperatives: General Information, Ordinary Partnership, General Terms about Trade Partners, Unlimited Liability Company, Limited Partnership, Joint-Stock, Open Joint-Stock Corporation, Limited Partnership Divided Into Shares, Limited and Holding Company and Cooperative] 386 (12.Baski Vedat Kitapcılık, Istanbul 2010) [12th ed. Vedat Kitapcılık Publishing, Istanbul 2010].

605 Article 385 has regulated this issue in the previous Commercial Code, which was in effect at the time when the book was published. The text of the previous version of the article was longer as it had extra explanations and definitions but the meaning was the same. The text of article 385 was as follows:

"D) Amendment of the Articles of Association
I-In General
1.Vested rights
Article 385: *Unless contrary is agreed in articles of association, general assembly can amend all provisions of the articles of association within the conditions below stated. However, vested rights that individual shareholders have due to their titles cannot be amended without their consent.*

Vested rights are the rights which are not subject to the resolutions of the general assembly or the board of directors; or arising from the right of attending the general assembly meetings in accordance with law or articles of association such as rights of membership, voting, filing action for annulment, receiving profit margin and liquidating dividend."

606 Before the enactment of the new Commercial Code, the previous version of the provision identified the vested nature of this right. While the new version of the provision is shorter, it still essentially identifies this right's vested character.

conclusion that the courts possess sole jurisdiction over actions for annulment; the vested character of these actions eliminates arbitration as an option. [607] He adds that provisions concerning the arbitration of the annulment of general assembly resolutions cannot be included in the articles of association; and, even if they are included, such provisions are invalid.[608] He asserts, finally, that neither arbitration nor settlement apply to actions for annulment of general assembly resolutions.[609]

Nomer argues that organs representing defendant corporations have no dispositive right over the content of such actions. Settlements regarding actions for the annulment of general assembly resolutions are, therefore, unavailable.[610] He highlights two reasons for the disallowance of settlements: settlements would affect everybody (*erga omnes*) and have a retrospective effect.[611] He contends that, because arbitration only affects parties bound by arbitration agreements, it cannot apply in such situations. [612]

2. Arguments on the Arbitrability of the Issue: A Synopsis

As the previous sections explain, the arbitrability of corporate-related disputes, including those arising from general assembly resolutions, is controversial. Scholars assert the inarbitrability of such disputes on various, overlapping grounds. Rationales for inarbitrability can be accurately divided into the following six categories:

- The compatibility with the criteria of the will of the parties;
- Judicial jurisdiction and the potential exclusivity of the rule in relation to public policy;
- Impact of decisions on shareholders and third parties not involved in the action;
- Vested right character and attendant outcomes;

---

607 Hasan Pulaslı, 6102 Sayılı Turk Ticaret Kanunu'na Gore Sirketler Hukuku Serhi [Annotated Corporations Law in Accordance with Turkish Commercial Code Numbered 6102] 865 (Cilt 1, Adalet Yayınevi Ankara 2011) [Vol.1, Adalet Publishing Ankara 2011].

608 *Id* at 864.

609 *Id* at 866.

610 Haluk N. Nomer, Kisi Birliklerinde Genel Kurul Kararlarının Gecersizligine Iliskin Temel Esaslar [Fundamental Principles regarding Annulment of General Assembly Resolutions in Private Companies] 176 (Beta Basım, Istanbul 2008) [Beta Publishing, Istanbul 2008].

611 *Id* at 177.

612 *Id* at 176-177.

- The effects of the imperative provisions principle in the Turkish Commercial Code on Arbitration;
- Procedural advantages and requirements stipulated by the law regarding court adjudication: consolidation of cases and other multiparty dispute mechanisms.

The next section of this chapter discusses each of these categories in detail.[613] At this point, the discussion has summarized the arguments for the inarbitrability of the annulment cases. It has included these perspectives to maintain objectivity. Going forward, the considerations will present counter-arguments in order to establish the framework for conclusion. Finally, the section will evaluate solutions that may alleviate deficiencies alleged to occur during the arbitration of corporate matters.

613 To be more precise, the book will refer to the related statutory rules and apply them to the matter in dispute for each of the categories. The statutory rules consist of:

- the rules relating to the general arbitrability of any dispute in Turkey, and
- the specific statutory regulations of corporate concepts included in the Turkish Commercial Code.

The subsequent headings will state the results of applying these rules to the issue in question. The book will then draw its general conclusion by synthesizing these individual results.

V. Counter Arguments

The controversy that surrounds the arbitrability of intra-corporate disputes is well-established: Turkish law does not explicitly regulate it and neither the courts nor legal commentators have reached a consensus regarding arbitrability. The previous chapter explored the grounds for inarbitrability asserted by some commentators. This chapter evaluates those assertions and presents counter-arguments.

A. Compatibility with the Criteria of the Will of the Parties

1. Essence of the Criteria: Dispositive Nature

The previous chapter explained that a dispute must be objectively arbitrable[614] to be resolved via arbitration. To be objectively arbitrable in Turkish law, the right in dispute must be subject to the will of the parties. Turkish law regards disputes as subject to the will of the parties when the parties have free disposition of the disputed right. [615] The previous chapter also established the relationship between the availability of settlement and the free disposition requirement. This section examines whether general assembly resolutions can be considered as subject to the will of the parties.

Some commentators argue that disputes arising from the general assembly resolutions of joint-stock corporations are inarbitrable. They assert this on the ground that such disputes fail to meet the arbitrability requirement in Article 408[616] of Turkish Code of Civil Procedure. This article stipulates that a dispute must be subject to the will of the parties.[617] These scholars contend that the plaintiffs and defendants in such cases cannot *settle* their disputes without court

614 The definition of 'objective arbitrability' in civil law jurisdictions corresponds to the 'subject-matter arbitrability' in Anglo-Saxon jurisdictions.

615 *See supra* Chapter II (A) 1. (a) for further explanations.

616 Or article 1(4) of Turkish International Arbitration Code, which has the same requirement for international disputes.

617 Erdogan Moroglu, Anonim Ortaklıkta Genel Kurul Kararlarının Hukumsuzlugu, p. 262.
Mehmet Helvacı, pp. 200–201.
Mehmet Bahtiyar, Anonim Ortaklık Sozlesmesi, p. 209.

decisions. [618] Moroglu, for instance, argues that because disputes arising from general assembly resolutions cannot be settled, they are not subject to the will of parties, and— therefore not arbitrable—.[619]

No specific regulation in Turkish law supports this definitive conclusion. The law contains provisions related to the issue in question, but does not explicitly regulate it. Those who adopt this line of reasoning, then derive their conclusion from an interpretation of the law. This section examines whether an interpretation of the law could lead to a contradistinctive conclusion. This examination serves as a counter-argument to the position of inarbitrability. The contrary views both derive from the text of the law, so this section begins by considering the precise language of the relevant article. The relevant portion of Article 408 of Turkish Code of Civil Procedure, [620] states that the arbitrability of disputes depends on their "*being subject to the will of the parties.*" [621] The law does not refer to the requirement stated in the opinion about *settlements*.

Other statutory standards help determine whether a dispute is subject to the will of parties in Turkish law. The limits of arbitrability in Turkish law derive from one general principle:[622] the independence of *the power of disposition of the parties* regarding the disputed right.[623] The previous chapter identified the

618 Erdogan Moroglu, Anonim Ortaklıkta Genel Kurul Kararlarının Hukumsuzlugu, p. 262.
See supra note 553 for a related Supreme Court decision.

619 Erdogan Moroglu, Anonim Ortaklıkta Genel Kurul Kararlarının Hukumsuzlugu, p. 262.
Article 408:

"*Disputes arising from in rem rights on immovable property or, disputes that are not subject to the will of the parties' are not arbitrable*".

620 "*… disputes that are not subject to the will of the parties' are not arbitrable*".

621 One shall note that Turkish Code of Civil Procedure governs domestic arbitration. Turkish International Arbitration Code governs the disputes with international character. The latter is the subject of this paper. Article 1 (4) of Turkish International Arbitration Code states that:

"*This Code shall not apply to the … disputes that are not subject to the will of the parties*".

This provision contains the same requirement. The courts and scholars mostly refer article 408 because it is more general. The explanations, therefore, remain valid for Turkish International Arbitration Code.

622 *See supra* Chapter II (A) 1. (a) for more information on criteria and approaches for a matter of dispute to be evaluated as subject to the will of the parties.

623 Rasih Yegengil, Tahkim: (L'arbitrage) [Arbitration: (L'arbitrage)] 152 (Istanbul, 1974).

right of disposition as an imperative principle for the civil judiciary system in Turkey.[624] The Turkish Code of Civil Procedure also emphasizes this principle.[625] Parties' power and opportunity of independent disposition extends from the pre-dispute interval through the submission of the dispute to the jurisdiction and hearings before the court.[626] The will of the parties, therefore, applies to the commencement of adjudication, the determination of subject matter, and the *settlement of the matter in dispute*.[627] The previous chapter explained that settlement is one of the rights that parties acquire *as a consequence of* having the power of disposition over the matter in dispute.[628] The right of settlement is, therefore, neither equivalent to nor a pre-requisite for the power of disposition. Parties can freely resolve disputes through settlements without court decisions. This strongly *indicates* that parties have the power of disposition in disputes, making disputes subject to the will of parties.[629]

In sum, parties can conclude a dispute through settlement without a court decision because they have the right of disposition. The availability of a settlement results from the dispositive character of the right in dispute. It may confirm a dispute's dispositive character in the absence of other indications. Dispositive character, however, generates the settlement option, not vice versa. Other circumstances can indicate a dispute's dispositive character even when the settlement option is not present. Drawing accurate conclusions regarding arbitrability requires the consideration of factors beyond the possibility of settlement. The statutory regulation explicitly refers to the 'disposition of the parties',

---

624 *See supra* note 52 and accompanying text for further explanation.

625 Article 24 of Turkish Code of Civil Procedure:

> "...Parties' right of disposition on a matter in dispute, which has a dispositive nature, remains *post litem motam*."

626 *See supra* note around 65 (Chapter II (A) 1. (a)).

627 *See supra* note 65 *et seq*. (Chapter II (A) 1. (a)).

628 *See supra* note 70 (Chapter II (A) 1. (a)).

The chapter has designated the meaning of the parties' power of disposition, and clarified what it corresponds to in Turkish Law with the following statement:

> "...the right of disposition of the parties on the matter in dispute remains *post litem motam* in accordance with the same provision. For this reason, parties are free to reconcile, mediate, settle or waive the lawsuit in terms of the matter in dispute, which follows the filing of the case."

629 *See supra* note 71 and accompanying text. (Chapter II (A) 1. (a)).

not settlements. [630] Doctrinal opinion, as opposed to the law, identifies settlement as an indicator of dispositive character. Inferring that parties lack the power to dispose of the right in question merely because they cannot resolve the dispute with a settlement is simply wrong. Disposition of the parties, not the possibility of settlement, determines arbitrability.

This section examines the disposition of the parties in the context of general assembly resolutions. Whether disputes arising from the annulment of general assembly resolutions are within the disposition of the parties is the crucial question. Several factors influence the dispositive nature of such disputes. The fact that resolutions passed in a general assembly came into existence as a consequence of the will of the members is beyond doubt.[631] It bears highlighting as well that: "*It is one of the fundamental principles of law that an authorized agency of a legal entity is entitled to amend or revoke a decision that it has made.*"[632] A general assembly can, therefore, amend or revoke any previous general assembly resolution subject to annulment action with a new resolution.[633] If the court has not settled the annulment action in such a case, it will dismiss the action as lacking a real contest because the plaintiff no longer possesses a legal interest in need of protection.[634] Members, thus, have the unequivocal right to revoke at any time a general assembly resolution for which an annulment has been filed before a court. This is possible when the corporation adopts a second contrary resolution until the court issues a final judgment, which makes the pending adjudication lacking in any subject matter.[635]

Resolutions are a declaration of the will of assembly. General assemblies have absolute power of disposition regarding resolutions they render.[636] Even when a court adjudicates an action for annulment of a general assembly resolution, the

---

630 Burak Huysal, p. 312.

631 *Id* at 313.

632 Burcin Yıldırım, p. 56.
Reha Poroy, Unal Tekinalp & Ersin Camoglu, para.615b.

633 Hasan Pulaslı, 6102 Sayılı Turk Ticaret Kanunu'na Gore Sirketler Hukuku Serhi, p. 866.

634 *Id* at 866 & n.649.

635 Burak Huysal, p. 313.
Reha Poroy, Unal Tekinalp & Ersin Camoglu, p. 394 (para 747).

"*The doctrine puts emphasis on whether the general assembly can amend annullable resolutions prior to the decision of annulment is rendered about them. This capability is generally accepted.*"

636 Mehmet Tas, p. 52.

general assembly has the explicit power of disposition regarding the resolution; it can reverse, amend, or revoke the resolution until the court settles the case with the final judgment.[637] This fact introduces another express factor for determining the disposition of the parties.

Prior to court involvement and during court proceedings, the parties possess dispositive power regarding general assembly resolutions.[638] The following two factors, in summary, satisfy this requirement:

- the general assembly issues the resolution in accordance with its own will,

and

- it is possible to revoke the related resolution by adopting another resolution until a court order annuls it.

Together, these two factors demonstrate the existence of will of the parties necessary for the recourse to arbitration. [639] The presence of an explicit dispositive character means that no other indication is necessary including the availability of settlement. For the annulment of general assembly resolutions, the will of the parties is explicit and sufficient. The Commercial Code contains no rule impeding arbitration in this regard, so annulment of general assembly resolutions should be considered arbitrable in accordance with Article 1(4) of Turkish International Arbitration Code or Article 408 of Turkish Code of Civil Procedure. [640]

Huysal adds a degree of interpretive nuance by approaching the issue from another point of view. He points out that, in Turkish law, the criterion that parties should have the power of disposition over arbitrated disputes is relevant in both procedural law and substantive law. [641] Arbitrability in procedural law connotes the ability to pursue procedural processes—settlement, acceptance, and renunciation—on the subject matter of the case.[642] In substantive law, arbitrability means that parties possess the authority of disposition over the right disputed in the case. *Huysal* concludes:[643]

---

637 *Ibid.*
638 *Ibid.*
639 Burak Huysal, p. 313.
640 *Ibid.*
641 Burak Huysal, p. 312.
642 *Ibid.*
643 *Ibid.*

...Those two senses of arbitration frequently overlap; in some exceptional cases, parties may be able to dispose in the field of substantive law despite being unable to settle before a court. On such occasions, the criterion of disposition, which refer to substantive law, prevail and the criterion for settlement will not be taken into consideration on account of the explicit regulations of Article 1(4) of Turkish International Arbitration Code and Article 408 of Turkish Code of Civil Procedure...

The way other countries approach the arbitration of the annulment of general assembly resolutions are illuminating. German Law, for example, has ceased to recognize the absence of the power of disposition on the matter in dispute as an impediment to arbitration.[644] The German Code of Civil Procedure [645] § 1030 no longer stipulates the power of disposition as a requirement for arbitration. Even before the removal of this stipulation, the German legal system had stopped recognizing this rationale.[646] Scholars who defend the inarbitrability of the annulment of general assembly resolutions on the grounds that such resolutions are not at the disposition of parties' lack substantive support. The purpose of the annulment action is to remove a general assembly resolution and it is possible to remove the resolution only by will of parties.[647] The existence of an arbitration agreement in the articles of association substantiates the dispositive power of the parties.[648] Settlement need not be available to satisfy the requirement of dispositive character. The progress of German law should serve as a model for Turkish law.

This sub-chapter concludes that disputes on the annulment of general assembly resolutions are arbitrable because they are subject to will of the parties as a matter of course. The statutory regulation explicitly refers to the notion of the 'disposition of the parties' rather than settlements.[649] Dispositive nature should, therefore, determine arbitrability. Evaluation of the annulment cases show sufficient indications of the dispositive nature of such disputes. This section has established that such cases are arbitrable because they are subject to will of the parties.

---

644 Haluk N. Nomer, pp. 178–179.
645 Zivilprozessordnung.
646 Haluk N. Nomer, p. 179.
647 *Ibid.*
648 *Ibid.*
649 Burak Huysal, p. 312.

2. Assessment of Settlement

The previous sub-chapter argued for the arbitrability of disputes arising from the annulment of general assembly resolutions. It identified requirements for determining whether a dispute is subject to will of the parties. It highlighted that compatibility with the settlement requirement is a subsidiary indication of arbitrability, not the main consideration. This sub-chapter further examines the availability of settlements. It establishes that even if one adopts the possibility of settlement as the main criterion, disputes arising from the annulment of general assembly resolutions remain arbitrable.

Some doctrinal commentators argue that the annulment of general assembly resolution proceedings is subject to the will of the parties.[650] They also maintain that settlements are undoubtedly available for such actions.[651] [652] They add that arbitration serves in two ways as a possible resolutory method for such disputes:

- through a clause included in the articles of association during the establishment of the company, or
- through a subsequent amendment of the company's articles of association.[653]

Turkish statutory law lacks an explicit regulation on this issue, so this analysis relies on the opinions of commentators. The availability of a settlement is not the only indicator of dispositive authority over the right in question.[654] A general assembly has the right to amend annullable resolutions by issuing another resolution before a court's annulment decision. This would make an annulment irrelevant. The parties, thus, clearly possess dispositive authority before the filing of the case.

The time after the filing of such cases merits its own examination. The defendant in an annulment action is the legal entity of the corporation. Plaintiffs in such actions can be shareholders, boards of directors, or individual members of the board of directors.[655] When shareholders file the action of annulment, the board of directors represents the corporate legal entity. The legal entity of the corporation is a party to the action for annulment; the board of directors plays a

650 Mehmet Helvacı, p. 200.

651 *Ibid.*

652 The commentator finds the annulment action inarbitrable in the final evaluation. He, however, assesses the factor related to settlement irrelevant.

653 Mehmet Helvacı, pp. 201–202.

654 Mehmet Tas, p. 51.

655 Possible plaintiffs were listed in article 446 of Turkish Commercial Code under the heading of "Persons Who Can File an Annulment Action" as:

deciding role in the establishing the character of the resolution.[656] [657] The board of directors can exercise powers supplied by procedural law in adjudication. The board of directors, therefore, has the power to finalize the annulment action by settling with the plaintiff party.[658] Corporations, thus, retain the right to accept cases or enter into extrajudicial settlements with plaintiffs. This serves as a sufficient indication of dispositive authority.

Those who assert that parties do not have a right to settle cases for the annulment of general assembly resolutions, make those cases inarbitrable. Annulment cases are subject to the will of the parties because parties have dispositive authority over those cases. None of the arguments mentioned above suffice to prove the inarbitrability of annulment cases. This means that parties in such cases should be able to resolve their disputes through international commercial arbitration in Turkey.

B. Judicial Jurisdiction: Potential Exclusivity of the Rule and Involvement of Public Policy

In a conference held in 1974 about antitrust law, commentators pointed out that the content and grounds of exclusive jurisdiction vary from jurisdiction to jurisdiction.[659] They also highlighted that a clearer definition of this concept

---

"

- *Shareholders who are present at the meeting, who dissented, and whose dissent is included in the minute,*
- *Shareholders who claim that the invitation was not made in due form; the agenda was not announced properly; persons who are not authorized to attend the general assembly -or their agents- attended the meeting and voted; they were unjustly not allowed to attend the general assembly and vote; and those abovementioned violations had an impact on issuing the general assembly resolution, regardless of the shareholder's presence at the meeting or having dissenting vote,*
- *Board of directors,*
- *Each of the members of the board of directors who will be subject to personal responsibility in the event of fulfillment of the resolution".*

656 The authority to represent the legal entity of corporation is one of the exclusive authorizations of the board of directors.

657 Mehmet Tas, p. 52.

658 *Ibid.*

Even though the board of directors may cause problems for the corporation by exercising this power, such problems would fall within the concern of the internal operation of the corporation

659 Richard W. Pogue, *Exclusive Jurisdiction*, 43 Antitrust L. J. Twenty – Second Ann. Spring Meeting Washington, D.C. (1974). pp. 314–315.

is needed.[660] Courts or practitioners have, indeed, used several '*nominative phrases*' to describe this concept, such as "primary jurisdiction", "*exclusive competence,*" "*exclusive primary jurisdiction,*" "*exclusive pre-liminary jurisdiction,*" "*primary original jurisdiction,*" "*ordinary primary jurisdiction,*" "*exclusion,*" and yet others.[661] Several areas of law may be affected by this concept of subject areas including anti-trust law, commercial law and criminal law, making for a long list.

The definition of exclusive jurisdiction also remains ambiguous in more recent comparative legal studies. *Uzelac* points out that interpretations on this issue vary, and the extent of the "exclusion" is unsettled.[662] *Exclusion* is demonstrated by the following examples:

- *"excluding default jurisdiction (e.g., jurisdiction according to domicile);*
- *excluding any foreign jurisdiction;*
- *excluding jurisdiction of courts of particular type;*
- *excluding courts which are territorially not competent; excluding any prorogation agreement or some of them;*
- *excluding arbitration (domestic or foreign); excluding any other option but the jurisdiction of a single body.*"[663]

This ambiguity arises from the absence of a universal definition of the concept. Many jurisdictions lack a direct and explicit regulation defining and governing exclusive judicial rules.[664] This necessitates legal interpretation which naturally (almost obligatorily) results in conflicting points of view. The problem explored in this section essentially arises from excessive interpretations concluding that an exclusive judicial jurisdictional rule makes a dispute inarbitrable. This section evaluates this problem by examining the related statutory regulations and their particular interpretations in Turkish law. Judicial jurisdictional regulations in Turkish law are one of the most frequently cited grounds for the inarbitrability of disputes arising from the annulment of general assembly resolutions. The relevant provision in the Commercial Code lies at the core of this debate. This section

660 Richard W. Pogue, pp. 315–316.
661 *Ibid.* (The list narrowed down as some phrases are related to anti-trust law.)
662 Alan Uzelac, p. 463.
663 *Ibid.*
664 *Ibid.*

examines Article 445 of the Commercial Code[665] to determine if the code aims to allocate sole authority to the national courts such as to exclude arbitration.

Article 445 provides:

> The persons identified in Article 446 can file annulment actions against general assembly resolutions that violate the law or articles of incorporation, particularly good faith, *before the commercial court of first instance in the location of the company headquarters,* within 3 months from the date of the decision.

The text of the article points out a specific court in a specified location for annulment actions. This has led some doctrinal commentators to conclude that those disputes can only be submitted to the specified court. They consider the regulation a mandatory exclusive judicial jurisdictional rule, identifying the authorized court as the commercial court closest to the company headquarters.[666] They also argue against the availability of arbitration as a mechanism of resolution for such disputes. This serves as the critical point for all arguments about the arbitrability of disputes arising from the annulment of general assembly resolutions in Turkish legal doctrine.[667] These arguments focus on whether the rule granting authorization to the court closest to the company headquarters has a mandatory character in a public policy context.[668]

1. Jurisdictional Rules and the Extent of Their Effect in Turkish Law

The previous chapter mentioned that[669] no statute in Turkish law definitively stipulates that a dispute must be heard before a court—thereby prohibiting other dispute resolution mechanisms including arbitral tribunals. Whether a rule stipulating jurisdictional exclusivity disables arbitration must be determined on a case-by-case basis by evaluating the general rules of procedural law. Mandatory rules of national legal systems may proceed from procedural rules rather than substantive rules. "Jurisdictional" rules, in which States establish an exclusive judicial authority for specific courts exemplify this phenomenon. To determine

---

665 The related regulation of the previous Commercial Code was Article 381.The sources written during that Code, therefore, refers to Article 381 instead. *See supra* note 566 for a further explanation.

666 Mehmet Bahtiyar, Ortaklıklar Hukuku [The Law of Corporations] 163 (7. Basım, Beta Basım) [7th ed. Beta Publishing 2012].

667 Sami Karahan, p. 529.

668 *Ibid.*

669 *See supra* Chapter II (B) (1).

the effect of such rules on the arbitrability of a dispute, one must determine whether the exclusive judicial jurisdiction rule is mandatory.

Such cases may occur in two ways in Turkish law: either through an explicit statement of 'exclusive judicial jurisdiction' in the related codes or through the expression of a 'court order' requirement in general. The previous chapter included this brief overview but did not examine the specific rules in the Turkish Commercial Codes.[670] Those rules are more relevant to this chapter's exploration of corporate issues. This chapter applies general information about exclusive judicial jurisdictional rules from the previous chapter to the issue of the arbitrability of the annulment of general assembly resolutions. The question is whether the regulation in Article 445 has mandatory jurisdictional authority resulting from either an explicit statement of jurisdictional exclusivity or a 'court order' requirement (which would mean that the exclusive authority of the national courts would exclude any possibility of arbitration).

The relationship between jurisdictional rules and arbitration merits clarification. Two major factors related to jurisdictional regulations may initiate debates about inarbitrability:

- jurisdictional rules that have explicit statements of 'exclusive judicial jurisdiction' in the related codes,

and

- the expression of a 'court order' requirement.

The regulation in Article 445 stating that parties can file actions for the annulment of general assembly resolutions before the commercial court closest to the company headquarters may relate to the first factor. This section analyzes the regulation in the context of explicit statements of 'exclusive judicial jurisdiction' in the related code.[671] Jurisdictional regulations contain both mandatory and non-mandatory rules. Non-mandatory rules are general jurisdictional rules. These rules may give the plaintiff the right to file a lawsuit either before a general court or before a specific court prescribed in the code.[672] Certain jurisdictional rules, on the other hand, may deem that court jurisdiction is a matter of public policy. Mandatory rules exclusively authorize a specific court. Doctrinal commentators

---

670 *See supra* Chapter II (B).

671 *See supra* Chapter II (B) 1 for further information.

672 *See supra* note 134 and accompanying text for further information. (Chapter II (B) 1)

denominate the latter *exclusive judicial jurisdictional rules* or *mandatory rules based on public policy.*

Jurisdictional rules need not be considered exclusive unless that attribute is explicitly stipulated. As a rule, in Turkish law, court jurisdiction does not relate to public policy.[673] This chapter previously listed jurisdictional regulations that authorize specific courts 'exclusively' as a matter of public policy.[674] Article 445 is not among the listed rules. The analysis of related general principles of procedural law suggests, therefore, that this rule should not impede arbitration.[675] Certain authors in Turkish legal doctrine nonetheless conclude that the jurisdictional regulation in Article 445 *exclusively* authorizes the court in the location of the company headquarters. This leads them to argue that actions for the annulment of general assembly resolutions are inarbitrable.[676] Such scholarly opinions are highly contestable. The wording of the law contains no indication of the rule's jurisdictional exclusivity. Certain other articles, meanwhile, make the jurisdictional exclusivity clear in the text of the article.[677] The existence of rules in which lawmakers explicitly prescribe jurisdictional exclusivity means that assertions of exclusivity in Article 445, which contains no such prescription, are based on excessive interpretation.

2. Exclusive Judicial Rules and Arbitrability

For the sake of argument, this section treats the jurisdictional rule in Article 445 as exclusive and examines how exclusivity affects arbitrability; it shows that even the jurisdictional exclusivity of Article 445 would not make annulment cases inarbitrable. This additional argument is justified because certain doctrinal scholars continue to assert the rule's exclusive character and because this chapter aims to cover all the arguments about the inarbitrability of these disputes due to jurisdictional exclusivity. Even if Article 445 included the term 'exclusive' and was designated as a jurisdictional rule involving public policy, it would not make

---

673 *See supra* note 140 for further information. (Chapter II (B) 1)

674 Chapter II (B) 1.

675 Neuchâtel Canton Court has decided that arbitrators can hear a case concerning annulment of a general assembly resolution when the articles of incorporation have an article stating, "disputes between the corporation and the shareholders can be arbitrated." in 1977.
Baki Kuru, Vol.VI, p. 5950–5951.

676 *See* discussions *supra* Chapter IV (C) 1.

677 *See* the list of rules with exclusive judicial jurisdiction *supra* note 143 *et seq*. (Chapter II (B) 1)

disputes regarding the annulment of general assembly resolutions inarbitrable. No judicial rule in Turkish law suggests that such disputes must be heard solely before courts and cannot be heard before other dispute resolution authorities such as arbitral tribunals.[678] [679] Arbitral agreements or clauses, moreover, are not exceptions to the mandatory nature of jurisdictional rules.[680]

Certain scholars use 'exclusive jurisdiction based on public policy' to describe situations in which the court designated in the Code must hear a case exclusively. This practice, however, only applies in domestic law.[681] Identifying all exclusive judicial jurisdictional rules in Turkish domestic law as matters of public policy—and thus making related disputes inarbitrable—would have an irreversible impact on international commercial practice. A distinction between international and domestic commercial practice is, thus, inevitable. Recent alterations to doctrinal approaches and court practices in comparative law support such a distinction.

For example, in their comparative study, *Poudret & Besson*[682] argue that:

> *The arbitral tribunal must in all events respect the exclusive jurisdiction of the courts of the country of the seat if they form and obstacle to arbitrability. However, it may be the case that such rules only apply to domestic matters and do not have the same effect in international arbitration. As we have said above,*[683] *we do not think that the arbitral tribunal is bound by the exclusive jurisdiction rules of another country, unless it characterizes such rules as a part of international public policy.*

Numerous examples in comparative law demonstrate a shift toward the belief that jurisdictional exclusivity does not prevent arbitrability. In German law, even matters recognized as subject to the 'judicial monopoly' of the courts by legislators—matters over which the court retains exclusive authority—cannot be designated as

678 Burak Huysal, p. 250.

679 *See supra* Chapter II (B) 1 for more information.

680 Jean-François Poudret & Sébastien Besson, p. 295 (*Citing* Yves Donzallaz, 3 La Convention De Lugano pp. 770–77 (Berne 1998)).

681 Baki Kuru, Vol.I, p. 549.

682 Jean-François Poudret & Sébastien Besson, p. 295.

683 *Id* at p. 294

It was stated about Swiss Law that:

> "*In international matters, arbitrability is exclusively governed by Federal Law, so that cantonal rules of jurisdiction no longer apply. In addition, only Federal rules of international public policy can form an obstacle to arbitrability.*"

inarbitrable.[684] Past debates in German law mirror the one taking place in Turkish law. § 246(3) of the German Corporate Law gives authority to the court in the same location as the company headquarters.[685] Legal scholars in Germany strongly opposed the notion that the jurisdictional rule in § 246(3) should prohibit arbitration. The German Federal Court responded to these criticisms and acknowledged the contemporary understanding of arbitration in 1996 by rejecting the use of jurisdictional rules as a basis for inarbitrability. This action confirmed the arbitrability of disputes arising from the annulment of the general assembly resolutions.[686]

The modern approach contradicts the traditional approach. *Yıldırım*[687] points out that relegating a dispute to the exclusive jurisdiction of national judges does not make the dispute inarbitrable. Exclusive authorization can eliminate arbitrability only if the legislator intends to endow the national courts with sole judicial power over the dispute.[688] Scholars of Swiss Law,[689] likewise, *"do not think the rules of PILS*[690] *which provide for the exclusive jurisdiction of a Swiss judge or restrict the freedom of the parties to conclude a jurisdiction agreement (PILS, Arts 97, 114(2) and 151(3)) apply to arbitration."*

The application of an exclusive jurisdictional rule to a dispute does not change the main criterion for determining arbitrability. The dispute must be subject to the will of the parties. The satisfaction of this criterion must be determined on a case-by-case basis. A dispute can, for instance, be considered subject to the will of parties if it is at the free disposition of the parties.[691] An arbitral clause would remain valid if the matter in dispute is at the free disposition of the parties' despite the application of a judicial jurisdictional rule.[692] Assuming that the presence of an applicable judicial jurisdictional rule makes a dispute inarbitrable is misleading. Doctrinal commentators point out another exclusive judicial jurisdictional rule.

---

684 Burak Huysal, p. 253. (*Citing* Klaus Peter Berger, *The New German Arbitration Law in International Perspective*, 26 FORUM International 7 (July, 2000)). *See supra* note 214. (Chapter II (B) 1)

685 Burak Huysal, p. 310.

686 *Ibid.*

687 Burcin Yıldırım, p. 36 & n.11 (*Citing* Olivier Caprasse, Les Societes et l'Arbitrage 23 (Bruxelles 2002)).

688 *Ibid.*

689 Jean-François Poudret & Sébastien Besson, p. 294.

690 Swiss Private International Law.

691 *See supra* Chapter II (A) 1 for further explanations on dispositive nature.

692 Rasih Yegengil, p. 174. (*See supra* note 196 and accompanying text). (Chapter II (B) 1)

The law about *in-rem* rights exclusively stipulates courts in specific locations.[693] However, the law exclusively authorizing the court in a specific location does not disqualify arbitrators from resolving the dispute. Rules stipulating territorial jurisdiction "(*ratione loci*)" do not normally prevent the arbitrability of disputes.[694]

The matter involving public policy in this rule about the location of the court is conceivably, valid only if parties decide to resolve the dispute through litigation.[695] This has no bearing on arbitration. As previously mentioned, parties possess the authority of disposition on the subject matter.[696] The notion that jurisdictional rules impede arbitration, therefore, clash with the general understanding of civil procedure and international law. Comparative law also confirms that the limitations embodied in foreign law may only apply with respect to claims: "*when their adjudication is 'exclusively' submitted to a court jurisdiction on the basis of provisions which must be taken into consideration from a public policy point of view.*"[697]

Even if one accepts the argument that the judicial jurisdictional rule in Article 445 is exclusive and involves public policy, granting the courts exclusive authority over arbitration requires additional circumstances in Turkish law.[698] Nothing in the article indicates that legislators intended to exclude arbitration when they delegated authority to domestic courts.[699] Turkish law identifies issues subject to the will of the parties as arbitrable. The exclusive authority of the courts, therefore, comes into question only when a valid arbitral agreement does not exist.

The protection of legal interests is a basis for public policy intervention.[700] Some may question whether this is the rationale behind the judicial jurisdictional rule in Article 445. Some types of disputes that fall within the ambit of particular areas of law are inarbitrable[701]—disputes relating to family law or law

---

693 See *supra* note 195. (Chapter II (B) 1 (a))

694 Jean-François Poudret & Sébastien Besson, p. 295.

695 Baki Kuru, Vol.VI, p. 5947.

696 *See supra* note 200. (Chapter II (B) 1 (a))

697 Jean François Poudret & Sébastien Besson, p. 294.

698 Burak Huysal, p. 311.

699 *Ibid.*

700 *See supra* note 86 and accompanying text for an example. The law protects the legal interest of a renter, who is a weaker party as a matter of public policy. *See* also *supra* note 351 *et seq.* and accompanying text for the examples related to consumers and employees. (Chapter II (C) 2 (a) 1)

701 See *supra* Chapter II (C) 2 (a) 1 for further information on issues considered as non-arbitrable due to public policy in domestic law.

of persons,[702] for example. The law requires that judges protect the children at risk in custody cases because the duty of protection also indirectly concerns the public.[703] Disregarding the will of the parties to resolve their disputes through arbitration and obligating them to submit their dispute to national courts based on a controversial judicial jurisdictional rule protects no similar significant legal interest.[704]

Some Turkish doctrinal commentators argue that the intervening rule in Article 445[705] of the Turkish Commercial Code, which *exclusively* authorizes the court in the location of the company headquarters, does not comply with the concept of arbitration.[706] The previous section evaluated the exclusivity factor of the judicial jurisdictional rule's subject matter in the context of Turkish procedural law. This evaluation briefly concluded that the judicial jurisdictional rule is not an exclusive rule because exclusive rules are enumerated, making the application of the designation to other rules inappropriate. As a result, even if this rule fit the category of exclusive rules, this categorization would not automatically exclude arbitration; to reach such a conclusion would require evaluation of additional abovementioned factors.

3. Other Counter-Arguments against Inarbitrability based on Judicial Jurisdictional Rules

Additional corporate perspectives deepen the analytical considerations. *Zafer Saka*'s opinion on arbitrability, for instance, directly relates to the cases on the annulment of general assembly resolutions. *Saka* argues that lawsuits are requests for legal protection through the adjudicatory authority.[707] He adds that courts possesses such adjudicatory authority *as a rule* and arbitrators possesses it *as an exception.*[708] Parties can submit the annulment of general assembly resolutions to arbitration on the condition that the articles of association contain a clause stipulating recourse to arbitration or that they subsequently insert such a clause into articles of association. *Saka* points out that, while the law recognizes the

702 *See supra* note 379 and accompanying text.
703 Burak Huysal, p. 311.
704 *Ibid.*
705 *See supra* note 566.
706 Erdogan Moroglu, Anonim Ortaklıkta Genel Kurul Kararlarının Hukumsuzlugu, p. 262.
707 Zafer Saka, Anonim Ortaklıklarda Genel Kurul [General Assembly in Joint Stock Corporations] 286 (Vedat Kitapcılık, Istanbul 2004) [Vedat Publishing, Istanbul 2004].
708 Zafer Saka, p. 286.

right to file an action for annulment as a *vested right*[709] and states the effects of the annulment judgment,[710] it does not draw a clear distinction between litigation and arbitration.[711] The law, in other words, grants court jurisdiction over cases when parties have not chosen arbitration.[712]

The Turkish Code of Civil Procedure regulates adjudicatory proceedings in the domestic civil courts. The courts are the official judicial organs of the State, so this Code contains legal provisions intended to govern adjudicatory proceedings pursued.[713] The Code also includes Articles—407 to 444—that govern arbitration as a private dispute resolution mechanism for some specific types of disputes.[714] Procedural law thus designates the courts as the *general* and usual dispute resolution authority while recognizing arbitration as an *exceptional* adjudicatory mechanism.[715]Codes that consist of substantive law provisions, like Contract or Commercial Codes, inevitably identify the courts as general resolution authorities while disregarding arbitration or arbitrators.[716] Substantive law regulations

---

709 Article 452 of Turkish Commercial Code:

> "*General assembly can amend all provisions of the articles of association in compliance with the conditions stipulated in the Statute unless otherwise provided; with the reservation of vested and inalienable rights.*"

It was article 385/II in the previous Commercial Code.

710 Effect of the Decision:
Article 450:

> "(1) *A court decision pertaining to annulment or nullity of general assembly resolution inures to the benefit of all shareholders after it is finalized...*"

It was article 383 in the previous Commercial Code.

711 Zafer Saka, p. 286.

712 *Ibid.*

713 Mehmet Tas, p. 58.

714 CHAPTER 11
Arbitration
Scope of Application
Article 407:

> "(1) *The provisions that take place within this Chapter apply to the disputes which do not consist of a foreign element in accordance with the Turkish International Arbitration Act dated 06/21/2001 and numbered 4686; and designates the place of arbitration as Turkey.*"

715 Mehmet Tas, p. 58.

716 *Ibid.*

thus do not specifically refer to arbitration for each issue. This, however, does not necessarily mean that the Codes intend to prohibit arbitration.

The Turkish Commercial Code contains substantial rules of law focused primarily on litigation. The fact that the code refers only to a specific court does not mean it intends to bar arbitration as a resolutory method. Article 445 of Turkish Commercial Code does not stipulate an exclusive jurisdiction. It only has a regulatory and territorial function if parties file the case before the court.[717] The fact that the article stipulates the authorized court does not, therefore, prohibit the arbitrability of such disputes. *Uzelac* describes the confusion between the national legal regulations on exclusive jurisdiction and arbitrability as follows:

> *The issue whether certain dispute should be submitted to a certain court obviously surpasses the questions of arbitrability.*[718]

Exclusive jurisdictional rules may have several functions. These functions may differ from one jurisdiction to another. *Uzelac* points out this distinction,[719] outlining possible consequences at different levels of the legal system:

- *the level of national courts' jurisdiction, where it raises the questions regarding jurisdiction of courts of different type, level and territorial competence;*
- *the level of distributing jurisdiction for particular cases among the public courts of different national jurisdictions*

and finally;

- *the level [that] distinguishes court jurisdiction from out-of-court dispute resolution methods, including arbitration* (*whereby, again, the sub-topic may be related to the seat of such dispute resolution methods.*)

The exclusive jurisdictional rule must belong to the last level in order to exclude arbitration as a dispute resolution option. Granting, for the sake of argument, the exclusive character of the judicial jurisdictional rule in Article 445, the applicability of the third level remains dubious. Turkish legal doctrine states that this rule was established to corroborate the judicial jurisdictional rule in Article 9 of the old Turkish Code of Civil Procedure numbered 1086.[720] The repealed Article

---

717 *Id* at 59.

718 Alan Uzelac, p. 453.

719 *Ibid*. (*See supra* note 167 and accompanying text for further information). (Chapter II (B) 1).

720 Burak Huysal, p. 311. (*Citing* Hakan Pekcanitez, *Anonim Ortaklıklarda Denetciler Tarafından Acılacak Davalar* [*Cases to be Filed by Auditors in Joint-Stock Corporations*]

9[721] stated that:

> *Every case should be heard before the court in the location where the defendant lived at the time of the filing in accordance with the Turkish Civil Code unless otherwise is implied by the law…*[722]

---

in Prof. Dr. Kudret Ayıter'e Armagan [Dedication for Prof. Dr. Kudret Ayıter] 482 (Ankara, 1998)).

721 Turkish Code of Civil Procedure numbered 6100 and dated 01/12/2011has replaced Turkish Code of Civil Procedure numbered 1086, which is why this article number has changed. The article 9 currently corresponds to multiple other articles about judicial jurisdiction including articles 6,7 and 9.

The related articles of the new Code are as follows:

"Court with General Jurisdiction
Article 6:

(1) *The court where the defendant real or legal person reside at the time of the filing of the case has general jurisdiction.*
(2) *Place of residence is determined in accordance with the Turkish Civil Code numbered 4721 and dated 11/22/2001.*

Jurisdiction in the Event of More Than One Defendants
Article 7:

(1) *If the defendant is more than one, the case can be filed before the court where either of them resides. However, if the law designates a court having a mutual jurisdiction for all the defendants depending on the ground of the action, the case shall be heard before this court.*
(2) *In the event of more than one defendant, if it is understood from evidences or indications that the case is filed with the sole intent of bringing one of the defendants to another court, the court decides rejection of venue by severing the case against him on the plea of the related defendant.*

Jurisdiction in the Event of Absence of a Place of Residence in Turkey
Article 9:

(1) *The court in the location of the last habitual residence of the defendant in Turkey has the general jurisdiction about the ones who lack a place of residence in Turkey.*

…"

722 Article 9 continues as follows:

"…*In the event that the place of domicile is not certain, the case should be heard before the court in the location of the last habitual residence in Turkey.*

This is one of the most longstanding general rules in Turkish procedural law for 'real' persons. One can, therefore, infer that the rule in Article 445 intended to affirm the judicial jurisdictional rule in civil procedural law for companies. The jurisdictional rule in Article 445 authorizing the court of a specific location aims to indicate the territory and the type of court. The content of the rule thus falls within the first of the three listed levels.[723] Some authors may assume that it is impossible to eliminate the authority of the court, or authorize another court[724] through an agreement or a general assembly resolution because of the exclusiveness of the jurisdictional rule in Article 445.[725] Such an assumption would, however, wrongly place Article 445 in the third level listed above. Such an interpretation would be excessive.

Even if the rule were exclusive and included in the assumed level, however, jurisdictional exclusivity would apply only when the parties prefer adjudication. This rule, in other words, only applies if the parties have not entered into an arbitral agreement. Disregarding the will of the parties to resolve their disputes through arbitration and obliging them to submit their disputes to judges on the grounds of a judicial jurisdictional rule would not protect any legal interest.

Supporting court decisions illustrate this point. Article 12 of the Turkish Code of Civil Procedure[726] is similar to Article 445. The article stipulates that cases involving immovable properties should be heard before courts in the location of the immovable property. This is an exclusive judicial jurisdictional rule.

If the defendant is more than one, the case can be filed before the court where either of them resides. In so far, if the law designates a court having a mutual jurisdiction for all the defendants depending on the ground of the action, the case shall be heard before this court.

However, if it is understood from indications or other evidences that the case is filed with the sole intent of bringing one of the defendants to another court, the court decides rejection of venue by severing the case against him.

For the divorce and judicial separation cases, the court in the location where the defendant resides or the last time spouses has resided together for 6 months prior to the case has jurisdiction."

723 *Supra* note 719 and accompanying text.

724 Than the court in the location of the company headquarters as stipulated in the article.

725 Mehmet Helvacı, p. 194.

726 It was article 13 in the previous Turkish Code of Civil Procedure numbered 1086. In the new Turkish Code of Civil Procedure numbered 6100, article 12 governs this issue. The court refers to article 13 because the previous Code was in effect at the time of this decision. The article states as follows:

Jurisdiction for the Cases Arising from *In Rem* Rights on Immovables

Article 12:

Confirming Article 12's status as an exclusive jurisdictional rule, the Court has found some cases to be inarbitrable.[727] The Turkish Supreme Court has also, however, confirmed the arbitrability of disputes arising from *in rem* rights on immovable property,[728] despite rules like Article 12 exclusively authorizing specific courts for the purposes of adjudication. This result contradicts the general view. The relevant Supreme Court decision[729] reads as follows:

> *Articles of 407–444 of Turkish Code of Civil Procedure[730] regulate arbitration in Turkish law. The courts are authorized to resolve any kind of dispute between the parties and within the jurisdiction of the civil or criminal judiciary as a general rule. It is, however, possible for two parties, who are in dispute over a right, to agree on submitting this dispute, which is not related to public policy, to private persons rather than the courts. Resolution of a dispute by arbitrators is a private judicial remedy in our Procedural Code. Arbitration is possible in the event that the laws explicitly and implicitly allow it. In such cases, parties may, of their own volition, choose to resolve the dispute between them by way of an arbitral tribunal. Restitution of an immovable property share and having the required adjustment proceedings in the land registry within the provisions of the construction contract dated 08/07/1972 between the parties derive from acts in law that parties may implement freely. The court deems such acts as subject to the will of the parties. Settling disputes by way of arbitration here shall not be regarded as a contravention of law. Such disputes do not relate to public policy.*

This decision establishes that, even if the law exclusively stipulates a court in a specific location for a dispute, the general rules of arbitrability remain applicable. Certain doctrinal scholars have also commented on instances in which the law requires parties to file cases before specific courts. *Ustundag*[731] states that, in such cases, a

---

"*The court in the location of the immovable has the "exclusive authority" for the cases related to in rem rights on immovables or cases that may cause a change in the ownership of in rem rights and cases related to possession or right of detention of the immovable.*"

727 Turkish Supreme Court 14th Civil Circuit decision dated 06/11/2010 numbered 2010/5842E and 2010/6880 K.

The Supreme Court stipulated that parties should file cases arising from the passage of the title of an immovable property before the court in the location of the immovable property. The court identified this rule as mandatory in nature and involving public policy. Supreme Court, therefore, has concluded that an agreement for authorization of another court despite this mandatory rule is invalid.

728 *See* further explanation and cases cited *supra* note 202. *See* also *supra* Chapter IV (A).

729 Turkish Supreme Court 15th Civil Circuit decision dated 05/31/1979 numbered 1195/1330.

730 The decision originally states articles 516–536 because the previous Code was effective at the time of the decision.

731 Saim Ustundag, Medeni Yargılama Hukuku [Civil Procedure Law] 942 (Alfa Yayınları, 6. baskı, Istanbul 1997) [Alfa Publishing, 6th ed. Istanbul 1997].

dispute can be arbitrated as long as it is subject to the will of the parties. This general criterion,[732] therefore, still prevails in terms of the determination of arbitrability. Even *procedural* regulations about the resolution of private law disputes, such as statements of the exclusive judicial jurisdiction of a specific court, do not hold up as grounds for inarbitrability.[733] This applies to the Article 445 of the Commercial Code[734] as well. The notion that the rule specifying a particular court for the resolution of an intra-corporate dispute impedes arbitrability thus proves to be inaccurate.

The requirement that disputes must be subject to the will of the parties to be arbitrable applies to international disputes as well as domestic disputes.[735] The law must also take into consideration the need for flexibility in international disputes. To meet the expectations of contemporary investors, it should recognize the dynamic character of the commercial practice. The modern practice runs contrary to the traditional approach: the former tends to conclude that regulating a dispute within the ambit of the exclusive jurisdiction of the national judges does not exclude the possibility of arbitration.[736] Contemporary arbitral regulations and practices recognize that the appointment of a special court to resolve a dispute does not, on its own, suffice to bar arbitration. For disputes regarding matters at the free disposition of parties to be heard exclusively by courts requires specific intent on the part of legislators.[737] In comparative practice, *Uzelac* makes the following summary assessment:[738]

> *...Extensive limitations of arbitrability by means of 'exclusive jurisdiction doctrine' ... were not only practically unacceptable, but also theoretically untenable, since they imposed restrictions there, where in the new circumstances of the market economy and political democracy, founded on the rule of law, there were no convincing legal or political grounds.*

---

732 Which is whether the subject matter of the dispute is subject to the will of the parties.
Article 408 of the Turkish Code of Civil Procedure addresses the general criterion of arbitrability in Turkish Law.:

"*...disputes that are not subject to the will of the parties' are not arbitrable.*"

733 Mehmet Tas, p. 59.

734 Article 445. *See supra* note 566 for full text.

735 Article 408 of Turkish Code of Civil Procedure governs this criterion in parallel to article 1(4) of Turkish International Arbitration Code. The former governs the domestic arbitration while the latter governs arbitration with international character. *See supra* Chapter II (B) 1 (a) for further information.

736 Burcin Yıldırım, p. 36.

737 Burak Huysal, p. 310 & n. 1053.

738 Alan Uzelac, n.19 (*Citing* Alan Uzelac, *New Boundaries of Arbitrability Under the Croatian Law on Arbitration*, 9 Croatian Arb. Y.B. (2002), p. 150.)

C. Impact of the Decision on Shareholders not a Party to the Action, and Third Parties

This sub-chapter evaluates the effects of the decision for the annulment of general assembly resolutions. The core arguments focus on the regulation in Article 450 of Turkish Commercial Code. This regulation states that, once the court renders an annulment[739] of a general assembly resolution, the decision applies to all shareholders.[740] Once finalized, such court decisions have a *definitive*[741] effect on plaintiffs and all shareholders and corporate departments. First, the final annulment of general assembly resolutions applies to all shareholders.

---

739 Or nullity.

740 *"A court decision pertaining to annulment or nullity of general assembly resolution inures to the benefit of all shareholders after it is finalized..."*

741 The reason why the text stated the term "*definitive*" judgment effect instead of *Res Judicata* is the differences between Anglo-Saxon and Turkish Law. *Res Judicata* corresponds to the French term *chose jugée*, whereas *definitive judgment effect* here corresponds to the French term *judgment definitive.*

See Kemal Gozler, *Res Judicata'nın Turkcesi Uzerine* [*On the Turkish Translation of Res Iudicata*] Ankara Universitesi Hukuk Fakultesi Dergisi 2007, Cilt. 56, Sayı. 2 [Ankara University Faculty of Law Journal 2007, Volume.56, Issue.2] for further information about the translation of Res Judicata. The current regulations do not have a direct translation although it is mistranslated as definitive judgement from time to time. The article also disregards the distinction of procedural and material definitive judgement effect. The fact that whether a decision is definitive is only one of the requirements for *Res Judicata is underlined.*

See also:

Jack Friedenthal, Mary Kane & Arthur Miller, Friedenthal, Kane and Miller's Civil Procedure 684 (4th ed. Hornbook Series W. Academic Publ'g 2005).

"*...The second requirement of Res Judicata is that it can be based only on a final judgement...*"

and

Thomas Penberthy Fry, *The Finality of Judicial Decisions,* [2 (1)] U. of Queensl. L. J. (1952) p. 9.

"...

(2) *THE DOCTRINE OF RES JUDICATA.*

(i) The Nature of the Doctrine.

If any judicial tribunal in the exercise of its jurisdiction delivers a judgment which is in its

nature final and conclusive, the judgment is res judicata.

...".

However, the regulation only stipulates this effect in regard to "litigation." Turkish law contains no equivalent regulation for arbitral awards. The absence of an explicit regulation for arbitration leads to conflicting interpretations of the law. Given the possible effects of a decision on third parties, this lack of clarity also undermines the certainty of the arbitrability of such disputes.[742] Whether the regulation for litigation applies to arbitral proceedings remains controversial in Turkish law. This section examines the legal nature of arbitral agreements and assesses relevant doctrinal opinions to reach a conclusion on the issue.

Annulment of general assembly resolution decisions have a constitutive and regulatory character.[743] The annulled resolution ceases to have an effect starting from the date of its inception. In other words, decisions of annulment have *definitive* effects that bind all shareholders and corporate departments both retrospectively and prospectively;[744] therefore, the extent of the final award's effect is significant. Arbitral awards, *per contra*, have a *definitive* effect as a rule only on the parties[745] to the arbitral agreement.[746] Arbitral agreements have an *inter partes* impact and do not bind third parties in principle.[747] In a decision dated 09/23/1975 and numbered 1975/6158E and 1975/1055K, the Turkish Supreme Court[748] ruled as follows:

> *...Arbitral agreements have effect only on the parties of it, like any other agreement. Agreements do not have any consequences for or against the ones who are not party to them. Arbitrators are authorized to hear the cases which are between the parties of the arbitral agreement....*[749]

---

for an illustration of the comparative aspect. One should, therefore, note that the explanation above is also the rule itself in comparative law with regard to the difference of *res judicata* and the definitive (final) effect of a judgment. The text aimed at underlining this nuisance considering the mistranslation in Turkish legal doctrine that uses those two terms interchangeably. Explanations on *res judicata* effect will follow in terms of multiparty issues below.

742 Burcin Yıldırım, p. 37.

743 Burcu Zengin, p. 108 & n.66.

744 *Ibid.*

745 And their singular and complete successors.

746 Zafer Saka, p. 287.

747 *Ibid.*

748 Turkish Supreme Court 4th Civil Circuit decision dated 09/23/1975 and numbered 1975/6158E and 1975/1055K. *See* Yargıtay Kararları Dergisi, Agustos 1976, s.1128 [Journal of Supreme Court Decisions, August 1976, p. 1128].

749 Zafer Saka, p. 287.

The Turkish Commercial Code regulation on the effects of decisions, *ipso facto*, raises an issue regarding arbitration. Is it legitimate that the final award affect shareholders not party to the arbitral case or some other third parties? Arbitral proceedings for annulment cases are typically conducted between a plaintiff, who has only a partial share of the corporation, and the defendant, who is the joint stock corporation. The arbitral tribunal appointed by these parties renders the arbitral award. Certain commentators assert that binding all shareholders and organs of the corporation with such an award is not legally acceptable.[750] Some arguments against the arbitrability of cases for the annulment of general assembly resolutions emerge from this position. The Article 450 rule about the effects of the annulment of general assembly resolution decisions, therefore, carries collateral consequences. Third party shareholders, departments of the corporation, and even possible third-party creditors may experience these consequences. Even though these parties would be uninvolved in the arbitral proceedings, they would still be bound by the arbitral decision.

Comparative law and Turkish law have both hesitantly approached the issue of the impact of annulment decisions on third parties.[751] To begin with, the 'third parties' component of the issue merits clarification. The analysis of the effects of arbitral awards, indeed, depends on this clarification. The 'third parties' with a stake in the arbitrability of annulment decisions include creditors or debtors who are not part of the corporation.[752] Some shareholders and corporate organs may also not be party to an annulment case. Some believe, on one hand, that arbitral awards would give rise to a *definitive* effect on all corporate shareholders and departments.[753] These intra-corporate actors, therefore, are not considered among third parties. Such determinations, on the other hand, bear examination because they are controversial.

Various terminological categorizations defining third parties take place in comparative studies. *Brekoulakis*, for instance, contends that there are different *groups* of third parties that are possibly affected by an arbitral

750 *See supra* Chapter IV (C) 1 for detailed arguments asserted about this in the doctrine.
751 Burak Huysal, p. 313.
752 *Id* at 313–314.
753 Burak Huysal, p. 314.
Reha Poroy, Unal Tekinalp & Ersin Camoglu, p. 386.
Mehmet Tas, p. 60.
Zafer Saka, p. 288.

award. [754] "*False third parties*" constitute one of those groups. The author explains the reason why this group is named *false third parties*:

> *...they are neither real parties nor pure third parties who are complete strangers to the arbitration between the two real parties....*[755]

This group of third parties, on one hand, is not a party to an arbitral agreement. On the other hand, they have cogent legal or financial benefits firmly connected to contractual relationships with the real parties, and the legal proceedings will influence them as well as the real parties.[756] *Guarantors,*[757]*subcontractors,*[758] or *teams of stockholders*[759] are such groups of third parties.[760]

The multiparty nature of corporate disputes, in a nutshell, requires a two-fold distinction between the 'false' third parties and other third parties. The former refers to the intra-corporate actors such as shareholders or corporate departments. The latter refers to the other third parties outside of the corporation such as creditors, debtors or sub-contractors. The subsequent sections will, therefore, evaluate the impact of arbitral awards on third parties according to the distinction of:

- Third parties who are intra-corporate persons or departments[761]; and,
- Third parties who are not intra-corporate persons or departments.[762]

---

754 Stavros Brekoulakis, *The Effect of An Arbitral Award and Third Parties in International Arbitration: Res Judicata Revisited*, 16 Am. Rev. Int'l Arb. (2005) p. 12.

755 Stavros Brekoulakis, p. 13.

756 *Ibid.*

757 Who "*...may remain outside the arbitration between the creditor and the principal debtor. This is so despite the fact that this arbitration may well determine that the guaranteed debt has been extinguished, in which case the guarantor would cease to be liable.*"

758 Who "*...may not take part in the arbitration between the owner and the contractor, although this arbitration may well determine that the project effectively delivered by the subcontractor is defective*".

759 Who "*...may not take part in the arbitration between the corporation and another party, although the arbitration may find against the corporation with considerable financial repercussions for the stockholders.*"

760 Stavros Brekoulakis, p. 13.

761 Such as other shareholders or organs of the corporation who are not party to the adjudicatory proceeding.

762 Such as creditors, debtors or sub-contractor.

1. Third Parties Who are Intra-Corporate Actors

This section's approach to the effects of arbitral awards varies according to the abovementioned categories. In particular, the section treats the argument for inarbitrability due to the possible effects of an arbitral award on third parties as noteworthy only for the latter category, not the former. Several reasons underlie this approach. First of all, the Commercial Code explicitly stipulates that the court decision will have an impact on the former group of third parties although no such regulation exists for the latter group. Once finalized in accordance with Article 450, indeed, a court decision on the annulment or nullity of a general assembly resolution will have a binding effect on *all* shareholders.[763] In this regard, comparative law suggests this rule should remain valid regardless of shareholder participation in the court proceedings. Spanish Law[764], in which an almost identical provision exists, describes this rule in a straightforward formula

> *...to recognize erga omnes effect to the award in the same terms as provided for court decisions under Article 222(3) Civil Code of Procedure. Although, some other problems might arise, those do not affect the arbitrability of the dispute but rather the procedure.*[765]

In Italy, lawmakers have gone a step further, stipulating mandatory proceedings including for international disputes. [766]

The analogous application of such rule to arbitral awards is highly desirable. Arbitral awards on annulment must have *definitive* effect on the first group of third parties. In other words, such awards must be binding for all shareholders and departments of the corporation regardless of being a party to the annulment case. This position is based on several reasons. First of all, the *exceptional* character of arbitration *vis-à-vis* litigation in Turkish legal doctrine needs to be reiterated.[767] The courts have the general authority while arbitrators have exceptional

---

763 Article 450

Effect of the Decision:

"(1) *A court decision pertaining to annulment or nullity of general assembly resolution inures to the benefit of all shareholders after it is finalized...*"

764 "*...in the validity of shareholders' meetings where Article 222(3) Spanish Civil Code of Procedure recognizes that a decision of a Court binds all the shareholders even those that did not participate in the court proceedings...*"

765 Loukas A. Mistelis & Stavros L. Brekoulakis, Arbitrability p. 289.

766 *Ibid.*

767 *See supra* note 715 *et seq.*

authority depending on arbitration agreements entered into by the parties.[768] Unsurprisingly, the rules in the national codes governing substantive matters[769] mention *courts*[770] and not arbitrators. Only specific parts of the procedural codes[771] govern arbitration as an alternative dispute resolution mechanism. Assuming that the arbitral award does not have the same effect as a court decision because the relevant article does not mention arbitral awards seems to be an excessive position. The provision in the Turkish Commercial Code indicates that lawmakers indeed intended the extension of the effect of a decision on annulment of general assembly resolutions. Although the provision only mentions the decision of the courts, can be extended to govern arbitral awards.[772] Nothing in the law indicates that the lawmakers intended to exclude arbitral awards from this regulation and reserved the application of Article 450 only to court decisions.[773]

The use of arbitration to resolve corporate disputes has grown rapidly. One should likely regard the fact that the effect of arbitral awards is not governed to include all shareholders as a legal gap in this particular area. Legislation of this issue for arbitral award by lawmakers would surely be the absolute solution to this problem. A clear regulation on the extent of the effect of arbitral awards would eliminate the controversy resulting from the conflicting interpretations. Until such an amendment is enacted, a consistent ruling on the case by the courts would also provide practice with clarity. The courts should acknowledge the legal gap. The rule stipulating the effects of court decisions on the annulment of general assembly resolutions should, by way of self-integration, fill the legal gap in the same way.[774] Indeed, filling such a gap by analogy has grounds in the principle of equality as a necessity of fairness—namely, similar outcomes (irrespective of the method of dispute resolution) ought to receive similar treatment.[775]

768 Mehmet Tas, p. 58.
769 Such as Turkish Commercial Code.
770 Or 'court decisions' while indicating a decisions or award.
771 Articles 407–444 of Turkish Code of Civil Procedure.
772 Burcu Zengin, p. 109.
773 *Ibid.*
774 Which can also be deemed as 'self-integration'.
See Maria José Falcón y Tella, Equity and Law 108 (Peter Muckley trans., Martinus Nijhoff Publishers 2008) for further information.
775 Cigdem Kırca, *Ortulu Bosluk ve Bu Boslugun Doldurulması Yontemi Olarak Amaca Uygun Sınırlama* [*Tacit Legal Gap and Reduction in Accordance with the Purpose as a Gap Filling Method*] Ankara Universitesi Hukuk Fakultesi Dergisi 2001, Cilt. 50, Sayı. 1 [Ankara University Faculty of Law Journal 2001, Volume.50, Issue.1] p. 100.

Turkish law, however, currently lacks a clear statutory regulation and consistent court precedent. Other suggestions and justifying grounds[776] for this group of third parties will, therefore, follow.

Corporate actors can conclude agreements to arbitration in several different ways. They can, for instance, insert the provision regarding arbitration for the resolution of a dispute in the articles of association during the establishment of the legal corporation. As some scholars, including *Poroy*, [777] [778] propound that, such an action implies all shareholders have consented to the arbitral proceeding. Alternatively, corporate actors can conclude such an agreement to arbitrate through a subsequent unanimous decision of the shareholders. Such an agreement would have the same influence as one included in the articles of association.[779] [780] Arbitral clauses accepted unanimously for the nullity of the general assembly resolutions are deemed acceptable on the grounds that they will serve the best interests of parties in terms of the procedural flexibility arbitration engenders.[781] A specific decision made by the Swiss courts bears mentioning. In 1959, the Geneva Canton Superior Court accepted an arbitral clause based on unanimity. By virtue of the advantages it provides, especially for

---

776 Supporting that the third-party effect does not result in inarbitrability of annulment cases for this group of third parties.

777 Reha Poroy, Unal Tekinalp & Ersin Camoglu, p. 386.

778 Also, Zafer Saka, pp. 287–288.

"...*On the condition that the provision exists or is inserted to the articles of association, cases for annulment of general assembly resolutions can be submitted to arbitration*...."

779 Reha Poroy, Unal Tekinalp & Ersin Camoglu, p. 386.

780 Some scholars do not support the opinion that a subsequent decision to be made unanimously would also have the same influence even though they support the arbitrability of annulment of general assembly resolutions. *Saka*, for instance, also agrees that cases for annulment of general assembly resolutions are arbitrable on the condition that the related provision is given place in the articles of association. He objects, however, the idea that this can also be achieved by a subsequent association decision even if it is unanimous. The author expresses the reason is that the articles of association would bind all the parties because it is a private law agreement while a decision is not an agreement.
Zafer Saka, pp. 287–288.

781 Reha Poroy, Unal Tekinalp & Ersin Camoglu, p. 386.

joint-stock corporations with a small number of shareholders, [782] legal scholar Robert*Patry*[783] supports such a decision.

Authors on Turkish doctrinal law also support such decisions. A related arbitral provision inserted in the articles of association enables the arbitration of general assembly resolutions. Association is mainly a private law agreement that generates rights and obligations.[784] Therefore, when obtained, an arbitral award regarding the annulment of a general assembly resolution should be effective and binding for the legal entity and all shareholders of the association in accordance with Article 450 of the Turkish Commercial Code.[785] Indeed, while pointing out the effects of the decision of annulment, the statute does not distinguish between courts and arbitrators.[786] Beyond that, the expanding effect of a court decision or arbitral award mainly stems from the nature of the case for the annulment of general assembly resolutions. One of the parties in such cases is the association itself and the regulation in the statute reflects this status.

Scholars have also accepted that shareholders who are party to an arbitral clause in articles of association have assented to multiparty arbitration.[787] Parties involved in the arbitration agreement can assert that they are not bound by the arbitral decision even if they have joined the arbitral proceedings to intervene in the arbitral process. This would, however, constitute an indication of a breach of the obligation to act in good faith.[788] Therefore, this section initially regards arbitral award as binding for the parties to the arbitral agreement without resorting to further interpretation.[789] Some scholars assert that, once finalized, arbitral awards acquire definitive effect; thus, like a court decision, an award with this effect becomes binding between the parties in Turkish law. [790] In the following statement, *Huysal*[791] provides a useful description of this rationale:

---

782 *Ibid.*

783 Robert Patry, La Nullité des Decisions des Organes dans la SA 230 (Melanges Roger Secrétan Lausanne 1964).
Reha Poroy, Unal Tekinalp & Ersin Camoglu, p. 379 & n. 717.

784 Zafer Saka, p. 288.

785 *Ibid.*

786 *Ibid.*

787 Burcin Yıldırım, p. 38.

788 *Ibid.*

789 *Ibid.*

790 Burak Huysal, p. 315.

791 *Ibid.*

> *...At this point, the essence of the court's decision should be given importance because the decision of annulment has its effects only against the corporation in principle. Namely, the annulment decision of the court does not inure to the benefits of other shareholders. The fact that the decision here affects the shareholder is a natural consequence of the corporation's status as a legal entity. In fact, the shareholders of the corporation, not the corporation, have made the resolution subject to the annulment. The resolution annulled by the court is, therefore, the will of shareholders reflected outside of the legal entity. Turkish Commercial Code Article 450*[792] *provides an explanation of the situation and reflects this rational approach. The same situation is also valid with regard to arbitral awards...*

Arbitral awards annulling general assembly resolutions address the legal entity of the corporation. The resolution is a declaration of the will of the shareholders. Authorized by the arbitral agreement, arbitrators can render the decision of annulment. Arbitrators, therefore, annul the declaration of the will of the persons who authorized them.[793]

The *inter partes effect* of the arbitral award is the core of this sub-chapter's argument. Arbitral awards annulling the resolutions also affect other shareholders that are not party to the litigation. For this group of third parties, however, this should be considered independent from the *inter partes* effect.[794] More precisely, in accordance with Article 423[795] of Turkish Commercial Code, when a general assembly issues a resolution, that resolution binds all shareholders, even those who do not attend the meeting or who voted against it. When the court annuls the general assembly resolution, that annulment remains definitive for shareholders who are not a party to the litigation.[796] Such a decision would, therefore, affect shareholders who have not attended the meeting or voted against the proposal. This is a natural consequence of the legal character of the corporation. [797]

Finally, it bears emphasizing that, after acquiring the status of legal entity, a corporation has an identity and will independent from its shareholders and it reveals its will through the agency of its departments.[798] Therefore, the

---

792 The author says article 383 because the previous code was in effect at the time of the text. In the current code, it corresponds to the article 450.

793 Burak Huysal, p. 315.

794 Mehmet Tas, p. 60.

795 "VII- *Effect of the Resolutions*

Article 423(1): *Resolutions issued by the general assembly are also valid for shareholders who do not attend the meeting or have dissenting vote.*"

796 Mehmet Tas, pp. 60–61.

797 *Id* at 61–62.

798 *Id* at 61.

corporation itself has the capacity to act as a legal entity independent of the personality of its departments. The legal acts of the corporation, thus, naturally affect the shareholders. This also complies with one of the fundamental principles of corporate law.[799] As widely recognized in comparative law, the arbitral awards annulling general assembly resolutions bind shareholders and corporate departments irrespective of their involvement in arbitral cases.[800]

A similar discussion took place in German law prior to a 1996 German Federal Court decision.[801] The latter illustrates a final point. The regulation at issue in German law was very similar to Article 450 of Turkish Commercial Code[802]. Section 248 of the related law stipulated that litigated annulment decisions affected all shareholders. In the 1996 decision, the German Court determined that this regulation could not apply analogously to arbitral awards; thus, this rule merits evaluation along with the rule authorizing the court in the location of the corporate headquarters contained in § 246(3).[803] The Court also emphasized the participation of all shareholders to the choice of arbitrators.[804] It stressed the particular importance of providing shareholders with the opportunity to be a party to the case. The most significant consequence of the decision was that arbitrators could hear annulment cases as long as the content of the concluded arbitral agreement complied with those rules.[805]

Corporations should, therefore, carefully draft their arbitral agreements to eliminate the risk that the absence of a definitive effect on third parties will render an annulment case inarbitrable. Even if the court finds it risky to arbitrate a matter as a result of procedural concerns, it may still accept the matter's arbitrability in the event that the arbitral clause is effectively drafted to eliminate those risks. *Trittmann and Hanefeld*[806] summarize the importance of drafting arbitral agreements in German arbitral law, which parallels Turkish regulations, as follows:

---

799 Burak Huysal, p. 315.
Mehmet Tas, p. 61.

800 Burak Huysal, p. 315.

801 *Id* at 314.

802 Article 383 in the previous Commercial Code.

803 Identical to the article 445 in Turkish Commercial Code.
Burak Huysal p. 314.

804 Burak Huysal p. 314.

805 *Ibid.*

806 Rolf Trittmann & Inka Hanefeld, Part II – Commentary on the German Arbitration Law Chapter II –Arbitration Agreement, § 1030, p. 120 *in* Arbitration in Germany: The Model Law in Practice.

...Shareholders' resolutions in commercial companies involve an economic interest. Consequently, disputes arising from them are arbitrable. The actual practical problem lies in the drafting of the arbitration clause...Furthermore, it has to ensure that the binding effect of the award extends to all shareholders and to the company itself. Therefore, the parties have to resort to drafting techniques developed for these specific circumstances. Under these circumstances, disputes about shareholder resolutions may be subject to arbitral proceedings....

This sub-chapter has shown, as a result, that intra-corporate actors such as shareholders and corporate departments are not considered third parties to the arbitration process. The effect of the related arbitral award on these 'false' third parties should not result in inarbitrability. In addition, effective drafting of the arbitral clause or agreement is vital to eliminate the risk of inarbitrability.

2. Third Parties Other Than Intra-Corporate Actors

Arbitral awards may affect two types of third parties who were not being a party to the arbitral proceeding. *Mistelis* and *Brekoulakis* defines those parties as:

...shareholders that did not participate in the process although they were parties to the arbitration agreement, or third parties that are not even parties to the arbitration agreement, such as creditors.[807]

The previous sub-chapter has already discussed the first group of third parties—actors inside the corporation. The second group is of a greater importance. Some Turkish legal scholars even consider the true third parties in debates about arbitrability only those included in this second group.[808] The first group of third parties, which includes shareholders and corporate departments, is naturally bound by the arbitral agreement. The fact that arbitral agreements affect this group in contrast to the *inter partes* principle of arbitral awards proves irrelevant to the arbitrability of general assembly resolutions. The previous section concluded that, subject to the discussion of Article 450, the third parties affected by court decisions or the awards of arbitral tribunals should consist of indirectly affected parties—namely, those who are not shareholders or departments of the corporation. This section will examine this group of third parties. This second group of the third parties is likely to produce more unanticipated consequences than the first group. The significance of claims against the *inter partes* effect of arbitral awards can also increase.

Third parties categorized as part of the second group are neither parties to arbitral agreement nor corporate actors in a close relationship to the corporation.

807 Loukas A. Mistelis & Stavros L. Brekoulakis, p. 289.
808 *See supra* Chapter V (C).

Awards can affect this group of third parties because of contractual or commercial relationships with the corporation—for example a creditor or sub-contractor of the parties to the arbitration or the arbitration agreement. Hypothetically, those involved in the case may intentionally or unintentionally preclude this group of third parties simply by not informing them about arbitral proceedings. The ultimate result that an arbitral award binds a person or legal entity even if that person or legal entity was not a party to the original arbitral agreement may seem unfair. Such unfairness may cause third parties to file additional lawsuits to resolve the same dispute. This could lead to conflicting decisions.

Turkish law lacks a clear and unequivocal resolution to the problem of uninformed third parties. No flawless solution mechanism has yet been offered. Multiparty arbitration continues to suffer the problems that inhere to its practice. This is not specific, however, to Turkish law; the matter has received considerable attention in comparative law. It remains one significant disadvantage of arbitration. Different legal systems have examined the problem in-depth. Despite the complications of arbitration, submission of disputes to the national courts may prove more disadvantageous than arbitration for variety of reasons, including the issue of objectivity. Based on a careful risk analysis, an individual foreign investor or representative legal entity may choose to disregard the possible effects of an arbitral award of annulment on third parties. In such cases, they may still prefer arbitration as an alternative dispute resolution mechanism.[809] To address such instances, the section below will present possible counter-arguments and suggestions to minimize the risk in Turkish law.

First of all, general assembly resolutions bind intra-corporate actors such as shareholders and the departments of a corporation. This factor leads to the conclusion that the possible effects of annulment of general assembly resolutions on third parties are very limited.[810] One can also explicitly infer this from the grounds[811] for annulment contained in Article 445.[812] The general assembly's status

809 Burak Huysal, p. 315

810 *Ibid.*

811 "*...violates the law or articles of incorporation and especially good faith...*" (Article 445) "*...invitation was not made in due form; the agenda was not announced properly; persons who are not authorized to attend the general assembly or their agents have attended the meeting and voted; he was not allowed to attend the general assembly and vote unjustly... and those abovementioned violations have an impact...personal responsibility in the event of fulfillment of the resolution...*" (Article 446)

See supra Chapter IV (B) for the full texts of these articles.

812 Article 381 in the previous Commercial Code.
Burak Huysal, pp. 315–316.

as an *internal* department of the corporation also bears mentioning. Because of this status, general assembly resolutions issued by this internal department will be internally-oriented. Cases in which resolutions have an external-oriented effect—namely, on third parties—remain exceptional.[813] There are only few examples of those exceptions with external effect on third parties. For instance:

- ratification of takeover or purchase proceedings in accordance with Article 356[814],

and

- sales of active asset in liquidation in accordance with Article 538 (2).[815]

---

813 Reha Poroy, Unal Tekinalp & Ersin Camoglu, p. 377.

814 It was article 311 in the previous Commercial Code.

C) *Fraud Against Law*

"Article 356:

(1) *Agreements with regard to takeover or leasing of a business organization or asset in return for a consideration exceeding ten per cent of the capital stock are not in effect within the two years from company registration unless being ratified by the general assembly and registered to the trade registry. Any type of act, which is including payments made with the purpose of their performance, prior to the ratification and registration of those agreements are invalid.*

...

(4) *Agreement is registered and announced by the ratification of the general assembly.*

..."

815 "3. Authorization for the Sale of Active Asset

Article 538:

(1) *Liquidating agents may sell the company's active asset by bargain, too, unless contrary is agreed by the general assembly.*
(2) *For the sale of active asset at considerable amount, general assembly resolution is required. Third and fourth sub-articles of article 421 applies to this resolution.*"

"V-Meeting and Resolution Quorums for the Amendments of Articles of Association Article 421

...

(3) *Following decisions on amendments to articles of association are made by affirmative votes of the shareholders or their agents of the shares that constitute at least seventy-five per cent of the capital stock:*

Issuing bonds, that Article 423 of the previous Commercial Code[816] regulated, was also another example. The current Commercial Code, however, does not include this provision.

Even in the two exceptional cases in which an external effect results, the general assembly does not implement the legal process. The authorized department in charge of the representation and execution of the joint-stock corporation executes the processes in those cases. Either the board of directors as the authorized department or liquidating agents hold the executive power.[817] The Commercial Code addresses general assembly resolutions involving third parties just to validate the process. In other words, the executory act of the board of directors would not become valid in the absence of the general assembly resolution requirement.

Apart from the above exceptions, the general assembly cannot represent the corporation or issue resolutions that affect external relations. Likewise, the articles of association cannot give the general assembly this type of power. The general assembly may only receive authorization for approval of some of the board of directors' decisions. According to the Turkish Commercial Code, the board of directors has the authority to manage external operations and represent the corporation. The general assembly may issue a resolution that relates to third parties through a directive to the board of directors. For instance, it may issue a resolution to sell some of the corporation's immovable property. In such a case, the board of directors can render a decision binding the joint-stock corporation

---

a) *Amendment of the company's field of operation completely.*
b) *Establishing privileged share.*
c) *Limitation of assignment of registered shares.*

(4) *In the event that the quorums foreseen in sub-articles two and three are not met in the first meeting, the same quorums are sought in the following meetings.*

..."

Reha Poroy, Unal Tekinalp & Ersin Camoglu, p. 377.

816 Article 423 of the previous Code:

"3. General Assembly Resolution
Article 423:
Even if the articles of association allow bond issue, a general assembly resolution is required in this regard… The resolution rendered by the general assembly cannot be enforced unless it is registered and announced."

817 Reha Poroy, Unal Tekinalp & Ersin Camoglu, p. 377.

as against third parties.[818] A general assembly resolution, however, does not give a third party the right to make a claim against the corporation. In such instances, the general assembly's status as an internal department that issues internally-oriented resolutions becomes apparent.[819] Cases in which the possible effect of an annulment decision on third parties leads to the inarbitrability of disputes arising from a general assembly resolution are, therefore, very rare.

There are statutory regulations in Turkish law that may alleviate the pitfalls of this issue. The obligation to register and announce the general assembly resolutions is among those applicable statutory requirements. The Turkish Commercial Code supports the counter-argument against claims of inarbitrability on the grounds of the effects of the arbitral award on third parties. It is, indeed, stipulated by Article 422 (2) that:

> *The board of directors is charged with giving a notarized copy of the minutes to the trade registry directorate promptly. It shall have the matters which are subject to registration and announcement in these minutes registered and announced. The minutes shall also be uploaded to the web-site of the corporation immediately.*

The Turkish Commercial Code requires official announcement of general assembly resolutions through registration in the trade registry. This requirement ensures that third parties related to the corporation can access resolutions that may affect them. Importantly, the Code also requires the publication of resolutions online in publicly available venues. The Code regards this requirement for the board of directors as so important that it stipulates it as a condition for the validity of a general assembly resolution.[820] The legislator thus render registration and announcement essential with regard to third parties.[821] The additional requirement that, as a general security measure, companies promptly submit minutes related to the resolutions to the trade registry further indicates the legislative intent and purpose. As a result of the Code's regulations, one can find all general assembly resolutions and related hearing minutes in the Trade Registry Gazette. Therefore, substantiating claims that third parties are completely uninformed of a general assembly resolution and deliberately barred from intervention proves difficult.

---

818 *Ibid.*

819 *Ibid.*

820 The consequence of this nuisance is that if the board of directors does not meet this requirement, the resolution will not be valid.
Reha Poroy, Unal Tekinalp & Ersin Camoglu, p. 377.

821 Reha Poroy, Unal Tekinalp & Ersin Camoglu, p. 377.

In addition, Article 450 of Turkish Commercial Code specifically requires registration and announcement in the event that a general assembly resolution is annulled or nullified. It is well-established that a copy of the decision of annulment of the general assembly resolution has to be registered in the trade registry by the board of directors immediately. It is also required to be uploaded to the company website, which makes it available to any third parties conveniently. Applied to arbitral cases, this requirement may serve as a partial solution of the issue.[822] At the time the company files the action for annulment, furthermore, it must announce and upload the resolution to its website and include the date of the hearing in the announcement. [823] This may also help third parties learn about the filing of a case for a resolution that can affect them. This regulation has the additional potential advantage of enabling third party involvement in the case in its early stages.

To conclude, this chapter analyzes the effect of the annulment of awards in two groups of third parties. The previous section discussed the impact of the annulment of general assembly resolutions on the first group of third parties—intra-corporate actors. The awards of annulment of general assembly resolutions will almost certainly bind this group. Shareholders and departments of the corporation are the natural parties to the arbitration agreement.[824] There is no possibility that the annulment of a general assembly resolution can unfairly affect this group of 'third parties'. The argument that the annulment decision will have an effect beyond the *inter partes* principle because third parties are not parties to the arbitration agreement is not substantiated. It also bears noting that the corporation itself is one of the parties in the arbitral proceeding. The first group of third parties is, therefore, included in one of the parties to the arbitration, and indirectly related to it. As a result of the corporate structure and the decision-making mechanisms of the general assembly in a corporation, these third parties can access the resolutions as well as the decisions of annulment of resolutions. An arbitral award of annulment will have a definitive effect upon all shareholders and corporate departments provided that the arbitral agreement stipulates this effect.[825]

---

822 While the code applies this rule to court decisions, the resolution method is not the primary concern. The rule regulates annulment decisions and it should therefore apply to arbitral awards as well.

823 "I-Announcement, Security and Right to Appeal

Article 448: (1) *Board of directors duly announces the filing of an action for annulment or nullity, the date of the hearing, and uploads to the company web-site.*"

824 Burak Huysal, p. 316.

825 Burak Huysal, p. 316.

Reha Poroy, Unal Tekinalp & Ersin Camoglu, p. 386.

For the second group of 'third parties', however, the *inter partes* effect of the arbitral award plays a more active role. Reaching a straightforward result for this group proves difficult in Turkish law. A general assembly resolution subject to the annulment award may pertain to a previously concluded contractual relationship between a third party and the corporation. The annulment award may, therefore, affect this third party, even though the third party—being neither an intra-corporate actor nor a department—would not be a party to arbitral agreement. Thus, for this group of third parties, one cannot assume with certainty that the *inter partes* principle applies. Exceptions in this regard may occur that result in a violation of the principle. Such cases, though, remain exceptional in the daily operations of on-going businesses. These cases do not occur outside the specific instances described above. Because of the internally-oriented nature of general assembly resolutions, the previous examples described exceptional cases. Companies can take measures to avoid these possibilities by using website announcements and adhering to the trade registration requirements stipulated by law. In addition, through oral hearing announcements, companies can include potentially affected third parties in early stages of arbitration. Assuming the third parties are not involved in the arbitral process, the requirement for announcing the annulment decision would also minimize the impact of these exceptions. A deliberately drafted arbitral agreement can also diminish third-party effects.

Cases for annulment are not categorically inarbitrable. The doctrinal assertions on the inarbitrability of annulment of general assembly resolutions due to the effect of the *inter partes* principle on third parties should be rejected. Every situation should be decided on a case-by-case basis. In disputes about the annulment of general assembly resolutions with no or limited third-party involvement or significant litigation-related concerns (objectivity, time, or predictability), arbitration may still be the best option. In addition, even if third parties are a factor, an effectively drafted arbitral agreement combined with special attention to the trade registry and an announcement to facilitate third party involvement would minimize these risks. This approach can facilitate the rejection of potential third-party claims. It informs third parties of the arbitral proceedings from an early stage, which enables their participation in the proceedings. If the third parties subsequently resorted to another forum to avoid the arbitration, they would be *venire contra factum proprium*. Because Turkish law requires parties to act in good faith, this bad faith action would weaken their claims.

Mehmet Tas, p. 62.
Zafer Saka, pp. 287–288.

On the other hand, cases may occur in which resolutions relate to issues that involve a great number of third parties. For instance, a buyer, seller, or creditor could act as a third party in the sale of a property subject to a resolution. If the company resorted to arbitration intending to disregard deliberately the claims of a third party in the party's absence, the law would not protect the company. If circumstances prevent third party participation, arbitration may not be the best means of resolving the dispute. A case's arbitrability ultimately depends on the specific dynamics of the third-party situation. In cases in which the parties prefer arbitration despite some degree of third-party-related risk, the precautionary measures mentioned above may prove useful.

D. Vested Right Character and Its Consequences

One specific regulation in the Turkish Commercial Code poses a challenge to the arbitrability of disputes related to general assembly resolutions. Article 452 of Turkish Commercial Code states that:

> *The general assembly can amend all provisions of the articles of association in compliance with the conditions stipulated in the Statute unless otherwise provided; with the reservation of vested and inalienable rights.*

The current Commercial Code shortens this provision and makes it more limited and less significant. Additionally, the previous Turkish Commercial Code defined the vested rights in a related article as: "*the rights which are not subject to the resolutions of the general assembly or board of directors in accordance with law or the articles of association, or the rights arising from the right of attending the meetings of the general assembly such as membership, voting, filing an action for annulment, receiving profit margins and liquidating dividends.*"[826] Although the current Commercial Code does not include this explanatory part in the definition of vested rights, it is useful to elucidate the notion of the vested character.

As a consequence of these regulations of Commercial Code, two points need to be highlighted:

- First, vested rights are excluded from the content of the articles of association that the general assembly can amend,

and

- Second, filing an action for annulment of a general assembly resolution is categorized as a vested right.

826 Article 385 of the previous Commercial Code numbered 6762.

These regulations give rise to two specific arguments. The first asserts that, because the Code stipulates annulment as a vested right for shareholders, litigation is the sole means of engaging in annulment. The second contends that, because the Code defines annulment as a vested right and excludes the amendment of vested right-related provisions, the company cannot insert an arbitration clause concerning the annulment of a general assembly resolutions into the articles of association. The first argument's rationale for inarbitrability is that the Code only stipulates litigation as a means of resolving such disputes. Filing a case for annulment of a general assembly resolution is a *vested right* of the shareholders.[827] Proponents of this position, therefore, assert that parties can only file such actions before courts because submitting them to arbitration would violate the 'vested' character of the right. Although the law considers filing an annulment action a vested right for shareholders, it includes no stipulation that parties must file these actions before national courts.[828] The law also makes no distinction between litigation and arbitration regarding the vested right.[829] Such cases are, therefore, arbitrable and arbitration would not breach the vested right.[830] Claiming inarbitrability on the basis of this regulation amounts to an excessive interpretation.

The Code, indeed, designates the courts as the *general* and usual dispute-resolution authority and regards arbitration as an *exceptional* judicial method.[831] As a result, substantive rules such as Commercial Code provisions naturally refer to the "cases or courts" while regulating issues,[832] and they may not mention arbitration each time as an exceptional resolution method for disputes. The fact that a regulation does not refer to arbitration for a specific dispute does not mean the dispute is inarbitrable. For matters under civil jurisdiction, procedural rather substantive law determines whether exclusive judicial jurisdiction applies or whether the matter can be resolved via either the courts or arbitration.[833] The specific procedural codes recognize arbitration. The exceptional nature of

827 *See supra* note 606 *et seq.*
828 Reha Poroy, Unal Tekinalp & Ersin Camoglu, p. 386.
829 Zafer Saka, p. 286.
830 Reha Poroy, Unal Tekinalp & Ersin Camoglu, p. 386.
831 This argument overlaps with an ongoing argument. The shareholder's vested right raises the issue of the potential exclusive authority of the courts. Chapter II (B) explained the relevant arguments on exclusive judicial jurisdictional rules; this section will review the counter-argument to this specific issue.
832 *See supra* note 716 for further explanation.
833 Mehmet Tas, p. 58.

arbitration vis-à-vis litigation results in the litigation-oriented language of the regulations. This factor should not impede arbitration.

This section has demonstrated that the first argument stemming from Article 452 breaks down under scrutiny. The second argument relates to the regulation of general assembly amendments to the articles of association. Article 452 excludes vested rights from matters subject to amendment by the general assembly. Some argue that this exclusion precludes the insertion of arbitral clauses in the articles of association. Previous sections have mentioned several different ways of integrating arbitral clauses into corporate practice.[834] First and foremost, corporations can include an arbitral clause in the articles of association during the establishment of the legal corporation. Nearly all commentators agree that arbitration provisions are valid, regarding them as evidence that all shareholders consented to arbitral proceedings.

Once established, a corporation can add an arbitral agreement to the articles of association with a unanimous decision of the general assembly. Some commentators argue, however, against the validity of arbitral clauses retrospectively inserted into the articles of association. They claim that the general assembly cannot amend provisions related to vested rights, and they regard the action for annulment as an example such a provision. They argue that arbitral clauses serve the best interests of parties because of the procedural flexibility they provide.[835] The rationale of the regulation in Article 452 is enlightening. This article aims to prevent shareholders from being bound by amendments to the articles of association to which they do not consent.[836] The choice of arbitration does not change shareholder rights or obligations.[837] Thus, the argument on vested right character proves irrelevant and insufficient to assert the inarbitrability of this subject matter.

The vested right-related regulation does not make annulment cases inarbitrable. This regulation does not suffice to create the inarbitrability of annulment cases. This discussion emphasizes that, to be on the safe side, corporations should strongly consider including arbitral clauses in the articles of association from the early stages of the corporation's establishment. In the event of a subsequent insertion of an arbitral clause into the articles of association, the corporation should strive to pass the resolution unanimously.

---

834 *See supra* Chapter V (C).
835 Reha Poroy, Unal Tekinalp & Ersin Camoglu, p. 386.
836 Burcin Yıldırım, pp. 78–79.
837 *Ibid.*

E. Imperative Provisions Principle in Turkish Commercial Code and Its Effect on Arbitration

Chapter II (A) of this book examined the issue of imperative rules and their effects on arbitrability. That section also explained the relationship between imperative rules and public policy. This sub-chapter offers an additional, separate examination of imperative rules because these rules depend on a specific article in the Turkish Commercial Code. This article introduces the principle of imperative provisions to corporate matters with wide-ranging application that may extend to the arbitration of corporate disputes.

The Turkish Commercial Code establishes the imperative character of its provisions in Article 340.[838] The first sentence of Article 340 states that *articles of association cannot regulate an issue differently from Turkish Commercial Code unless the Code itself explicitly recognizes the difference.* The following sentence also mentions that *subsidiary provisions for articles of association that the other Codes allow are exclusively applicable to those codes.*[839] The article, therefore, attributes an imperative character to the provisions of the Turkish Commercial Code. The attribution is of core importance to Turkish commercial practice for many reasons. This article has caused significant controversy since the enactment of the new and current Commercial Code numbered 6100. The section below will analyze the practical consequences of the first and second sentences of Article 340, and then examine their potential impact on the arbitration of corporate disputes.

---

838 2. Imperative Provisions

Article 340

(1) Articles of association may differ from the provisions of this Code with regard to the joint stock corporations on the condition that the Code explicitly recognizes the difference. Subsidiary articles of association provisions stipulated by the other codes are exclusively applicable for those codes.

839 Article 340 foresees these regulations for joint stock corporations. Article 579 includes a similar regulation regarding limited liability companies. The article states that regulations for limited liability corporations may differ from the provisions of the Turkish Commercial Code on the condition that the Code itself explicitly recognizes the difference. The provision for subsidiary regulations stipulated by other codes also applies to limited liability corporations.

1. *The Explicit Recognition* Limitation of Article 340

The first sentence[840] of Article 340 governs situations in which a regulation in the articles of association prohibits effect of a provision of the Turkish Commercial Code. The Code must explicitly recognize such a regulation for it to be valid. This regulation appears in the new Turkish Commercial Code numbered 6102. The previous Commercial Code numbered 6762 was effective prior to the current new code. According to this previous code, *any issue which was not explicitly forbidden by the law could be regulated by the articles of association as a matter of principle.*[841] The validity of provisions in the articles of association that prohibit the effect of the Turkish Commercial Code, therefore, becomes an important issue of analysis. Article 339 points out[842] the content and limitations

---

840 "*Articles of association may differ from the provisions of this Code with regard to the joint stock corporations on the condition that the Code explicitly recognizes the difference...*"

841 Rauf Karasu, *6102 Sayılı Turk Ticaret Kanunu'na Gore Anonim Sirketlerde Emredici Hukumler Ilkesi* [*Principle of Mandatory Provisions in Joint Stock Corporations in Accordance with Turkish Commercial Code numbered 6102*], Marmara Universitesi Hukuk Fakultesi Hukuk Arastırmaları Dergisi, Ozel Sayı Cilt:18, Sayi:2 Legal Yayıncılık (2012) [Marmara University Law Faculty Legal Researches Journal, Special, Vol.: 18, Issue: 2 Legal Publishing (2012)] p. 312.

842 IV- Articles of Association
1. Content
Article 339

(1) *Articles of association of the joint stock corporations have to be concluded in writing; and all the founding shareholders' signatures have to be approved by the notary or the articles of association has to be signed before the trade registry manager.*

(2) *Following matters are written in the articles of association:*
  a) *Trade name of the company and the place where the headquarters will locate.*
  b) *Field of operation essential points of which are specified and defined.*
  c) *Company capital and nominal value of each share; formal requirements and conditions of their payment.*
  d) *Certificate of bearer share or certificate of registered share; privileges granted to specific shares; transfer restriction.*
  e) *Rights and assets apart from money invested; their value; number of shares to be given in return for them; value of a business or asset in the event of taking over, and the value of assets and rights bought on behalf of the company by the founder shareholders; value of payment, allowance or award to be given to the ones who serve for the foundation of the company.*

of the articles of association. This provision lists the matters to be included in the articles of association, and that list does not include arbitration.

Based on the innovation introduced by the current Code, some authors deduce that the '*Principle of Imperative Provisions*' supersedes the '*Principle of Freedom of Contract*' for joint stock corporations and limited liability corporations in Turkish corporate law.[843] Since the release of the draft of this Code, commentators have criticized the necessity and possible outcomes of these regulations. Even prior to its enactment, certain commentators took the position that this regulation restricted the principle of freedom of contract, [844] which is the main principle of contracts law, beyond the accepted limits.[845] Limits to the principle of freedom of contract in Turkish law can be illustrated as follows[846]:

---

f) *Dividends to be provided for the founders and members of board of directors and others.*
g) *Number of the members of the board of directors, authorized signatories of them.*
h) *The way to call a meeting of general assemblies; the voting rights.*
ı) *Duration if the company is time-limited.*
i) *The way to make the announcements of the company.*
j) *Types and values of the shares undertaken by the shareholders.*
k) *Accounting period of the company.*
(3) *First members of the board of directors are nominated by articles of association.*

843 Rauf Karasu, *Emredici Hukumler Ilkesinin Kapalı Tip Anonim Sirketler ve Limited Sirketler Acısından Dogurdugu Sorunlar ve Cozum Onerileri* [*The Issues Arising from the Principle of Imperative Provisions in Closed Type Corporations and Limited Liability Companies and Proposals for Solutions*] *in* I. Ticaret Hukuku Uluslararası Sempozyumu [I. Commercial Law International Symposium], Ticaret ve Fikri Mulkiyet Hukuk Dergisi (2015/1) [Commercial and Intellectual Property Law Journal (2015/1)] p. 116.

844 *See supra* Chapter I (A) for more detail about the dominance of this principle in Turkish Law.

845 Erdogan Moroglu, Turk Ticaret Kanunu Tasarısı ile Yururluk ve Uygulama Kanunu Tasarısı Taslagı: Degerlendirme ve Oneriler [Turkish Commercial Code Draft and Enforcement and Implementation Code Draft: Evaluation and Suggestions] 145 (Turkiye Barolar Birligi Yayınları, 4. Bası, Ankara 2006) [Turkish Bar Association Publishing, 4th Ed., Ankara 2006).

Erdogan Moroglu, Turk Ticaret Kanunu Tasarısı ile Yururluk ve Uygulama Kanunu Tasarısı Taslagı: Degerlendirme ve Oneriler [Turkish Commercial Code Draft and Enforcement and Implementation Code Draft: Evaluation and Suggestions] 141–142 (Vedat Kitapcılık, 6. Bası, Istanbul 2009) [Vedat Publishing, 6th Ed. Istanbul 2009].

846 Erdogan Moroglu, Turk Ticaret Kanunu Tasarısı, p. 146.

"*Terms of contracts may freely be determined by the parties within the limits of the law.*";[847]
"*Agreements which are contrary to the imperative rules of law, morality, public policy, personal rights, or the subjects of which are impossible are null and void.*"[848]
"*No person may waive his or her capacity to have rights or capacity to act, even partially. No person may waive his or her freedoms or restrict them against the law or morals.*"[849]

The regulation in Article 340, however, expands this limited list by stating "*Articles of association may differ from the provisions of this Code with regard to the joint stock corporations on the condition that the Code explicitly recognizes the difference.*" Thus, the list can extend beyond the boundaries of freedom of contract stipulated in Turkish Contract Law and the Turkish Civil Code. To be regarded as valid, discretionary regulations made in the articles of association must not only satisfy the imperative rules, public policy and morality, or personal rights criterion, but also be "*explicitly recognized by the* (Turkish Commercial) *Code.*"[850]

Doctrinal commentators consider this an excessive restriction, which will prevent the development of corporate law. It also conflicts with other provisions in corporate law.[851] Commentators engaged in additional criticism of this regulation. For closed joint-stock corporations in particular, they argued that the regulation violates the principle of proportionality and freedom of contract.[852]

---

847 As stated by article 26 of Turkish Code of Contract.

848 As stated by article 27 of Turkish Code of Contract: "*The nullity of the terms of the agreement partly does not affect the validity of the rest of the terms. However, the contract is deemed as null and void completely if it is understood that the contract could not have been concluded without the terms considered void.*"

849 As stated by article 23 of Turkish Civil Code. The article continues as:

"*Upon written consent extraction, vaccination and transfer of biological substances of human origin are legitimate. However, no claim may be raised against the person under the obligation of giving biological substance, to fulfill his or her obligation; no claim may be raised for compensation of physical and spiritual damages.*"

850 Erdogan Moroglu, Turk Ticaret Kanunu Tasarısı, p. 146.

851 And limited liability companies due to article 579.

852 *See* Rauf Karasu, p. 329 for further explanations on the negative impacts of those regulations on closed corporations. In short, although imperative provisions principle aims at maximum protection for the stockholders of the corporations, stockholders of close corporations do not prefer this. These stockholders are likely to desire an active role in the management of the corporation and avoid alienation within the corporation. Imperative provisions principle in Turkish Commercial Code, however, restricts the effectiveness of stockholders who are not part of the corporate management, to a large extent.

While lawmakers based the regulation on a German law regulation for joint stock corporations,[853] its enactment led to confusion because they only partially adopted the German regulation and also altered its meaning.[854] Critics of the regulation further argued that it gives the will of shareholders, expressed through the articles of association, a very restricted impact.[855] Finally, early criticism of the regulation highlighted both its potential homogenizing effect on articles of association and how it would likely confuse the process of identifying unimperative regulations.[856] These criticisms are very persuasive. The regulation, however, has become the law in the current Turkish Commercial Code and has several noteworthy consequences. First of all, all Turkish Commercial Code regulations regarding joint-stock corporations are imperative in nature and any deviation from the Code in the articles of association requires an 'explicit recognition.'[857] The following questions, then, merit attention: Does the imperative provision principle bar arbitration agreements for the resolution of disputes within corporations? Does it bar corporations from inserting arbitral clauses into the articles of association? To address these questions, the section below will examine the effect of the principle of imperative provisions in Article 340 on the arbitration of corporate disputes.

Commentators have criticized the wording of the article and many find the boundaries of the restriction vague. They argue that the situations considered are distinct from the Code and the requirements for explicit allowances remain unclear. To analyze the effects of the imperative provisions principle on arbitration, this section first clarifies the types of situations that qualify as deviations from the Code and explains how the law defines explicit recognition. The following related parts of the law's preamble provide some clarification in this regard:

> *...In the event that whether a regulation can 'differ' from the Code is not clear, the following instances shall qualify satisfying 'the explicit recognition of the Code':*
>
> - *falling within the ambit,*
> - *not conflicting with methodological discipline,*

---

853 Aktiengesetz § 23/V (Grundsatz der Satzungsstrege).

854 Hasan Pulaslı, 6102 Sayılı Turk Ticaret Kanunu'na Gore Yeni Sirketler Hukuku Genel Esaslar [Corporations Law in Accordance with The New Turkish Commercial Code Numbered 6102 General Principles] 364 (Adalet Yayınevi Ankara 2012) [Adalet Publishing Ankara 2012].

855 Sami Karahan, pp. 349–350.

856 *Id* at 350.

857 Hasan Pulaslı, Sirketler Hukuku Serhi, Vol. 1, pp. 567–568.

- *being based on satisfactory rationales,*
- *having fair consequences, and*
- *the difference can gain justification based on the balance of interests.*

In the event that the law is silent for a concrete case, methodological rules with regard to filling the legal gap apply.

Even though the Code does not clarify the content of an explicit recognition, the law's preamble includes a directive that fulfills the requirement. In other words, the Code does not explicitly stipulate that a corporation can include an arbitration agreement in its articles of association. Such an action, however, satisfies the criteria for "explicit recognition" listed in the Code's preamble (and reproduced above). A joint stock corporation's decision to resolve disputes via arbitration 1) falls within the ambit, 2) does not conflict with methodological discipline, 3) has a good rationale, 4) has fair consequences, and 5) preserves the balance of interests. Applying this rule to a concrete issue, the balance of interest factor proves applicable to arbitration when the parties have previously agreed on arbitration for the resolution of their disputes. Regarding the will of parties about forum selection also constitutes a satisfactory rationale and assures fair consequences. There is, therefore, no indication of conflict with methodological discipline. Thus, the absence of an explicit recognition in the Code does not invalidate an arbitration agreement in articles of association. Such cases completely fulfill the various requirements stipulated in the preamble's explanation of the restriction.

Turkish doctrinal scholars agree that a dispute's relationship to issues regulated by imperative provisions should not bar that dispute from resolution via arbitration.[858] The imperative provisions principle regulated in Article 340 does not constitute an impediment to conclude arbitration agreements because arbitrators also have to apply imperative provisions in the resolution of such disputes.[859] An arbitrator, for instance, can rule on the issue of whether the articles of association of the joint-stock corporation comply with the imperative provisions of the Turkish Commercial Code.[860] Finally, the explanations for the

858 Rauf Karasu, Turk Ticaret Kanunu Tasarısına Gore Anonim Sirketlerde Emredici Hukumler Ilkesi [Mandatory Provisions Principle in Joint Stock Corporations in Accordance with Turkish Commercial Code Draft] 155 (Yetkin Yayınları, Ankara 2009) [Yetkin Publishing, Ankara 2009].

859 *Id* at 156.

860 *Ibid.*

relationship between imperative provisions and public policy bears highlighting in brief.[861] The fact that imperative provisions regulate a given area does not automatically mean that the area involves public policy.[862] Corporate law does not generally aim to protect public interests, so identifying intra-corporate disputes as inarbitrable on this basis is likely to amount to excessive interpretation. [863]

2. Limitation of Article 340 on Subsidiary Provisions

The foregoing section mentioned that the second part[864] of Article 340 refers to another restriction about subsidiary regulations. The provision states that subsidiary provisions in other Codes regarding the articles of association apply exclusively for those codes when they govern. They do not override Commercial Code regulations. A Code other than the Commercial Code may, for instance, allow corporate parties to insert items into the articles of association that the Commercial Code does not allow. This regulation stipulates that such an allowance would be valid only for that other Code; it would have no bearing on the Commercial Code. Commentators have leveled several criticisms at this part of Article 340.[865]. They claim that, in practice, it will cause discord and confusion.[866] Existing regulations in areas including Capital Market Law, Banking Law, and Financial Leasing Law already affect the corporate world. They claim the regulation causes ambiguity in cases in which special codes and public codes simultaneously apply to the same corporate issue. The pertinent question vis-à-vis this regulation, however, has to do with the arbitration of corporate matters covered by the Turkish Commercial Code. While the Turkish Commercial Code does regulate corporate issues, it does not govern arbitration. Other Codes, such as the International Arbitration Act, perform this function. This section will refer to subsidiary provisions of other special codes governing international arbitration in Turkey. The effect of the regulation in Article 340 regarding subsidiary provisions of special codes on arbitrability provisions will prove important in this regard.

---

861 *See supra* Chapter II (A) for more information.
862 Burcin Yıldırım, p. 30.
863 *Ibid.*
864 *"Subsidiary provisions for articles of association allowed to be foreseen by the other codes are effective exclusively for those codes."*
865 For joint stock corporations and article 579 for limited liability corporations.
866 Erdogan Moroglu, Turk Ticaret Kanunu Tasarısı, p. 146.

The regulation in Article 340 gives subsidiary provisions regarding the articles of incorporation in Codes other than the Commercial Code regulatory power exclusively in the context of those other codes. This regulation aims to authorize the special Codes only within the framework of their specific subject matter.[867] This should not cause ambiguity about the application of special codes such as Capital Market Law, Banking Law, or Financial Leasing Law to related matters of corporate law. In light of the principle of "*lex specialis derogat legi generali,*" this part of Article 340 proves unnecessary.[868] The special code would have priority in practice because lawmakers enacted it for the purpose of solving concrete problems. Furthermore, Article 330 of Turkish Commercial Code explicitly states that the provisions of Turkish Commercial Code apply only when related provisions do not exist in the special codes. This means that special code provisions supersede any contrary provisions in Turkish Commercial Code.[869] Despite the changes initiated by Article 340 in the current Turkish Commercial Code subsidiary provisions allowed by the special codes remain valid.

As previously mentioned, the Turkish Commercial Code designates litigation as the major dispute resolution system, and the substantive codes do not explicitly regulate arbitration in general. Other specific codes, however, do regulate arbitration. The International Arbitration Code, for instance, regulates the arbitration of disputes with an international character in Turkey. Thus, this Code's subsidiary provisions regarding corporate matters addressed in the Turkish Commercial Code remain valid and, on these grounds, the regulation in Article 340 should not result in inarbitrability.

F. Multiparty Issues and Procedural Regulations for Law favoring Court Adjudication: Suggestions for Arbitral Proceedings

This section discusses the procedural difficulties of multiparty arbitral cases—the final grounds for assertions of inarbitrability. These procedural matters, including the consolidation of cases, are regulated in the context of court adjudication. In the context of arbitration, however, the potential problems specific to

867 Rauf Karasu, Emredici Hukumler Ilkesinin Kapalı Tip Anonim Sirketler ve Limited Sirketler Acısından Dogurdugu Sorunlar, p. 120.

868 A statutory law governing a specific subject matter (*lex specialis*) prevails a statutory law that just governs general matters (*lex generalis*).
Ibid.

869 Ibid.

multiparty disputes are not frequently regulated. Examining the various potential problems in such cases, and providing solutions will minimize future risks for Turkish law. The topic of the arbitral resolution of multiparty disputes is indeed complex. The list of possible problems on this matter is long. Most, however, are not peculiar to Turkish law. These general issues have received significant attention in comparative law.[870]This section will, therefore, address issues that pertain more specifically to Turkish law. It will also suggest ways to minimize potential risks associated with the current regulations. These suggestions will refer to comparative works as needed. In contrast to a purely theoretical assessment, this section's practical approach assures the originality of the considerations.

Disputes between corporate actors commonly involve a considerable number of parties.[871] The actors in such disputes most frequently include shareholders. As corporate actors, shareholders are typically involved in various associated or unassociated contracts—articles of incorporation, letters of intent, promises to sell shares, guarantee agreements related to their workflow, and they may even possess shares of diverse corporations.[872] Corporate disputes frequently involve multiple parties, so the issues related to the multiparty factor are the crux of this examination of the arbitrability of corporate disputes.[873] Statistics related to overall arbitral cases under the ICC illuminate the importance of multiparty disputes. In 2004, 31% of the cases filed with ICC were multiparty disputes.[874] The approximate number of parties in these multiparty disputes was five.[875] In 2009, 233 multiparty arbitrations took place, 28.5% of all ICC arbitrations that year.[876] [877] The proportion of multiparty arbitral cases rose from 31% to 33% in

870 "*Since the now infamous 1992 Dutco decision there has been a recognized need to specifically accommodate multi-party arbitrations in arbitral rules.*"
Stefan Michael Kröll et al., International Arbitration and International Commercial Law: Synergy, Convergence and Evolution 307 (Kluwer Law Int'l 2011).

871 Alexis Mourre, p. 302.

872 *Id* at 306.

873 Burcin Yıldırım, p. 93.

874 Loukas Mistelis, *International Arbitration – Corporate Attitudes and Practices,* p. 532.

875 *Ibid.*

876 Stefan Michael Kröll et al., International Arbitration and International Commercial Law: Synergy, Convergence and Evolution, p. 307.

877 It was also specified that 206 (88.4 %) of those cases involved between three and five parties, 21 (9 %) involved between six and 10 parties, and six (2.6 %) involved more than 10 parties. One case filed in 2009 had 19 different parties.

2012.[878] A third of the 2,222 cases filed in 2014 also involved more than two parties.[879]

The institutional statistics clearly demonstrate that a significant proportion of arbitral cases involve more than two parties. Many jurisdictions, however, lack specific and detailed regulations for the arbitration of multiparty disputes. This makes the multiparty factor worth examining in the context of arbitration. Turkish law does regulate procedural issues that arise in multiparty disputes if the disputes are submitted to national courts. Neither corporate nor arbitral statutory law in Turkey, however, regulate these procedural issues when multiparty disputes are submitted to arbitrators.[880] Whether and to what extent rules for the litigation of multiparty disputes can be applied to arbitration remain open questions.

To answer these questions, this section first defines the procedural issues that arise in multiparty disputes. It then describes relevant litigation regulations and examines the compatibility of those regulations with the fundamental principles of arbitration. Some jurisdictions and arbitral institutions in comparative law incorporate regulations for the arbitration of multiparty disputes that are different from those in Turkish law. This section concludes by mentioning regulations from comparative law that may have useful application in Turkish law.

1. Possible Issues in Multiparty Arbitration

Certain general principles, such as being subject to the will of the parties, equality of the parties in selection of arbitrators, and the equal treatment principle, govern any adjudicatory proceeding. National statutes enforce such principles for litigation, but they also must be adopted in arbitration.[881] Adopting these principles in arbitral proceedings may create problems. These problems include the constitution of the arbitral tribunal;[882] the equal selection of arbitrators;[883] the conduct of arbitrators;[884] the status of the parties in arbitral

---

878 No. 1, 25 2013 Statistical Report 2 (ICC Int'l Court of Arbitration Bulletin 2014).

879 No. 1 2014 Statistical Report 1 (ICC Int'l Court of Arbitration Bulletin 2015).

880 Ziya Akıncı, Arbitration Law of Turkey, p. 105.
Mehmet Tas, p. 63.

881 Mehmet Tas, p. 63.

882 Bernard Hanotiau, Complex Arbitrations: Multiparty, Multicontract, Multi-Issue and Class Actions 199 (Kluwer Law Int'l 2006).

883 Richard Bamforth & Katerina Maidment, *All Join In" or Not? How Well Does International Arbitration Cater for Disputes Involving Multiple Parties or Related Claims?*, 1 Kluwer L. Int'l ASA Bull. (2009) p. 6.

884 Mehmet Tas, p. 64.

proceedings;[885] the effect of the arbitral award on the parties;[886] and the communications between parties and arbitrators.[887]

2. Definition and Content of Multiparty Disputes and Related Concepts

Defining multiparty arbitration in a comprehensive manner is difficult.[888] Put simply, the presence of more than one parties on one or both sides in one arbitral case, meaning *the position of the parties is polarized*, is the key point in multiparty arbitration.[889] When a single case involves multiple parties, various problems and concepts may arise. These include the designation of the parties in the arbitral clause, the extension of the arbitral clause, the extension, participation, and joinders of parties or causes for intervention, etc.[890] Multiparty issues are thus extensive and complex, involving several other concepts.

Some commentators view multiparty arbitration as reflecting the concepts of "joinder of parties," "intervention in the case," and "the consolidation of cases" in the context of international commercial arbitration.[891] One major concern in multiparty arbitral cases, on the one hand, is the flawless conduct of arbitral proceedings. The three related concerns—joinder of parties, intervention in the case, and consolidation of cases—, on the other hand, illuminate the problematic nature of such proceedings. The section below explains how Turkish law regulates these issues in judicial proceedings to determine their applicability to arbitral cases and concludes with proposals to minimize risks.

3. Examination of Related Concepts and Their Applicability

This section examines the following concepts in the order they are listed:

- *joinder* of the parties, including mandatory and optional perspectives;

---

885 Bernard Hanotiau, Complex Arbitration, p. 7.

886 Mehmet Tas, p. 64.

887 Thomas E. Carbonneau & William Elliott Butler, p. 997

888 Nimet Ozbek, *MTO Kuralları Isıgında Yeni Bir Tahkim Turu ve Sartı Olarak Cok Taraflı Tahkim* [*A New Kind of Arbitration: The Multiparty Arbitration in the Light of ICE Rules*] BATIDER, Cilt 20, Sayi 2, 1999 [BATIDER Journal Volume 20, Issue 2, 1999] p. 100.

889 Julian D. M. Lew, Loukas A. Mistelis & Stefan Michael Kröll, Comparative International Commercial Arbitration 179 (Kluwer Law Int'l 2003).

890 Bernard Hanotiau, Complex Arbitration, p. 2–4.

891 Nimet Ozbek, pp. 97–100.

- *intervention*, including primary and secondary perspectives; and
- *consolidation* of cases.

Turkish arbitration law does not regulate either joinder of parties or intervention through statutes. The section, therefore, refers to statutory regulations for litigation to generate suggestions for the regulation of arbitral adjudication.

a) Joinder of Parties

Joinder of parties is a procedural mechanism in Turkish law that relates to the resolution of multiparty disputes. This mechanism applies in situations involving multiple parties as defendants or plaintiffs,[892] and its application may be optional or mandatory. Turkish arbitration law does not specifically regulate joinder of parties; this section examines relevant litigation regulations to determine their applicability in arbitration.

(1) Optional Joinder of Parties

Multiple parties may file a lawsuit or be sued together in the following circumstances:[893]

a) The right or obligation at issue between the plaintiffs or defendants in the lawsuit is mutual for reasons other than joint ownership.
b) They all have a right or obligation in common as a result of a mutual transaction.
c) The facts and legal reasoning of their individual cases are the same or similar.

Cases involving optional joinder of parties remain independent from each other, and individual parties act independently.[894] Although courts conduct such cases together, they evaluate and judge causes of actions, preliminary objections, conditions of time limits, etc., separately. Courts render one decision at the end of the case for all of the optional joinder of parties, but this decision can involve different content and directions for each of them.[895] The joinder of parties mechanism thus results in procedural economy. For the concept of optional joinder of parties to apply in arbitral cases, parties must be bound by an arbitral agreement

---

892 Pelin Akın, *Tahkimde Cok Taraflılık* [*Multiparty Dispute in International Arbitration*] Gazi Universitesi Hukuk Fakultesi Dergisi C. 18, Y. 2014, Sayi 3–4 [Gazi University Law School Journal Vol. 18, Year 2014, Issue 3–4] p. 323.

893 Article 57 (1) of Turkish Code of Civil Procedure.

894 Article 58 (1) of Turkish Code of Civil Procedure.

895 Pelin Akın, p. 327.

or a clause, or by a subsequent agreement. Cases conducted separately can, then, be heard together. Parties are not, however, required to act together. Each party has the right to make specific individual claims and defenses and to select ratification or amicable settlement. Time limits and objections also only influence the related party.[896] All of the parties are, therefore, independent at all levels of the arbitral case, which is very advantageous in multiparty disputes, especially considering the consensual nature of arbitration.

(2) Mandatory Joinder of Parties

The Turkish Code of Civil Procedure specifies situations in which mandatory joinder of parties applies.[897] These include when multiple people use a right or have a claim made against them together,[898] and substantive law requires a single decision for all of them. The difference in mandatory joinder of parties is the fact that parties must act together.[899] For this mechanism to apply in arbitral cases, parties must be bound by arbitral agreements or clauses. Parties can also file an arbitration plea stating that the parties prefer arbitration to court litigation on the basis of the exercise of their will.[900] Consent becomes crucial at this point. To avoid the case's dismissal and achieve the mandatory joinder of cases, parties must be bound by an arbitral agreement and they must join the case within the time allowed by the arbitral agreement.[901] [902] This factor is essential to

---

896 *Ibid.*

897 Article 59 (1).

898 For instance, cases concerning joint ownership of an asset or a right, cases requiring evacuation of rented property based on renting contracts with more than one landlord or renter.

899 "The *Position of Mandatory Joinder of Parties in the Case*

Article 60 (1): Mandatory joinder of parties can file a lawsuit together or be filed a lawsuit against together. Parties have to act together in this type of joinder or parties. However, procedural actions taken by the parties who appear for the oral hearing shall take effect on the parties who do not appear for the oral hearing despite a due invitation."

900 Pelin Akın, p. 325.

901 If all the mandatory joinder parties are not party to arbitral agreement, they cannot join the arbitration unless the defendant consents; which means that the requirement of the case to be filed by all of the mandatory joinder of parties; and thus, the arbitral agreement will result in voidness due to article 11(3) of New York Convention. For instance, if a dispute will be submitted to arbitration against a joint venture, it is required to file this case against all the parties of joint venture. If the arbitral agreement was concluded by only some of those parties, it may result in voidness of the arbitral agreement.

902 Pelin Akın, p. 325.

understanding the procedural mechanism of mandatory joinder of parties in a multiparty arbitral case.

b) *Intervention*

Under Turkish civil procedural law, third parties can intervene in ongoing cases. The regulations do not, however, dictate whether such an action can be taken in arbitral cases. This legislative silence suggests the procedure's applicability to arbitration. The concept of intervention allows multiple parties in a case to submit their dispute to arbitration to the extent that it complies with the specifications of international arbitration.[903] The next section examines the limits and conditions of the application of intervention concept to arbitration. The Turkish Code of Civil Procedure[904] dictates that intervention in a case can be either primary or secondary. The option of notice of the proceeding is also statutorily enabled. Primary intervention is when a third-party files a case claiming to have a right related to the subject of an ongoing case between two parties. Secondary intervention is an intervention by a third party whose legal situation will be affected by the case's decision.[905]

(1) Primary Intervention

The latest version of the Turkish Code of Civil Procedure[906] explicitly regulates intervention for the first time. A third person who claims a partial or complete right on a matter or right in an ongoing case may file a lawsuit against the parties of the case before the same court by claiming that this circumstance exists. This action can be filed until a decision is rendered.[907] The plaintiff and defendant of the main case, then, become the defendants of the new counter case,[908] while the third party becomes the plaintiff.[909] The fact that the court adjudicates and concludes the primary intervention case and the main case together is the core of the issue for arbitration.[910] In the context of arbitration, decisions in intervention

903 *Id* at 314.
904 Between articles 61–69.
905 Nimet Ozbek, p. 125.
906 Numbered 6100 and dated 1/12/2011.
907 Article 65 (1).
908 Similar to abovementioned mandatory joinder of parties except they do not have to act together.
909 Pelin Akın, p. 319.
910 Article 65 (2).

cases are, indeed, conclusive for parties in the main cases who have consented to arbitration, within the limits they have established. Compelling those parties to approve another case and party, which would expand the time and resources expended in the main case, may prove risky.[911] Parties' consent to the third-party action becomes the only means of approval; because the original parties' approval seems unlikely, the mechanism is an ineffective solution to possible third-party claims in ongoing arbitrations.

(2) Secondary Intervention

Secondary intervention is possible when a third party has a legal interest in the outcome of a case for a given party.[912] [913] The intervention must also help that party. The intervenor must aim to improve its position or prevent it from worsening after the case is decided.[914] Such intervention is possible only prior to the end of the discovery phase.[915] Article 67 dictates that third parties who demand intervention must meet specific requirements to petition the court.[916] The Article adds: "*... The parties of the case shall be notified of the petition for intervention. The court invites the third party along with the parties if needed, and decides on the demand of intervention even if they don't appear....*"[917] The Article also contains additional provisions about the intervenor's organization in such cases, including his position and the effect of the case.[918]

911 Pelin Akın, p. 320.
912 Article 66 (1).
913 Ufuk Aydin &Haluk Konuralp, p. 81.
914 *Ibid.*
915 Article 66 (1).
916 "Demand and Examination of Secondary Intervention
Article 67 (1): Third party who demands to intervene makes an application to the court through a petition indicating the party that he wants to be at the side of, the reason for intervention and the bases of this."
917 Article 67 (2).
918 "The Position of the Secondary Intervenor

Article 68 (1): *Intervenor can pursue the case only starting from the current stage in the event of that the demand for intervention is approved. Intervenor can use the claim and defense means in favor for the party at the side he intervened for; can take any actions not against that party's transaction and explanations.*

(2) *Court notifies the intervenor of the actions that the parties are informed starting from the point of intervention.*"

"Effect of Secondary Intervention

In the context of the arbitration, the fact that the regulation does not stipulate the parties' consent proves important. The regulation entitles the court to approve the intervention of third parties without the original parties' consent on the condition that the intervention meets the legal requirements.[919] This may raise issues related to confidentiality and party equality of position—fundamental requirements in relation to the right to a fair trial,[920] which a third-party intervention may affect. Arbitration is a dispute settlement mechanism that is subject to the will of the parties, which adopts those principles. Considering the importance of these principles and the intent of the parties, the direct application of this mechanism to arbitration may not be a solution. The intervention of a third party in an arbitral case, however, remains possible for third parties with legal interests in cases in which the parties make a demand in this direction. Such interventions require the consent of the parties involved in the arbitration.[921]

A third party, for instance, qualifies as a secondary intervenor on the side of the parties in an arbitration if:

- the parties have integrated a multiparty arbitration clause in their contract; or
- the parties or arbitrators do not object to intervention in the absence of such a clause; or
- the parties agree to the intervention despite not having a multiparty arbitration clause because it accords with the will of the parties.[922]

In such an instance, the secondary intervenor participates in the case as an aid to the parties. He does not, however, qualify as a party; his participation will not affect the legal dynamics of the case for the original parties. This participation will not jeopardize confidentiality because the original parties consent to the third

---

Article 69 (1): *In the main case that intervenor takes place, too, the decision is given about the parties.*

(2) *Secondary intervenor's claim challenging the decision given about dispute of the main case cannot be listened in recourse relation with the party. However, the intervenor can claim that the party he is at the side of conducts litigation incorrectly indicating that he has joined the case late due to not being informed of the proceeding on time; or that party has prevented the use of claim and defense means; or the intervenor could not use the facilities of claim and defense not known by him due to gross negligence of that party."*

919 Pelin Akın, p. 318.

920 Viladimir Tochilovsky, Jurisprudence of the International Criminal Courts and the European Court of Human Rights 274 (Martinus Nijhoff Publishers 2008).

921 Burcin Yıldırım, p. 96.

922 Pelin Akın, p. 319.

party's involvement. The additional requirement of consent proves rational for arbitration. The parties who prefer arbitration over litigation, indeed, mainly rely on the procedure's consensual nature.[923] Consent is, therefore, a crucial matter in this regard.

(3) Notice of the Proceeding

Another mechanism related to multiparty disputes in procedural law is notice of the proceeding. Legal commentators construe this mechanism as a type of secondary intervention[924] for the following reasons:

> The Turkish Code of Civil Procedure states that: "*A party can give notice of proceedings to a third person if he believes that third person will hold him liable, or that the third person will be held liable if he loses the lawsuit until investigation is completed…*"[925]

The person who receives notice of the proceeding can join in the lawsuit on the side of the party with whom his legal interests align.[926] Additional procedural regulations related to the notice of proceeding are applicable. These regulations may aid parties who intend to adopt this mechanism as part of their arbitral agreements, or use it as a solution to their multiparty disputes.[927] In the context of arbitration, the mechanism's aim corresponds to the secondary intervention of

---

923 *Ibid.*

924 Nimet Ozbek, p. 125.

925 Article 61 (1).

It is possible that the person given the notice of proceeding to give the notice of proceeding to another person under the same conditions and the notice can be furthered in this way (Article 61 (2)).

926 Article 63 (1).

927 These regulations are in the following articles of Turkish Code of Civil Procedure:

"Form of the Notice

Article 62 (1): *The notice is given in writing; it is required to indicate the reason of the notice with rationales and the stage of the lawsuit.*

(2) *The hearing cannot be adjourned due to the notice and a delay is not granted except the compulsory situations such as sequence of the notice.*

Effect of the Notice

Article 64 (1): Article 69 (2) applies by analogy about the decision's effect on the person giving the notice in the case of notice of proceeding."

Article 69 (2) mentioned in this article is:

"*Secondary intervenor's claim challenging the decision given about dispute of the main case cannot be listened in recourse relation with the party. However, the intervenor can claim that the party he is at the side of conducts litigation incorrectly indicating that he*

third parties with legal interests. One nuisance warrants highlighting. One of the parties in the case must initiate third party involvement instead of the third party himself. This raises the question of whether the consent of the parties requirement holds for this mechanism. When the parties in the case file the demand, does this satisfy the requirement of their consent?

Turkish legal doctrine provides contradicting answers to this question. Some authors assert that this mechanism can apply to arbitration as well as litigation. Others assert that it cannot apply in arbitral cases because it will contradict the will of the parties.[928] The difference between this mechanism and the others serves as a starting point for determining its suitability for arbitral proceedings. The fact that the third party receives notice of the proceedings at the initiation of one of the parties in the arbitral proceeding indicates that this party provides its consent.[929] The opponent party in the arbitral case, however, may object to the participation of a third party for reasons such as confidentiality. After one party files a demand to deliver a notice of the proceedings to a third party, the opponent party must consent. This reduces the risk of initiating the procedure. After the third party receives notice of the proceedings in accordance with Article 63, he can join the case on the side of the party with whom its legal interests align. The consent of the opposing party should be sought prior to delivery of the notice. If granted entry, the third parties may join the case. This process ensures the consensus of all parties and eliminates potential ambiguity and misunderstanding.

Lastly, Article 448 of the Turkish Commercial Code includes a specific regulation regarding notice of the proceedings, which involves actions for the annulment of general assembly resolutions. The Article[930] states that a board of directors must promptly announce the filing of an action for annulment and include the date of the oral hearing in the announcement; the company must announce the case's initiation and the date of the oral hearing on its website and also make the announcement through the Trade Registry Gazette.[931] This regulation

---

has joined the case late due to not being informed of the proceeding on time; or that party has prevented the use of claim and defense means; or the intervenor could not use the facilities of claim and defense not known by him due to gross negligence of that party."

928 Pelin Akın, pp. 323–324.

929 *Id* at 323.

930 "Announcement, Security and Right to Appeal

448: (1) *Board of directors announces and uploads to the web-site of the company that action for annulment or nullity was filed and the date of the hearing duly….*"

931 Burak Huysal, p. 319.

mirrors the notice of the proceedings process for annulments of general assembly resolutions. It proves that adopting this process for specific actions should not pose a problem for arbitration.

c) Consolidation of Cases

Consolidation of cases is the last procedural mechanism that applies to the resolution of multiparty cases. One specific regulation in Turkish Commercial Code addresses the consolidation of cases. This regulation receives priority here because it relates to the annulment of general assembly resolutions. Article 448 (2) states that, when multiple annulment cases are filed before a court, the court will hear them in a consolidated fashion. This article applies specifically to annulment cases of the same general assembly resolution.[932] This commercial law regulation aims to prevent conflicting decisions and the loss of time and money that results from filing more than one cases against the same resolution.[933] No such rule aiming at procedural economy exists for arbitration and the regulation's application to arbitration remains controversial.

No other international arbitration regulation addresses the consolidation of cases, but references to related provisions of the Turkish Code of Civil Procedure[934] for domestic arbitration may help fill the gap. Article 166 regulates the consolidation of cases mechanism, including procedural organization.[935] According to this provision, cases with connections can be consolidated *on demand or per se.*

---

932 *Id* at 316.

933 *Ibid.*

934 Numbered 6100.

935 Full text of the provision in Turkish Code of Civil Procedure is as follows:

"Consolidation of Cases
Article 166:

(1) *Cases filed before the civil courts with the same level, title and judicial locality can be consolidated under the court that the first case was filed in the event of a connection between the cases at any stage per se or upon demand. The court that the second case was filed gives the decision of consolidation and this decision binds the other court.*
(2) *Consolidation due to connection can be demanded from the court where the second case is filed if the cases are filed before the courts that take place in the same judicial locality with the same level and title. The court where the first case is filed is bound by this as from the approval of demand and the finalization of the decision on consolidation of cases.*

Two particular requirements apply for the consolidation of multiparty disputes in Turkish law:[936] connection between the cases and consent of the parties. The section below examines regulations related to these two requirements to determine their applicability to arbitration.

(1) Connection between the Cases

Cases are connected when they arise for similar reasons or the decision in one affects the other.[937] These criteria apply to litigation; for arbitration, the connection between cases required for consolidation needs further research. Recent developments in comparative law regarding arbitral institutions and statutory regulations prove helpful. In 2012, the International Chamber of Commerce adopted new rules that include regulations for arbitration of multiparty disputes and the consolidation of cases. Article 10 of the ICC Rules of Arbitration includes statements that address the required connections between cases.[938] These statements include: "*…all of the claims in the arbitrations are made under the same arbitration agreement…*"[939]; and "*…the disputes in the arbitrations arise in connection with the same legal relationship…*"[940]—when the court identifies arbitral cases between the same parties based on multiple arbitration agreements that are "*compatible*".[941] These statements have more comprehensive and specific applications to the contractual side of arbitration than to the general regulation mentioned above.

---

(3) *The court where the first case is filed shall promptly be informed of the decision of consolidation.*
(4) *The connection is deemed to exist in the event that the cases arise from the same or similar reasons or the decision to be rendered for one case is such as to affect the other one.*
(5) *The cases, appellate examinations of which are required to be made before different chambers can also be consolidated in accordance with this provision. In this case, the regional court of justice that considers the decision with regards to the main legal relationship that causes the dispute in the consolidated cases makes the appellate review.*"

936 And generally, in comparative law.
937 *See supra* article 166(1) (4).
938 *Available at* http://www.iccwbo.org/products-and-services/arbitration-and-adr/arbitration/icc-rules-of-arbitration/
939 Article 10 (b).
940 Article 10 (c).
941 Article 10 (c).

The Istanbul Arbitration Centre enacted new rules in 2016 that also address consolidation of arbitral cases. In accordance with the related part of Article 11[942] of its Arbitration Rules, the Board of the Istanbul Arbitration Centre can consolidate two or more pending cases on the condition that "*…the disputes in the arbitrations arise in connection with the same legal relationship and the arbitration agreements are compatible…*" when the parties to the arbitrations requesting consolidation are the same and the claims in the arbitrations are based on more than one agreement. [943] Finally, in January 2015, the China International Economic and Trade Arbitration Commission (CIETAC) revised its arbitration rules to include a regulation for the consolidation of cases. These rules stipulate that to connect arbitrations conducted under multiple arbitral agreements, the arbitrations must "*…involve the same parties as well as legal relationships of the same nature….*"[944] Turkish domestic law clearly dictates the connections between cases necessary for consolidation in the context of litigation. Although no similar regulations explicitly address arbitration, this consideration of comparative law shows the requirements for litigation should apply in practice to arbitration.

(2) Consent of the Parties

Turkish law regulates the consolidation of cases in the context of litigation. The first regulation states that "*in the event that multiple annulment cases are filed, those cases shall be consolidated to be heard.*"[945] The second regulation states that "*Cases filed before the civil courts with the same level and title and in the same judicial locality, can be consolidated… per se or upon demand.*" Crucially for its application to arbitration, the regulation disregards whether parties consented to the consolidation of their cases; it thereby entitles the court to rule on the consolidation of cases *per se*, too.

The differences between arbitration and litigation are crucial, however, for designating the parties. The voluntary nature of arbitration means that only signatories to the arbitral clause or agreement can participate as parties in the arbitral proceeding; meanwhile, any third party with an interest in protection may join a case litigated before a court.[946] When determining the parties to

942 Article 11 (1) (b) (iii).

943 *Available at* https://istac.org.tr//wp-content/uploads/2016/02/ISTAC-Arbitration-and-Mediation-Rules-f.pdf

944 Article 1(b).
Available at: http://www.cietac.org/index.php?m=Page&a=index&id=106&l=en

945 Article 448 (2) of Turkish Commercial Code regulating the cases for annulment of general assembly resolutions.

946 Bernard Hanotai, Complex Arbitration, pp. 6–7.

arbitral agreements in comparative law, courts or arbitral tribunals mainly consider whether a party has given consent.[947] The consensual nature of arbitration only allows those who have consented to the arbitral agreement or clause to be party to the arbitral proceedings.[948] This crucial difference between litigation and arbitration makes it possible and rational for courts to consolidate two cases in their jurisdictions *per se* and even in the absence of demand from the parties. In arbitration, however, such an action would contradict the voluntary nature of arbitration. Non-voluntary consolidation of arbitral cases involves other parties in the arbitral proceedings, infringing upon the main parties' autonomy.[949]

This is a core concern in multiparty arbitral disputes. Avoiding undesired third-party involvement in an arbitral case is naturally preferable; meanwhile, by consolidating closely connected cases, parties can avoid conflicting decisions and procedural difficulties. This paradox is not specific to Turkish law. Legal systems of the world generally agree that the scope of multiparty disputes in arbitration needs improvement.[950] OECD's Work Program on Corporate Governance has addressed arbitration procedures for multiple parties.[951] As Howes and Stowell[952] put it, "*...the consolidation dilemma can be framed as a struggle between party autonomy and efficiency...*". In a nutshell, statutory regulations address two requirements for the consolidation of cases: connections between the cases and consent of the parties. The latter is key to minimizing any risk.[953] Scholars have criticized also major international arbitration institutions for failing to develop sufficient procedural regulations to govern multiparty arbitrations.[954] In this regard, recently adopted regulations warrant analysis.

Most recently, the ICC has integrated the concept of consolidation into its Rules of Arbitration. This regulation entitles courts to rule on party's

---

947 *Id* at 7.

948 Stavros Brekoulakis, *The Relevance of the Interests of Third Parties in Arbitration: Taking a Closer Look at the Elephant in the Room*, 113:4 Penn State L. Rev. (2009) p. 1166.

"*...Only persons who have unequivocally consented and signed and arbitration agreement can participate in arbitration proceeding and be bound by resulting arbitral award...*" Ziya Akıncı, Arbitration Law of Turkey, p. 104-105.

949 *Ibid.*

950 Loukas Mistelis, *International Arbitration – Corporate Attitudes and Practices,* p. 584.

951 Louis Bouchez & Alexander Karpf, p. 12.

952 B Ted Howes & Allison M Stowell, *The Consolidation Dilemma: Is There Finally a Pragmatic Solution?,* 10 Disp. Resol. Int'l (2016), p. 8.

953 Jean-François Poudret & Sébastien Besson, p. 209.

954 Ted Howes & Allison M Stowell, p. 4.

consolidation requests in the following circumstances: if the parties agree on consolidation; if the parties have made their claims under the same arbitration agreement; or if the parties have made their claims under more than one arbitration agreement but the parties in the arbitration are the same, the disputes have arisen from the same legal relationships, and the arbitration agreements prove compatible.[955] CIETAC also has a more recent set of rules regarding the consolidation of arbitrations. These rules stipulate that arbitrations may be consolidated after a party requests it and when all parties agree on consolidation or when the parties make their claims under the same arbitral agreement;[956] If the claims are made under multiple identical or compatible agreements, then arbitrations must involve the same parties and legal relationships of the same nature; multiple contracts must involve a main contract and its ancillary contracts.[957]

Article 11 of the Istanbul Arbitration Centre Rules also stipulates that arbitrations can be consolidated when a party requests consolidation and the cases meet certain conditions. These conditions include the agreement of the parties when the arbitrations involve different parties.[958] If the parties are the same, their

---

955 ICC Rules of Arbitration, Article 10. *Available at*: http://www.iccwbo.org/products-and-services/arbitration-and-adr/arbitration/icc-rules-of-arbitration/
Follows as:

"In deciding whether to consolidate, the Court may take into account any circumstances it considers to be relevant, including whether one or more arbitrators have been confirmed or appointed in more than one of the arbitrations and, if so, whether the same or different persons have been confirmed or appointed.

When arbitrations are consolidated, they shall be consolidated into the arbitration that commenced first, unless otherwise agreed by all parties."

956 Article 19 (1) (a), (d).

957 Article 19 (1) (b), (c).
Article 19 follows as:

"…2. In deciding whether to consolidate the arbitrations in accordance with the preceding Paragraph 1, CIETAC shall take into account the opinions of all parties and other relevant factors such as the correlation between the arbitrations concerned, including the nomination and appointment of arbitrators in the separate arbitrations.

3. Unless otherwise agreed by all the parties, the arbitrations shall be consolidated into the arbitration that was first commenced.

4. After the consolidation of arbitrations, the conduct of the arbitral proceedings shall be decided by the Arbitration Court if the arbitral tribunal is not formed, or shall be decided by the arbitral tribunal if it has been formed."

958 *Available at*: http://www.cietac.org/index.php?m=Page&a=index&id=106&l=en

agreement on consolidation suffices or the same arbitration agreement will govern all claims in the arbitrations; if not, and there are multiple arbitration agreements, consolidation requires that the disputes arise in connection with the same legal relationship and the arbitration agreements must be compatible.[959]

The institutional regulations suggest that consent of the parties is the key to consolidation despite the existence of other avenues such as connections between the cases. Existence of such consent may, in fact, suffice for consolidation.[960] In the context of arbitration, tribunals are not entitled to rule on consolidation of cases *per se* unless one of the parties requests it. If the parties prefer to utilize institutional rules for the consolidation of their cases, those rules will stipulate the consent of the parties and the requirement of the request of one of the parties. When drafting the arbitral clause independently, on the other hand, parties must actively integrate these rules because current Turkish law does not assume their inclusion.

This section has emphasized the absence of statutory regulations governing multiparty disputes in arbitral proceedings in Turkish law. It has introduced secondary sources that may influence arbitral proceedings involving multiple parties conducted under Turkish law. These include domestic law regulations of multiple party disputes in litigation and possible mechanisms that may resolve procedural issues arising from the multiparty character of such disputes. Because these regulations apply specifically to litigation, this section has also introduced several transnational institutional arbitral rules to identify possible contrasts with litigation. These institutional rules highlight the importance of the issue of consent of

---

Article 11 (1) (a). *Available at*: https://istac.org.tr//wp-content/uploads/2016/02/ISTAC-Arbitration-and-Mediation-Rules-f.pdf

959 Article 11 (1) (b).
Article 11 follows as:

"…*2. In deciding whether to consolidate, the Board considers any relevant circumstances, such as whether or not the arbitrators have been designated and, if so, whether the designated persons are the same or not. If the co-arbitrator of the respondent has not been designated at the time of the request for consolidation, the co-arbitrator of the respondent shall not be designated until the Board decides on the request for consolidation.*

3. The request for consolidation shall be submitted to the Secretariat. The Secretariat, after consulting with all of the parties, transmits the request for consolidation to the Board. If the Board decides to consolidate, the arbitrations shall be consolidated into the arbitration that commenced first, unless otherwise agreed by all parties…"

960 Pelin Akın, p. 311.

the parties in arbitral proceedings with multiple parties. The section below assesses the points made so far and concludes with practical suggestions that take into account the statutory regulations and mechanisms examined up to this point.

d) *Proposals for the Resolution of Multiparty Disputes through Arbitration in Turkish Law*

(1) *General Explanations of Multiparty Arbitration Proceedings*

The issues that arise from multiparty disputes are common in the corporate world because corporate agreements frequently involve more than two partners or shareholders.[961] Multiparty disputes occur particularly frequently in the construction and finance sectors in which corporations undertake enterprises—projects, loan agreements, etc.—together.[962] This section examines solutions to issues resulting from disputes in such multiparty arrangements.

Primary intervention best addresses multiparty issues in cases in which the groups of companies involved include joint ventures or consortiums.[963] The mechanisms of secondary intervention and notice of the proceedings are best suited to cases involving chain contracts, a situation in which a main contract dictates the execution of the service and multiple ancillary agreements drawn in association with the main contract. [964] The repercussions in contracts involving several parties and multiple intra-corporate actors, such as the shareholders of a company, in each legal entity may impede the performance of contracts. In such cases, the comparative advantages[965] of arbitrating versus litigating multinational cases may still justify submitting disputes to arbitration.[966]

In disputes involving more than two parties, consolidation provides various advantages, too. It avoids potential conflicting decisions from multiple arbitral tribunals and facilitates coordination between contractors, sub-contractors in

---

961 Julian D.M. Lew et al., Comparative International Commercial Arbitration, p. 378.

962 *Ibid.*

963 Nimet Ozbek, pp. 102–105, 125.

964 Examples of chain contracts are construction contracts with contractor and sub-contractors; chain sales with manufacturer, wholesaler, retailers and customer; and ship-owners, main charterer and sub-charterer as the contracts that involve "*repercussion*".
Id at 106–107, 125.

965 Alexis Mourre, p. 299.

966 Nimet Ozbek, p. 107.

chain or construction contracts, and shareholders.[967] Consolidation is also more financially and procedurally expedient.[968] In reality, arbitration of multiparty disputes has its own disadvantages, too. The presence of multiple parties may, for example, create procedural difficulties that delay a case's conclusion.[969] Arbitration agreements drafted to avoid possible pitfalls and satisfy the requirements for accurate and enforceable arbitral awards, however, may help overcome these procedural drawbacks.[970] The section below describes the keys to effectively drafting arbitration agreements and suggests strategies for avoiding the risks of multiparty proceedings.

Parties can refer to the rules of arbitral institutions to establish regulations regarding the resolution of disputes arising from consolidated arbitrations.[971] To avoid issues that might affect the enforceability of the final award, when establishing rules concerning consolidation, parties should clarify:[972]

- The content of the "connection" required for consolidation.
- The stage of the case at which consolidation is available.
- The process of consolidation;
- The designation of the contracts to be included in the event of multiple contracts such as chain contracts or group corporations.[973]

Because these issues are not statutorily governed, parties should draft their arbitration agreements to address them to avoid procedural mishaps or unwanted

967 Richard Bamfort, p. 4.

968 Due to conducting the hearings and taking of evidence jointly which saves time and expenses.
Fritz Nicklisch, *Multi-Party Arbitration and Dispute Resolution in Major Industrial Projects,* 11 J. Int'l Arb. (1994) p. 68
Ziya Akıncı, Arbitration Law of Turkey, p. 104.

969 Fritz Nicklish, pp. 68,69.

970 Nimet Ozbek, pp. 108–109.

971 *Id* at 120.

972 *Ibid.*

973 Other questions may gain currency if abovementioned participation of a third party is the case instead of consolidation of cases. In that case, it should be favorable to additionally indicate the following factors:

- Conditions of joinder,
- Type of joinder,
- Stage of the case, until which the consolidation is available,
- Rights of the joinder,
- Effect of the award on the party joined.

surprise. Consolidation cannot be mandated without the consent of the parties,[974] even if it is the most convenient solution in a multiparty dispute situation. Although Turkish law contains no explicit regulation, doctrine regards multiparty arbitration as possible only when all relevant parties consent.[975] To avoid potentially surprising consequences later on, parties must agree from the outset on the rules for the resolution of multiparty disputes. If they do not, that task will fall to arbitral tribunals or national courts, and the rules developed by these bodies may adversely affect the parties' freedom of contract.[976] Parties may also struggle to reach consensus regarding the resolution of their disputes once a dispute arises. This, again, highlights the importance of drafting arbitration agreements early in contractual relationships, especially in situations involving multiple parties whose consent will be required.[977]

Acquiring the consent of all relevant parties in a multiparty arbitration can be arduous given the complex legal relationships in chain contracts or between sub-contractors and shareholders. In certain circumstances, if the parties elect to do so, well-drafted arbitration provisions can include the related procedural mechanisms for future use, because predicting the exact parties in a possible dispute may be impossible. Integrating an 'umbrella' clause[978] that includes possible multiple parties and agreements may provide the widest possible coverage.[979] Significant issues can arise when connected contracts are covered by different arbitral clauses or the arbitral clauses are not effectively coordinated.[980]

---

974 Nimet Ozbek, p. 120.

975 Ziya Akıncı, Arbitration Law of Turkey, p. 105.

976 Nimet Ozbek, p. 120.

977 Ziya Akıncı, Arbitration Law of Turkey, p. 105.
Matthew D. Schwartz, *Multiparty Disputes and Consolidated Arbitrations: An Oxymoron or the Solution to a Continuing Dilemma,* 22 Case W. Res. J. Int'l L. (1990) p. 372.

978 "...*An umbrella arbitration agreement corresponds to a superior agreement in which several subsequent and interconnected contracts are referred to. Therefore, the clause spreads its effects and binds the parties to the related contracts. The first is where only the heads of agreement, or framework agreement, contains an arbitration clause to which the other related contracts refer...*"
Felipe Vollbrecht Sperandio, *The Reach of the Arbitration Agreement to Parties Involved in the Same Legal Relationship,* 11 REVIST@ E – Mercatoria 1 (2012) p. 175.

979 Bernard Hanotai, Complex Arbitration, p. 103.
Richard Bamforth, p. 20.
Ziya Akıncı, Arbitration Law of Turkey, p. 106.

980 Alexis Mourre, p. 306.

The consensual nature of arbitration can, thus, impede multiparty proceedings that involve divergent or contradictory arbitral clauses.[981] As a corporate policy, therefore, arbitral agreements or clauses should contain identical clauses for multiparty arbitration that cross-reference underlying contracts and use an umbrella clause to resolve possible conflicts.[982]

In a construction contract between an owner, contractor, and subcontractor, for example, the parties should consider two possible multiparty arbitration agreements: a single agreement between all three parties or separate agreements between each pair of parties[983] that integrate the multiparty arbitration clause into each main contract and connected sub-contract.[984] Such an arbitral clause can stipulate,[985] for instance, whether issues that arise under the main contract are the same or connected with the sub-contract; whether they are related to the facts between contractor and sub-contractor; or whether issues between a contractor and sub-contractor are of sufficient concern to be submitted to arbitration.[986]

(2) Explanations of Intra-Corporate Dispute Settlement in Specific and Conclusion

Turkish arbitration law does not establish which rules apply when parties in intra-corporate disputes confront problems in multiparty arbitration proceedings.[987] Relevant rules in domestic law for multiple parties nevertheless apply to arbitration provided they comply with the fundamental principles of arbitration.[988] The Turkish Code of Civil Procedure provisions and the mechanisms for

---

981 *Id* at 309.

982 Ted Howes, p. 4.

983 In particular, a main contract between the owner and contractor; and a second sub-contract between contractor and sub-contractor, both of which having a multiparty arbitration clause.

984 Okuma Kazutake, *Party Autonomy in International Commercial Arbitration: Consolidation of Multiparty and Classwide Arbitration*, 9:1 Ann. Surv. of Int'l & Comp. L. Article 212 (2003), *available at*: http://digitalcommons.law.ggu.edu/annlsurvey/vol9/iss1/9.

985 In addition to the matters abovementioned.

986 *See* Okuma Kazutake, pp. 212–213 & n.45 *citing* Model Form International Contract for Process Plant Construction drafted by the Japan Engineering Advancement Association (ENAA) for further explanations.

987 Mehmet Tas, p. 63.

988 *Id* at 65.

multiparty disputes examined above, therefore, apply to arbitrations conducted under Turkish law with the exceptions stated.[989]

The preceding section evaluated multiparty arbitration methods through examples such as chain and group contracts. This section concludes the discussion of the specific application of those rules to companies' internal legal relationships. All of the mechanisms examined above are available for the parties involved in the arbitration of an intra-corporate dispute. The choice of which mechanisms to adopt for intra-corporate disputes depends on the circumstances, the perspective of the shareholders, and the field of operations. Parties that intend to resolve their disputes through multiparty arbitration should consider methods for minimizing risks when they begin drafting the contract.

The application of the mechanisms for multiparty intra-corporate disputes can also be illustrated with examples of annulment cases. The mechanisms in the Turkish Code of Civil Procedure regarding multiparty disputes apply when multiple shareholders file a case for the annulment of a general assembly resolution. The joinder of parties mechanism, for instance, would apply in such a case.[990] Consolidation of cases also applies when multiple shareholders file for the annulment of a general assembly resolution. The two main requirements for consolidation of cases—*connection* between cases and *consent* of the parties—remain valid for the consolidation of the annulment cases.

For an annulment case to meet these requirements, the draft of the arbitration agreement should include the criteria[991] for establishing a *connection* sufficient for consolidation. Given the nature of general assembly resolutions, establishing the existence of a connection will likely require that the dispute arise from the same resolution.[992] If the dispute arises from different resolutions, establishing a connection will depend on the circumstances. Depending on the balance of the interests, conducting arbitrations before different arbitrators for different resolutions made in the same general assembly meeting remains a possibility.[993]

---

989 For instance, although the law foresees that courts can consolidate cases *ex officio*, a request from one of the parties and the consent requirement is essential in arbitration. *Ibid.*

990 Burak Huysal, pp. 316, 318.
Mehmet Tas, p. 65.

991 Such as the cases to be arisen from the same or similar reasons or the decision to be rendered for one case is such as to affect the other one.

992 Burak Huysal, p. 316.

993 Mehmet Tas, p. 66.

The key criteria for consolidation of the cases is the consent of the related parties. A specific provision in the Turkish Commercial Code requires consolidation—exclusively for actions of annulment—when parties file multiple cases.[994] Another regulation in Turkish law entitles national courts to order consolidation of cases *per se* as well as on demand.[995] These regulations govern litigation; they apply to arbitration provided that they comply with the fundamental principles and nature of arbitration. They simply aim to prevent the loss of time and money due to filing of various cases against the same resolution.[996] The regulations do not aim to force parties to consolidate their cases. It should not, therefore, result in the consolidation of cases against the will of parties. The parties' consent is important. Institutional arbitral rules confirm this view as indicated above. An arbitral tribunal, therefore, cannot decide on the consolidation of cases without the consent of related parties and the parties' authorization of the tribunal to make such a decision.[997]

No rule in Turkish law impedes the consolidation of cases in arbitration.[998] Multiple parties signing an arbitral agreement that explicitly governs the issue of multiparty arbitration signals that they consent to a possible multiparty arbitral proceeding.[999] When parties file multiple arbitration cases, they may consolidate those cases for a hearing before a single arbitral tribunal, provided consolidation accords with the will of the parties or a clause in the arbitral agreement stipulates this action.[1000] Parties included in an arbitration agreement in the articles of association should consent to multiparty arbitration.[1001] Including clauses stipulating multiparty arbitration in the arbitration agreement in the articles of association signals the consent of all shareholders and departments of the corporation;[1002] such clauses corroborate the arbitrability of disputes.

---

994 Article 448 (2):

> "…. *If more than one annulment action is filed, the actions shall be consolidated to be heard.*
> …"

995 *See supra* Chapter V (F) 3 (c).
996 Burak Huysal, p. 316.
997 *Id* at 317.
998 *Ibid.*
999 Julian D.M. Lew et al., Comparative International Commercial Arbitration, p. 379.
1000 Mehmet Tas, p. 66.
1001 Burcin Yıldırım, p. 38.
1002 Burak Huysal, p. 319.

Given the large number of shareholders and other corporate actors,[1003] conducting arbitration with the consent of all parties may seem untenable. Multiparty clauses in the arbitral agreement in the articles of incorporation, however, would bind previous, present, and future shareholders even in case of share transfers as long as such a clause exists at the time of the transfer.[1004] If the company concludes the arbitral agreement after the establishment of the corporation, the consent of all parties would indicate that the arbitration agreement binds all corporate actors. This means it would bind all the subsequent actors as well.[1005]

Arbitral clauses inserted into the articles of association should refer to disputes between shareholders and the corporation (and its departments), and to disputes between shareholders, the corporation and its representatives, who may not be shareholders,[1006]rather than only referring to disputes between shareholders.[1007] When a party files for the annulment of a general assembly resolution, the plaintiff is the legal entity of the corporation, meaning the risks of multiparty character only relate to the defendant.[1008] Companies should consider the complexity and consensual nature of arbitration and multiparty disputes when drafting arbitral agreements.[1009] The consent of all related parties is crucial in this regard. The inclusion of identical arbitral clauses in related contracts may also minimize possible risks.[1010] Regularizing proceedings including, to the extent possible, integrating applicable multiparty mechanisms in arbitral clauses for connected parties and claims will aid significantly in this process.[1011] During multiparty arbitration proceedings, "[s]*ometimes it is unsatisfactory drafting of the arbitration clause that raises problem*[s]..."[1012]; and thus, "[t]*he easiest and cleanest solution to the consolidation dilemma is to draft the right of consolidation...If*

1003 Joseph Lee, *Intra-Corporate Dispute Arbitration and Minority Shareholder Protection: A Corporate Governance Perspective*, Feb. 23, 2015 *available at* https://papers.ssrn.com/sol3/papers2.cfm?abstract_id=2736981 p. 10.

1004 Joseph Lee, p. 10.

1005 Burcin Yıldırım, p. xxii.

1006 Representatives shall also be requested to give consent to arbitration.

1007 Alexis Mourre, p. 299.

1008 Mehmet Tas, p. 63.

1009 Alexis Mourre, p. 309.

1010 Bernard Hanotai, Complex Arbitration, p. 102.
Alexis Mourre, p. 309.

1011 Alexis Mourre, p. 309.

1012 Bernard Hanotai, Complex Arbitration, p. 204.

such 'consolidation provisions' are drafted correctly, no party can argue it has not consented to consolidation at the time of the dispute...."[1013] Companies should, therefore, draft arbitral clauses to make the consent of the parties explicit and to delineate its content and boundaries.[1014]

Apart from joinder of parties and consolidation of cases, shareholders with legal interests may also intervene in arbitral cases based on the consent of the parties.[1015] Both Turkish and German law consider intervention to be a shareholder right and the mechanism's availability serves as a specific pre-requisite for arbitration.[1016] This right proves problematic only for persons who are not party to the arbitration agreement. Because all shareholders are party to arbitration agreements in annulment cases, however, the intervention of other shareholders and departments of the corporation is not a problem.[1017]

To minimize potential procedural difficulties, arbitration agreements should make the parties' consent clear.[1018] They should also include mechanisms related to the notification and participation of shareholders and regulate[1019] the selection of arbitral tribunals[1020] to ensure that all parties take an equal part in the process. The timing of the use of the multiparty arbitration mechanisms, including consolidation, joinder, etc., should also be considered. To insure the equality of parties throughout the arbitral proceeding, these issues should be clarified at the earliest possible stage when parties may still take part in the appointment of the arbitrators.[1021] Parties to arbitration agreements who do not join arbitration proceedings and claim not to be bound by the final award when they could have participated breach good faith.[1022] To avoid any confusion, the arbitration agreement should state that awards given in such cases will bind the parties to the arbitration agreement who do not join the arbitration despite having the opportunity to join.[1023]

1013 Ted Howes & Allison M Stowell, p. 8.
1014 Felipe Vollbrecht Sperandio, p. 172.
1015 Burcin Yıldırım, p. 96.
1016 Burak Huysal, p. 319.
1017 *Ibid.*
1018 Felipe Vollbrecht Sperandio, p. 172.
1019 Joseph Lee, p. 10.
1020 Thomas E. Carbonneau & William Elliott Butler, p. 701.
1021 *See* Felipe Vollbrecht Sperandio, p. 205 for further explanations on equality of parties.
1022 Burcin Yıldırım, p. 39.
1023 *Ibid.*

The three-month time limit[1024] for the commencement of oral hearings, specifically stipulated for the consolidation of annulment cases, should also apply to arbitration. This regulation dictates that oral hearings cannot commence before the lapse of time of three months[1025] in an action for annulment. Parties should also take this time limit into consideration during the proceedings. Article 449 of the Turkish Commercial Code contains another regulation regarding the Court's suspension of the execution of a general assembly resolution for which an annulment action is filed.[1026] The regulation stipulates that the court must consider the opinions of the board of directors to suspend the execution of the related resolution.[1027] To meet the procedural requirements for general assembly resolutions in Turkish law, therefore, drafts of the arbitral clause should also include such a requirement for arbitrators. Finally, Turkish law requires parties to be specific about disputes when agreeing on arbitration. The parties must be aware of all the types of disputes to be submitted for arbitration.[1028] The parties' agreement to submit a dispute arising from a specific agreement, for instance, qualifies as a sufficient level of specificity. Such an agreement could be a sales agreement, loan agreement, or articles of association. An agreement with the following wording: "*[a]ny type of disputes that arise between the parties hereupon shall be resolved through arbitration.*" will be ineffective because it does not specify the type dispute, making the agreement too general and abstract.[1029] Parties must also pay attention to this requirement while drafting because the degree of specificity regarding disputes affects the validity of the arbitral agreement.[1030]

Provisions governing multiparty arbitration in the arbitral clauses are crucial to internal corporate policy in transnational commercial relations or

---

1024 Article 448 (2) of Turkish Commercial Code.

1025 Three months foreseen in article 445.

"Article 445: (1) The *persons identified in Article 446 can file annulment actions against general assembly resolutions that violate the law or articles of incorporation, particularly good faith, before the commercial court of first instance in the location of the company headquarters, within 3 months from the date of the decision.*"

1026 "Suspending the Execution of the Resolution

Article 449: (1) *When an action of annulment or nullity against a general assembly resolution is filed, the court may decide to suspend the execution of the resolution subject to this action, after taking the opinion of members of the board of director.*"

1027 Article 449.

1028 Mehmet Bahtiyar, Anonim Ortaklık Sozlesmesi, p. 210.

1029 *Ibid.*

1030 *Ibid.*

within corporations with multiple corporate actors. At the outset of arbitration, plaintiffs and their counsel frequently discover the absence of such provisions for multiparty mechanisms even in some flawlessly drafted arbitral clauses. These omissions give "... *respondents the keys to cause mischief...*"[1031] Legal practitioners who serve as counsel for international commercial companies play an important risk-management role during the drafting period. They should be trained to keep arbitral agreements in intra-corporate documents and external corporate contracts consistent, and to ensure that they address the riskiest points of multiparty cases stated above. This will enable international corporate actors in developing countries like Turkey to have established legal practices in the area of arbitration.

Multiparty mechanisms such as the consolidation of cases have two sides in the context of arbitration. This is referred to as a "dilemma" in comparative law. Consent of the parties is crucial for assuring party autonomy as a fundamental principle of arbitration.[1032] It, therefore, poses risks in multi-party cases. Failing to consolidate similar cases, however, has considerable risks too, including the possibility of multiple proceedings for similar disputes, increased fees, and even conflicting decisions.[1033] At that point, 'proportional harmonization' always proves more effective than 'all or nothing' approaches that depend on the circumstances.[1034] No answer covers all possible scenarios. Corporate actors should evaluate their internal affairs and external commercial relationships and determine the most consistent and comprehensive corporate policy for the resolution of possible disputes. Arbitration in the Turkish legal system is still likely to provide faster and more neutral resolutions to intra-corporate disputes, as well as providing the necessary expertise. If corporations prefer arbitration, this preference should be reflected in arbitral agreements in the related documents such as articles of association. These agreements should address all the risks outlined above. Legal practitioners should be sensitive and careful throughout the process of drafting arbitral clauses. Only the contributions of legal and corporate practitioners make comprehensive arbitral

---

1031 Ted Howes & Allison M Stowell, p. 5.

1032 *Id* at 8.

1033 *Ibid.*

1034 Stavros Brekoulakis, *The Effect of An Arbitral Award and Third Parties in International Arbitration: Res Judicata Revisited*, p. 18.

clauses that include solutions for the potential procedural risks involved in multiparty cases possible.

G. Conclusion

Party autonomy is the key principle of arbitration. Turkish law contains multiple statutory regulations that uphold party autonomy, which demonstrate the law's general respect for the principle. Certain additional factors can affect the arbitrability of disputes. Imperative rules, for instance, may make a dispute inarbitrable. Exclusive judicial jurisdictional rules, similarly, can make disputes inarbitrable when the rules interdict arbitration. Public policy can also impact the arbitrability of disputes. Its broad application can, moreover, result in instances of excessive interpretation in the context inarbitrability. These are the main factors influencing arbitrability in arbitration Codes and other substantive and procedural areas of Turkish law.

Corporate disputes effectively exemplify how the general rules of arbitrability apply in practice. Corporate disputes—especially the ones arising from internal corporate affairs—benefit from arbitration in many ways. Corporate actors therefore frequently prefer arbitration to other dispute resolutions methods including litigation. Speed, efficiency, confidentiality, cost-effectiveness, neutrality, and expertise are among arbitration's benefits. No specific rules explicitly govern the arbitration of intra-corporate disputes in Turkish law. Case law and doctrinal comments also lack consistent approaches to the issue. This ambivalence results in confusion among practitioners.

Doctrinal commentators who argue against the arbitrability of intra-corporate disputes make their arguments on several grounds. All relevant concepts apply to annulment of general assembly resolutions cases, making such cases illuminating examples of the complexities of arbitrability. Grounds for inarbitrability in annulment of general assembly resolution cases include: judicial jurisdictional rules that assign exclusive jurisdiction to specific courts; imperative provisions of law or possible multiparty issues and procedural inconveniences; and vested right character for filing a case for annulment of the general assembly resolutions. One could expand this list by considering interpretations of the limited statutory and general rules of arbitrability.

The assumptions and interpretations of legal scholars vary regarding the arbitrability of corporate disputes; however, the law itself does not prohibit the arbitration of such disputes. The law seeks only one general standard for the arbitrability of a dispute: whether the disputed issue is subject to the will of the parties.[1035] Any dispute can be arbitrated as long as it is subject to the will of the parties. This must remain the prevailing standard for the arbitrability all disputes, including corporate-related disputes. Arguments that link other irrelevant procedural or substantive rules of law with inarbitrability will likely prove inaccurate. Arbitration is a private dispute resolution method recognized on an exceptional basis in Turkish Law. The Turkish Code of Civil Procedure governs arbitration domestically in Turkey. The Turkish International Arbitration Code, likewise, governs the arbitration of international disputes. Other Codes containing substantial rules such as Turkish Contracts or Commercial Codes do not incorporate arbitration-related regulations. These substantive Codes, therefore, designate the courts as the *general* and usual dispute-resolution authorities and regard arbitration as an *exceptional* judicial method. The exceptional nature of arbitration vis-à-vis litigation results in the litigation-oriented language of the regulations. The provisions of these codes naturally refer to courts and may not refer to arbitration in every case where it applies as an exceptional resolution method. This does not necessarily mean that these codes intend to prohibit arbitration in such cases.

The Turkish Commercial Code, which regulates corporate-related issues including annulment of general assembly resolutions, focuses primarily on litigation. The fact that the code designates specific courts for annulment cases, however, does not mean it intends to bar arbitration as a resolution method. This book has demonstrated that exclusive jurisdictional rules only have regulatory and territorial functions if parties file cases before the courts. The fact that the Turkish Commercial Code authorizes specific courts does not, therefore, interdict the arbitrability of such disputes. Even if the law exclusively stipulates a court in a specific location for a dispute, the general rules of arbitrability remain applicable. In such cases, a dispute can be arbitrated as long as it is subject to the will of the parties. Even *procedural* regulations regarding the resolution of private law disputes—such as the allocation of exclusive judicial jurisdiction to a specific court—do not hold up as grounds for inarbitrability.

This book provides several similar counterarguments to other rationales for inarbitrability asserted by commentators. It critically examines each argument, setting out to prove the validity of alternate interpretations of the law. The original rationales are not absolute impediments to the arbitration of corporate disputes. States can impose restrictions or protect their sovereignty in areas

1035 In addition to the specific rule of in-rem rights.

like criminal or administrative law. Turkish law, however, has no unfamiliar or extraordinarily restrictive regulations that differ significantly from other civil law jurisdictions. Attributing meanings to those regulations in a manner that widens their scope creates a significant disincentive to arbitrate. Regulations are more important than interpretations and no specific regulations impede the arbitration of corporate disputes. From the corporate point of view, conclusions of inarbitrability based on excessive interpretations are not beneficial. Corporate disputes do not necessarily fall within the ambit of those restrictions.

This book ultimately reaches the following conclusions. The arbitrability of corporate disputes remains a very vague issue in Turkish law. No consensus exists between the legislative, doctrinal, and adjudicatory dimensions of the law. Inconsistencies, moreover, confuse commercial practitioners and lawyers, creating dysfunction in civil law jurisdictions. Commercial actors demand consistency and predictability. Ensuring that the laws governing arbitration meet the needs of investors is particularly important for developing countries. The fair arbitration of intra-corporate disputes relies on agreement between legislation, court decisions, and scholarly opinion. All three must agree beyond a shadow of doubt that corporate actors should be allowed to resolve intra-corporate disputes through arbitration. While domestic laws include exceptions to the party autonomy rule, if all parties involved consent and follow the rules governing arbitration, intra-corporate disputes should not be considered one.

This book makes several suggestions to address the issues surrounding arbitration of intra-corporate disputes in Turkey. To begin with, new legislation is the ultimate solution to the current problems. A clear statutory law clarifying the arbitrability of such disputes is required. Case law and legal commentary must support such legislative action. Until the enactment of new legislation, interpretations exceeding current statutory law that lead to inarbitrability must be avoided. State policies should not determine the scope of court decisions and legal opinions. Turkey's approach to intervention in the arbitration of corporate disputes should be hesitant and selective. Instead of enforcing legislative regulations limiting arbitration, efforts should be exerted to make arbitration part of the discussion and attractive. Jurisdictions that have succeeded with arbitration have liberalized restrictions and trusted arbitral tribunals to act independently. Intra-corporate legal disputes frequently have an international character and require a great deal of flexibility. Turkey should therefore adopt more flexible and liberal rules that respect party autonomy and the will of parties to arbitrate. Such an approach would meet the needs and requirements of international commerce. The world has begun approaching the arbitration of corporate disputes in an increasingly flexible manner. This general tendency is evident in comparative law. Turkey should endeavor to follow this trend to maintain and bolster its position as location for investment and arbitration.

Turkey could achieve this in a number of ways. Adopting a more effective approach to arbitration in legal education and conducting seminars with corporate executives would be a good place to start. Court support is also crucial. The Supreme Court's ambivalent approach—characterized by conflicting decisions rendered by different chambers—warrants consideration. Establishing a special chamber with the mission of sustaining, supporting, and developing arbitration would help resolve this inconsistency. The Court must acknowledge that, even if it requires the surrender of some traditional legal functions, a strong arbitration system serves the best interests of Turkey; it should focus on how arbitration can help the legal system better serve the people's needs.

Until case law achieves consistency and further legislation is enacted, those opposed to international standards will continue to argue that corporate disputes cannot be arbitrated. This book includes a list of these arguments; it also elaborates counterarguments based on alternate legal interpretations that favor lifting the limits on arbitration. The book explains each of these counterarguments on statutory or adjudicatory grounds, and includes practical suggestions for addressing ambiguous matters to help corporate practitioners minimize risks. It can act as a guide for corporate practitioners until the law is completely clear for two reasons. First, it explains all the risks they may encounter during the arbitration of corporate disputes in Turkey. Second, it suggests ways to avoid those risks. This may enable practitioners who want to arbitrate corporate disputes in Turkey under current regulations to do so, and provide grounds to support their claims. Practitioners should thus take this book's risk analyzes and proposals into consideration during the drafting their arbitration agreements to avoid potential pitfalls.

VI. Bibliography

Books

A. Gunduz Okcun, Devletler Hususi Hukukunun Kaynakları ve Kamu Duzeni [Sources of International Public Law and Public Policy] 18 (Ankara, 1967).

Ahmet M. Kılıcoglu, Borclar Hukuku Genel Hukumler [The Law of Contracts General Provisions] 53 (Turhan Kitabevi, Ankara, 2007) [Turhan Publishing, Ankara 2007].

Alan Redfern et al., Law and Practice of International Commercial Arbitration 22 (4th ed. Sweet & Maxwell 2004).

Albert Venn Dicey, Lawrence Collins & John Humphrey Carlile Morris, 2 Dicey, Morris and Collins on the Conflict of Laws ¶ 32–004 (14th ed. Sweet & Maxwell 2010).

Ali Yesilırmak, Turkiye'de Ticari Hayatın ve Yatırım Ortamının Iyilestirilmesi Icin Uyusmazlıkların Etkin Cozumunde Dogrudan Gorusme, Arabuluculuk, Hakem-Bilirkisilik ve Tahkim: Sorunlar ve Cozum Onerileri [Reconciliation, Mediation, Arbitral Referee and Arbitration for the Effective Resolution of Disputes in Order for Optimization of Commercial Life and Investment Environment: Problems and Solution Suggestions] 85 (On Iki Levha Yayıncılık, 1. Baskı, Istanbul 2011) [On Iki Levha Publishing, 1st Ed. Istanbul 2011].

André Garnefsky, Public Policy in Soviet Private International Law (2nd ed. Springer).

Anton G. Maurer, Public Policy Exception Under the New York Convention 11 (Juris Publishing, Inc. 2013).

Aysel Celikel & Bahadır Erdem, Milletlerarası Ozel Hukuk [International Private Law] 149 (11. Basi, Beta Yayınları) [11th ed., Beta Publishing].

Baki Kuru, Hukuk Muhakemeleri Usulu [Civil Procedure] 5946 (6. baski, Cilt VI, Istanbul 2001) [6th ed., Vol. IV, Istanbul,2001].

Baki Kuru, Hukuk Muhakemeleri Usulu [Civil Procedure] 381 (6. baski, Cilt I, Istanbul 2001) [6th ed., Vol. I, Istanbul,2001].

Baki Kuru, Ramazan Arslan & Ejder Yılmaz, Medeni Usul Hukuku [Civil Procedure Law] 130 (Yetkin Yayınevi, 24. Baski, 2013) [Yetkin Publishing, 24th ed. 2013].

Bernard Hanotiau, Complex Arbitrations: Multiparty, Multicontract, Multi-Issue and Class Actions 199 (Kluwer Law Int'l 2006).

Bryan A. Garner, Black's Law Dictionary 124 (10th ed. W. Grp. 2014).

Burak Huysal, Milletlerarası Ticari Tahkimde Tahkime Elverislilik [Arbitrability in International Commercial Arbitration] 113 (Vedat Kitapcılık, Istanbul 2010) [Vedat Publishing, Istanbul 2010].

Cemal Sanlı, Milletlerarası, Ticari Tahkimde Esasa Uygulanacak Hukuk [The Law Applicable to the Substance in International Commercial Arbitration] ff. 105 (Banka ve Ticaret Hukuku Arastırma Enstitusu, Ankara 1986) [Banking and Commercial Law Research Institute, Ankara 1986].

Cemal Sanlı, Uluslararası Ticari Akitlerin Hazırlanması ve Uyusmazlıkların Cozum Yolları [Preparation of International Commercial Agreements and Ways for Resolution of Disputes] 241 (Beta Yayınevi, 3. basım, Istanbul 2005) [Beta Publishing, 3rd ed. Istanbul 2005].

Christian Bühring-Uhle, Lars Kirchhoff & Gabriele Scherer, Arbitration and Mediation in International Business pp. 70 (Kluwer Law Int'l 2006).

Constantine Partasides et al., Redfern and Hunter on International Arbitration para 2.116 (5th ed. Oxford Univ. Press 2009).

Devin Bray & Heather L. Bray, International Arbitration and Public Policy 41 & n.94 (Juris Publishing, Inc. 2014).

Douglas Shontz, Fred Kipperman & Vanessa Soma, Business-to-Business Arbitration in the United States: Perceptions of Corporate Counsel (Rand Inst. for Civil Justice 2011), *available at:* http://www.rand.org/content/dam/rand/pubs/technical_reports/2011/RAND_TR781.pdf.

Emmanuel Gaillard, Berthold Goldman & John Savage, Fouchard, Gaillard, Goldman on International Commercial Arbitration 312 (Kluwer Law Int'l 1999).

Erdogan Moroglu, Anonim Ortaklıkta Genel Kurul Kararlarının Hukumsuzlugu (6102 Sayılı Turk Ticaret Kanunu'na Gore) [Annulment of General Assembly Resolutions in Joint-stock Company (In Accordance with Turkish Commercial Code numbered 6102)], 12 Levha Yayıncılık, 6. Baskı, Istanbul 2012 [12 Levha Publishing, 6th Ed. Istanbul 2012], s.262 [p. 262].

Erdogan Moroglu, Turk Ticaret Kanunu Tasarısı ile Yururluk ve Uygulama Kanunu Tasarısı Taslagı: Degerlendirme ve Oneriler [Turkish Commercial Code Draft and Enforcement and Implementation Code Draft: Evaluation and Suggestions] 145 (Turkiye Barolar Birligi Yayınları, 4. Bası, Ankara 2006) [Turkish Bar Association Publishing, 4th Ed., Ankara 2006].

Erdogan Moroglu, Turk Ticaret Kanunu Tasarısı ile Yururluk ve Uygulama Kanunu Tasarısı Taslagı: Degerlendirme ve Oneriler [Turkish Commercial Code Draft and Enforcement and Implementation Code Draft: Evaluation and Suggestions] 141–142 (Vedat Kitapcılık, 6. Basi, Istanbul 2009) [Vedat Publishing, 6th Ed. Istanbul 2009].

Ergin Nomer, Nuray Eksi & Gunseli Oztekin Gelgel, Milletlerarası Tahkim Hukuku [International Arbitration Law] 40 (Cilt 1, Beta Yayıncılık, 4. Baski 2013) [Vol. 1, Beta Publishing, 4th ed. 2013].

Feyiz Erdogan, Uluslararası Hukuk ve Tahkim [International Law and Arbitration] 123 (Seckin Yayıncılık, 2004) [Seckin Publishing, 2004].

Fikret Eren, Borclar Hukuku Genel Hukumler [The Law of Contracts General Provisions] 18 (Beta Yayıncılık, 2010) [Beta Publishing, 2010].

Gerhard Kegel, 3 International Encyclopedia of Comparative Law; Chapter 3 Fundamental Approaches 7 (Kurt & eds., Brill Archive 1986).

Gulgoren Tekinalp, Milletlerarası Ozel Hukuku [International Private Law] 35 (Istanbul 1997).

Hakan Pekcanıtez, Oguz Atalay & Muhammet Ozekes, Medeni Usul Hukuku [Civil Procedure Law] 355 (Yetkin Yayınları, 14. baski, 2013) [Yetkin Publishing, 14th. ed. 2013].

Haluk N. Nomer, Kisi Birliklerinde Genel Kurul Kararlarının Gecersizligine Iliskin Temel Esaslar [Fundamental Principles regarding Annulment of General Assembly Resolutions in Private Companies] 176 (Beta Basım, Istanbul 2008) [Beta Publishing, Istanbul 2008].

Hasan Pulaslı, 6102 Sayılı Turk Ticaret Kanunu'na Gore Yeni Sirketler Hukuku Genel Esaslar [Corporations Law in Accordance with The New Turkish Commercial Code Numbered 6102 General Principles] 364 (Adalet Yayınevi Ankara 2012) [Adalet Publishing Ankara 2012].

Hasan Pulaslı, 6102 Sayılı Turk Ticaret Kanunu'na Gore Sirketler Hukuku Serhi [Annotated Corporations Law in Accordance with Turkish Commercial Code Numbered 6102] 864 (Cilt 1, Adalet Yayınevi Ankara 2011) [Vol.1, Adalet Publishing Ankara 2011].

Ilhan E. Postacıoglu, Medeni Usul Hukuku Dersleri [Lectures on Civil Procedure Law] 646 (6. Basi, Istanbul, 1975) [6th ed. Istanbul 1975].

Ismail Doganay, Turk Ticaret Kanunu Serhi [Commentary of Turkish Commercial Code] 734 (Beta Yayıncılık, Istanbul 2004) [Beta Publishing, Istanbul 2004].

Jack Friedenthal, Mary Kane & Arthur Miller, Friedenthal, Kane and Miller's Civil Procedure 684 (4th ed. Hornbook Series W. Academic Publ'g 2005).

Jacob Grierson & Annet van Hooft, Arbitrating Under the 2012 ICC Rules n.12 (Kluwer Law Int'l 2012).

Jean-François Poudret & Sébastien Besson, Comparative Law of International Arbitration 281 & § 326 (Sweet & Maxwell 2007).

Julian D. M. Lew, Loukas A. Mistelis & Stefan Michael Kröll, Comparative International Commercial Arbitration 179 (Kluwer Law Int'l 2003).

Karl-Heinz Böckstiegel, Stefan Michael Kröll et al., Arbitration in Germany: The Model Law in Practice § 139 (Kluwer Law Intl 2007).

Kemal Dayınlarlı, Milli- Milletlerarası Kamu Duzeni; Tahkime Etkileri ve Sonucları [Domestic and International Public Policy; Effects on Arbitration and Consequences] 148 (Dayınlarlı Hukuk Yayınları, 2. Baski 2011) [Dayınlarlı Legal Publishing, 2nd ed. 2011).

Kemal Gozler, Hukuka Giris [Introduction to Law] 142 (Ekin Basım Yayın Dagıtım 5. Baskı 2008) [Ekin Publishing 5th Ed. 2008].

Loukas A. Mistelis & Stavros L. Brekoulakis, Arbitrability: International and Comparative Perspectives 10 (Kluwer Law Int'l 2009).

Marco Ventoruzzo et al., Comparative Corporate Law 637 (1st ed. W. Academic Publ'g 2015).

Maria José Falcón y Tella, Equity and Law 108 (Peter Muckley trans., Martinus Nijhoff Publishers 2008).

Mauro Rubino-Sammartano, International Arbitration Law and Practice 110 (Kluwer Law Int'l 2001).

Mehmet Bahtiyar, Anonim Ortaklık Sozlesmesi [Articles of Association in Joint-Stock Corporations] 208 (Beta Yayıncılık 2001) [Beta Publishing 2001].

Mehmet Bahtiyar, Ortaklıklar Hukuku [The Law of Corporations] 163 (7. Basım, Beta Basım) [7th ed. Beta Publishing 2012].

Michael Hwang, Corporate Governance in Emerging Markets Enforcement of Corporate Governance in Asia (The Organization for Econ. Co-operation & Dev. 2007).

Mustafa Erkan, Milletlerarası Tahkimde Yetki Sorunları [The Issue of Jurisdiction in International Arbitration], 75 (Yetkin Basımevi, Ankara 2013) [Yetkin Publishing, Ankara 2013].

Nevhis Deren Yıldırım, Uncitral Model Kanunu ve Milletlerarası Tahkim Kanunu Cercevesinde Milletlerarası Tahkimin Esaslı Sorunları [Essential Concerns of International Arbitration within the Framework of UNCITRAL Model Law and International Arbitration Code] 13 (Alkım, Istanbul 2004) [Alkım Publishing, Istanbul 2004].

Osman Fazıl Berki, Devletler Hususi Hukuku, Kanun Ihtilafları [International Private Law, Conflicts of Law] 80 (Cilt 2, Ankara 1966) [Vol. 2, Ankara 1966].

Rasih Yegengil, Tahkim: (L'arbitrage) [Arbitration: (L'arbitrage)] 152 (Istanbul, 1974).

Rauf Karasu, Turk Ticaret Kanunu Tasarısına Gore Anonim Sirketlerde Emredici Hukumler Ilkesi [Mandatory Provisions Principle in Joint-stock Corporations in Accordance with Turkish Commercial Code Draft] 155 (Yetkin Yayınları, Ankara 2009) [Yetkin Publishing, Ankara 2009].

Register of Texts of CONVENTIONS AND OTHER INSTRUMENTS CONCERNING INTERNATIONAL TRADE LAW, Vol. II (United Nations, New York 1973) p. 13.

Reha Poroy, Unal Tekinalp & Ersin Camoglu, Ortaklıklar Ve Kooperatif Hukuku: Genel Bilgiler, Adi Ortaklık, Ticaret Ortaklarına Iliskin Genel Hukumler, Kollektif, Komandit, Anonim, Halka Acık Anonim, Sermayesi Paylara Bolunmus Komandit, Limited ve Holding Ortaklıklar ile Kooperatif [The law of Corporations and Cooperatives: General Information, Ordinary Partnership, General Terms about Trade Partners, Unlimited Liability Company, Limited Partnership, Joint-stock, Open Joint-stock Corporation, Limited Partnership Divided Into Shares, Limited and Holding Company and Cooperative] 386 (12.Baski Vedat Kitapcılık, Istanbul 2010) [12th ed. Vedat Kitapcılık Publishing, Istanbul 2010].

Robert Patry, La Nullité des Decisions des Organes dans la SA 230 (Melanges Roger Secrétan Lausanne 1964).

Saim Ustundag, Medeni Yargılama Hukuku [Civil Procedure Law] 942 (Alfa Yayınları, 6. baskı, Istanbul 1997) [Alfa Publishing, 6th ed. Istanbul 1997].

Sami Karahan, Sirketler Hukuku [Corporations Law] 529 & n.1 (1. Baskı Seckin Yayıncılık 2012) [1st ed. Seckin Publishing 2012].

Sanal Gorgun & Mehmet Kodakoglu, Medeni Usul Hukuku [Civil Procedure Law] 154 (Yetkin Yayınları, 2. baski, 2012) [Yetkin Publishing, 2nd. ed. 2012].

Sibel Ozel, Milletlerarası Ticari Tahkimde Kanunlar Ihtilafı Meseleleri [The Issues of Conflict of Laws in International Commercial Arbitration], 38 (Istanbul, 2008).

Stefan Michael Kröll et al., International Arbitration and International Commercial Law: Synergy, Convergence and Evolution 307 (Kluwer Law Int'l 2011).

Thomas E. Carbonneau, Carbonneau on International Arbitration: Collected Essays 118 (Juris 2011).

Thomas E. Carbonneau, Cases and Materials on Arbitration Law and Practice 27 (5th ed. W. Academic 2009).

Thomas E. Carbonneau & William Elliott Butler, International Litigation and Arbitration 573 (W. 2013).

Timucin Musul, Hukuk Usulu Muhakemeleri Kanunu ve Ilgili Mevzuat [The Code of Civil Procedure and the Related Regulations] 83 (Alfa Yayınları, 3. baski, Istanbul 2012) [Alfa Publishing, 3rd ed., Istanbul 2012).

Tugrul Ansay & Don Wallace, Introduction to Turkish Law 156 (Kluwer Law Int'l 2011).

Turgut Kalpsuz, Turkiye'de Milletlerarası Tahkim [International Arbitration in Turkey] 146 (2. Baski, Yetkin Yayınevi, Ankara 2010) [2nd ed. Yetkin Publishing, Ankara 2010].

Ufuk Aydın & Haluk Konuralp, Medeni Usul Hukuku [Civil Procedure Code] 66 (TC Anadolu Universitesi Yayını no.1706) [Republic of Turkey Anadolu University Publishing, number 1706].

Viladimir Tochilovsky, Jurisprudence of the International Criminal Courts and the European Court of Human Rights 274 (Martinus Nijhoff Publishers 2008).

Yavuz Alagonya, Kamil Yıldırım & Nevhis Deren Yıldırım, Medeni Usul Hukuku Esasları [Fundamentals of Civil Procedure Law] 83 (Beta Yayınları, 7. baski, Istanbul 2009) [Beta Publishing, 7th ed. Istanbul 2009]

Yavuz Alagonya, Medeni Usul Hukukumuzda Tahkimin Niteligi ve Denetlenmesi [Nature and Inspection of Arbitration in Our Civil Procedure Law] 84 (Fakulteler Matbaası, Istanbul 1973) [Faculties Press, Istanbul 1973].

Yves Donzallaz, 3 La Convention De Lugano pp. 770–77 (Berne 1998).

Zafer Saka, Anonim Ortaklıklarda Genel Kurul [General Assembly in Joint-Stock Corporations] 286 (Vedat Kitapcılık, Istanbul 2004) [Vedat Publishing, Istanbul 2004].

Ziya Akıncı, Arbitration Law of Turkey: Practice and Procedure 195 (Juris Net, 2011).

Ziya Akıncı, Milletlerarası Tahkim [International Arbitration] 77 (Vedat Kitapcılık, 3. Baski 2013) [Vedat Publishing, 3rd ed. 2013].

Ziya Akıncı, Milletlerarası Ticari Hakem Kararları ve Tenfizi [International Commercial Arbitral Awards and Recognition] 197 (Dokuz Eylul Universitesi Hukuk Fakultesi, Ankara, 1994) [Dokuz Eylul University, Faculty of Law, Ankara, 1994].

Articles

Alan Uzelac, *(In)Arbitrability and Exclusive Jurisdiction: Parallels that Matter, in* International Arbitration and International Commercial Law 453 (Kluwer Law Int'l 2011).

Alan Uzelac, *New Boundaries of Arbitrability Under the Croatian Law on Arbitration*, 9 Croatian Arb. Y.B. (2002), p. 150.

Alexis Mourre, *Arbitrage, conflits de juridictions et ADR dans la résolution des litiges entre actionnaires/Arbitration, Jurisdiction Conflicts and ADR for the Resolution of Disputes between Shareholders*, Rev. dr. aff. int./Int'l Bus. L.J. 299 (2004).

Andreas Bucher, *Court Intervention in Arbitration, in* International Arbitration in the 21st Century: Towards "Judicialization" and Uniformity? (Richard B. Lillich & Charles Nelson Brower eds., Brill – Nijhoff 1994) p. 38.

Antonio Monti, *Arbitration and Corporation in* Three Essays on International Commercial Arbitration, Ed. Antonio Monti, Francesco Trezzini & Francesco Wicki (2002) (*available at* www.montiswisslaw.com) pp. 60.

B Ted Howes & Allison M Stowell, *The Consolidation Dilemma: Is There Finally a Pragmatic Solution?*, 10 Disp. Resol. Int'l (2016), p. 8.

Burcu Zengin, *Sirketler Hukukunda Tahkime Elverislilikle Ilgili Temel Meseleler* [*Fundamental Issues Concerning the Arbitrability in Company Law*] Terazi Aylık Hukuk Dergisi, Cilt:9, Sayı:95, (Temmuz 2014) [Terazi Monthly Law Journal, Volume:9, Issue: 95, (July 2014)] p. 103.

Cemal Ruhi & Yavuz Kaplan, *Yabancı Mahkeme ve Hakem Kararların Tenfizi Acısından Kamu Duzeni* (*Ordre Public*) [*Public Policy in Terms of Enforcement of Foreign Judicial and Arbitral Decisions* (*Ordre Public*)] *in* Prof. Dr. Ergin Nomer'e Armagan; Milletlerarası Hukuk ve Milletlerarası Ozel Hukuk Bulteni [Dedication for Prof. Dr. Ergin Nomer; International Law and International Private Law Bulletin] 644 (Yıl: 22, Sayı: 2, 2002) [Year:22, Issue:2, 2002].

Cigdem Kırca, *Ortulu Bosluk ve Bu Boslugun Doldurulması Yontemi Olarak Amaca Uygun Sınırlama* [*Tacit Legal Gap and Reduction in Accordance with the Purpose as a Gap Filling Method*] Ankara Universitesi Hukuk Fakultesi Dergisi 2001, Cilt. 50, Sayi. 1 [Ankara University Faculty of Law Journal 2001, Volume.50, Issue.1] p. 100.

Derya Ates, *Irade Ozerkligi Kapsamında MK. M. 23/II Hukmu ve Karar Ozgurlugu* [*Article 23/II of Civil Code Within the Scope of Party Autonomy and Freedom of Decision*] Ankara Barosu Dergisi, Yıl: 65, Sayı: 2, Bahar 2007 [Ankara Bar Journal, Year: 65, Issue 2, Spring 2007] p. 136.

Derya Ates, *Sozlesme Ozgurlugu Yonunden Durustluk Kuralları* [*The Principle of Good Faith in Terms of Freedom of Contract*], Turkiye Barolar Birligi Dergisi, Sayı 72, 2007 [Turkish Bar Association Journal, Issue 72, 2007] p. 75.

Ejder Yılmaz, *Hukuk Muhakemeleri Kanunun Getirdikleri* [*Amendments by new Turkish Code of Civil Procedure*] Ankara Barosu Dergisi, 2011/2 [Ankara Bar Journal, 2011/2] p. 252.

Felipe Vollbrecht Sperandio, *The Reach of the Arbitration Agreement to Parties Involved in the Same Legal Relationship*, 11 REVIST@ E – Mercatoria 1 (2012) p. 175.

F. Hodge O'Neal, *Resolving Disputes in Closely Held Corporations: Intra-Institutional Arbitration*, 67 Harv. L. Rev. 290 (1954).

Francesco Trezzini, *The Challenge of Arbitral Awards for Breach of Public Policy according to Art. 190 para. 2 lit. e) of the Swiss Private International Law in* Three Essays on International Commercial Arbitration, Ed. Antonio Monti,

Francesco Trezzini & Francesco Wicki (2002) (*available at* http://www.montiswisslaw.com) § 11.

Fritz Nicklisch, *Multi-Party Arbitration and Dispute Resolution in Major Industrial Projects*, 11 J. Int'l Arb. (1994) p. 68.

Fusun Arsava, Yabancı Mahkeme Kararlarının Icrası ve Devletlerin Yargı Bagısıklıgı [Enforcement of Foreign Court Decisions and Judicial Immunity of States], Turkiye Adalet Akademisi Dergisi Cilt:1 Yıl:3 Sayı:8, (Ocak 2012) [Turkey Justice Academy Journal, Vol:1 Year:3 Issue:8, (January 2012)], p. 2.

Hakan Pekcanıtez, *Anonim Ortaklıklarda Denetciler Tarafından Acılacak Davalar* [*Cases to be Filed by Auditors in Joint-Stock Corporations*] *in* Prof. Dr. Kudret Ayıter'e Armagan [Dedication for Prof. Dr. Kudret Ayıter] 482 (Ankara, 1998).

Huseyin Ali Sadrolesrafi, *Devletler Ozel Hukuku'nda Genel Olarak Atıf Teorisi (Renvoi)* [*A General View: Theory of Renvoi in International Private Law*], Kudret Ayiter'e Armagan; Dokuz Eylul Universitesi Hukuk Fakultesi Dergisi Cilt 3 Sayı 1–4 Ankara, 1988 [Dedication for Kudret Ayıter; Dokuz Eylul University Faculty of Law Journal Vol.3 Issue 1–4 Ankara, 1988] p. 521.

Joseph Lee, *Intra-Corporate Dispute Arbitration and Minority Shareholder Protection: A Corporate Governance Perspective*, Feb. 23, 2015 *available at* https://papers.ssrn.com/sol3/papers2.cfm?abstract_id=2736981 p. 10.

Julie K. Bracker & Larry D. Soderquist, *Arbitration in the Corporate Context*, Colum. Bus. L. Rev. 1 (2003).

Karl-Heinz Bockstiegel, *Role of Party Autonomy in International Arbitration*, J. Disp. Resol. 25 & 30 n.3 (Summer 1997).

Kemal Gozler, *Res Judicata'nın Turkcesi Uzerine* [*On the Turkish Translation of Res Iudicata*] Ankara Universitesi Hukuk Fakultesi Dergisi 2007, Cilt. 56, Sayi. 2 [Ankara University Faculty of Law Journal 2007, Volume.56, Issue.2].

Louis Bouchez & Alexander Karpf, *The OECD's Work Programme on Corporate Governance and Dispute Resolution*, The Quality of Corp. L. & the Role of Corp. L. Judges 6 (2006).

Loukas Mistelis, *International Arbitration – Corporate Attitudes and Practices – 12: Perceptions Tested: Myths, Data and Analysis Research Report*, 15 Am. Rev. Int'l Arb. 540 (2004).

Matthew D. Schwartz, *Multiparty Disputes and Consolidated Arbitrations: An Oxymoron or the Solution to a Continuing Dilemma*, 22 Case W. Res. J. Int'l L. (1990) p. 372.

Mehmet Helvacı, *Anonim Ortaklık Genel Kurul Kararlarının Iptali Davalarının Tahkim Yargılamasına Uygunlugu Uzerine Dusunceler* [*Thoughts on Arbitrability of Lawsuit of Annulment of General Meeting Resolution of Companies*] *in* II. Uluslararası Ozel Hukuk Sempozyumu "Tahkim" [II. International Private Law Symposium "Arbitration"] 200 (Ankara 2009).

Mehmet Koseoglu, *Milletlerarası Ozel Hukuk ve Usul Hukuku Hakkında Kanun madde 31: Sozlesme ile Sıkı Iliskili 3. Bir Devletin Dogrudan Uygulanan Kurallarına Etki Tanınması* [*The Code on Private International Law and Civil Procedure article 31: Validating the Mandatory Rules of a Third State which is in Close Relationship with the Contract*], MHB Yıl 28, Sayı 1–2 (2008) [International Private Law Bulletin, Year 28, Issue 1–2 (2008)] pp. 149–150.

Mehmet Sarı, *Tahkime Elverislilik* [*Arbitrability*], Terazi Aylık Hukuk Dergisi, Yıl: 4, Sayı: 32, (Nisan 2009) [Terazi Monthly Law Journal, Year:4, Issue: 32, (April 2009)] p. 147.

Nevhis Deren Yıldırım, *Tahkim ve Objektif Acıdan Tahkime Elverislilik* [*Arbitration and Objective Arbitrability*] *in* Prof. Dr. Yavuz Alagonya icin Armagan [Dedication for Prof. Dr. Yavuz Alagonya] 59, 47 (Alkım Yayınevi, Istanbul 2007) [Alkım Publishing, Istanbul 2007].

Nimet Ozbek, *MTO Kuralları Isıgında Yeni Bir Tahkim Turu ve Sartı Olarak Cok Taraflı Tahkim* [*A New Kind of Arbitration: The Multiparty Arbitration in the Light of ICE Rules*] BATIDER, Cilt 20, Sayi 2, 1999 [BATIDER Journal Volume 20, Issue 2, 1999] p. 100.

Okan Demirkan & Burak Eryigit, *Developing Court Practice in Turkey Regarding Applications to Set Aside Arbitral Awards*, 26:4 Am. Rev. Int'l Arb. 596 (2015).

Okuma Kazutake, *Party Autonomy in International Commercial Arbitration: Consolidation of Multiparty and Classwide Arbitration*, 9:1 Ann. Surv. of Int'l & Comp. L. Article 212. (2003), *available at*: http://digitalcommons.law.ggu.edu/annlsurvey/vol9/iss1/9.

Paul Weitzel, *The End of Shareholder Litigation? Allowing Shareholders to Customize Enforcement Through Arbitration Provisions in Charters and Bylaws*, BYU L. Rev. 85 (2013), *available at*: http://digitalcommons.law.byu.edu/lawreview/vol2013/iss1/2

Pelin Akın, *Tahkimde Cok Taraflılık* [*Multiparty Dispute in International Arbitration*] Gazi Universitesi Hukuk Fakultesi Dergisi C. 18, Y. 2014, Sayi 3–4 [Gazi University Law School Journal Vol. 18, Year 2014, Issue 3–4] p. 323.

Pierre Lalive, *Enforcing Awards in 60 Years of ICC Arbitration: A Look at the Future* (ICC Publication no.412, 1984) p. 349.

Rauf Karasu, *Emredici Hukumler Ilkesinin Kapalı Tip Anonim Sirketler ve Limited Sirketler Acısından Dogurdugu Sorunlar ve Cozum Onerileri* [*The Issues Arising from the Principle of Imperative Provisions in Closed Type Corporations and Limited Liability Companies and Proposals for Solutions*] *in* I. Ticaret Hukuku Uluslararası Sempozyumu [I. Commercial Law International Symposium], Ticaret ve Fikri Mulkiyet Hukuk Dergisi (2015/1) [Commercial and Intellectual Property Law Journal (2015/1)] p. 116.

Rauf Karasu, *6102 Sayılı Turk Ticaret Kanunu'na Gore Anonim Sirketlerde Emredici Hukumler Ilkesi* [*Principle of Mandatory Provisions in Joint-stock Corporations in Accordance with Turkish Commercial Code numbered 6102*], Marmara Universitesi Hukuk Fakultesi Hukuk Arastırmaları Dergisi, Ozel Sayi Cilt:18, Sayı:2 Legal Yayıncılık (2012) [Marmara University Law Faculty Legal Researches Journal, Special, Vol.: 18, Issue: 2 Legal Publishing (2012)] p. 312.

Richard Bamforth & Katerina Maidment, *All Join In" or Not? How Well Does International Arbitration Cater for Disputes Involving Multiple Parties or Related Claims?*, 1 Kluwer L. Int'l ASA Bull. (2009) p. 6.

Richard W. Pogue, *Exclusive Jurisdiction*, 43 Antitrust L. J. TWENTY-SECOND Ann. SPRING MEETING Washington, D.C. (1974). pp. 314–315.

Seyda Dursun, *A Critical Examination of the Role of Party Autonomy in International Commercial Arbitration and an Assessment of Its Role and Extent*, Yalova Universitesi Hukuk Fakultesi Dergisi (2012/1) [1 Yalova University Faculty of Law Journal (2012)] p. 161.

Stavros Brekoulakis, *The Effect of An Arbitral Award and Third Parties in International Arbitration: Res Judicata Revisited*, 16 Am. Rev. Int'l Arb. (2005) p. 12.

Stavros Brekoulakis, *The Relevance of the Interests of Third Parties in Arbitration: Taking a Closer Look at the Elephant in the Room*, 113:4 Penn State L. Rev. (2009) p. 1166.

Stefan Grundmann, *Information, Party Autonomy and Economic Agents in European Contract Law*, 39 Common Mkt. L. Rev. 269 (2002).

Suha Tanrıver, Yabancı *Hakem Kararlarının Turkiye'de Tenfizi Baglamında Kamu Duzeninin Etkisi* [*Effect of Public Policy in The Context of Enforcement of Foreign Arbitral Awards in Turkey*] *in* Hukuk-Ekonomi Perspektifinden Uluslararası Tahkim ve Kamu Hizmeti [International Arbitration and Public Service from the Perspectives of Law-Economy] 83 (Liberte Yayınevi, 2001) [Liberte Publishing, 2001].

Suha Tanrıver, Yabancı *Hakem Kararlarının Turkiye'de Tenfizi Baglamında Kamu Duzeninin Etkisi* [*Effect of Public Policy in The Context of Enforcement of Foreign Arbitral Awards in Turkey*], MHB Yıl 17–18, (1997–98) [International Private Law Bulletin, Year 17–18 (1997–98)] p. 477.

Thomas E. Carbonneau, *Arguments in Favor of the Triumph of Arbitration*, 10 Cardozo J. Conflict Resol. 397 (2009).

Thomas E. Carbonneau & Francois Janson, *Cartesian Logic and Frontier Politics: French and American Concepts of Arbitrability*, 2 Tul. J. Int'l & Comp. L. 194 (1994).

Thomas E. Carbonneau, *The Exercise of Contract Freedom in the Making of Arbitration Agreements*, 36 Vand. J. Transnat'l L. 1198.

Thomas Penberthy Fry, *The Finality of Judicial Decisions*, [2 (1)] U. of Queensl. L. J. (1952) p. 9.

Unal Tekinalp, *Hakem Sozlesmesinin Hukuki Mahiyeti Uzerine Dusunceler* [*Thoughts on Legal Nature of Arbitration Agreement*], *in* IV. Ticaret ve Banka Hukuku Haftası, Bildiriler & Tartısmalar [IV.th Commercial and Banking Law Week, Notices & Discussions] 28 (Banka ve Ticaret Hukuku Arastırma Enstitusu, 1966) [Banking and Commercial Law Research Institute, Ankara 1986].

Yılmaz Altug & Mustafa Yasan, *Milletlerarasi Ozel Hukukta Kamu Duzeni* [*Public Policy in International Private Law*] *in* Prof. Dr. Ergun Onen'e Armagan [Dedication for Prof. Dr. Ergun Onen] 139 (Alkım Yayınevi, Istanbul 2003) [Alkım Publishing, Istanbul 2003].

Zhaohua MENG, *Party Autonomy, Private Autonomy, and Freedom of Contract*, 10:6 Canadian Soc. Sci. 215 (2014), http://www.cscanada.net/index.php/css/article/view/5155.

Dissertations

Burcin Yıldırım, Anonim Ortaklıklarda Sirket Ici Uyusmazlıkların Milletlerarası Tahkim Yoluyla Cozumlenmesi [Resolution of Intra-Corporate Disputes of Companies by International Commercial Law] (2012) (Yayınlanmamıs Yuksek Lisans Tezi, Galatasaray Universitesi, Sosyal Bilimler Enstitusu) [Unpublished LLM Thesis, Galatasaray University, Institute of Social Sciences].

Isadora Cipriani, The Public Policy Exception to the Enforcement of Foreign Arbitral Awards in Brazil (2012) (Unpublished LLM Thesis, Bucerius Law School) p. 25 (Available at: http://www.gbv.de/dms/buls/734889984.pdf).

Isılar Umut Mutlu, Yabancı Hakem Kararlarının Tanınmasında ve Tenfizinde Kamu Duzeni Etkisi [The Effect of Public Policy in Recognition and Enforcement of Foreign Arbitral Awards] (2003) (Yayınlanmamıs Yuksek Lisans Tezi, Ankara Universitesi, Sosyal Bilimler Enstitusu, Devletler Ozel Hukuku Ana Bilim Dali) [Unpublished LLM Thesis, Ankara University, Institute of Social Sciences, Department of International Private Law] p. 20.

Mehmet Tas, Turk Hukukunda Anonim Sirket Genel Kurul Kararlarının Iptali Davalarının Milletlerarası Ticari Tahkimde Gorulmesi [Settlement of the Lawsuit of Annulment of General Meeting Resolution of Companies Before International Commercial Arbitration in Turkish Law] (2007) (Yayınlanmamıs Yuksek Lisans Tezi, Istanbul Universitesi, Sosyal Bilimler

Enstitusu) [Unpublished LLM Thesis, Istanbul University, Institute of Social Sciences].

Sulbha Rai, How Do or Should Arbitrators Deal with Domestic Public Policy or Regulatory Issues? Does It Affect Arbitrability? (2009) (Unpublished LLM Thesis, King's College, London) p. 8 (Available at: http://ssrn.com/abstract=1433799).

Reports

No. 1 2014 Statistical Report 1 (ICC Int'l Court of Arbitration Bulletin 2015).

No. 1 25 2013 Statistical Report 2 (ICC Int'l Court of Arbitration Bulletin 2014).

Cases

Mitsubishi Motors Corp. v. Soler Chrysler-Plymouth 473 U.S. 614, 628 (1985).

Benteler v. Belgium, Journal des Tribunaux, Bruxelles, No. 5289, 31 March 10984.

Wauquier et Cie v. Government of Turkey et al (1930), 10 Recueil des Decisions des Tribunaux Arbitraux Mixtes, 65 (1930); 1929–30 *Annual Digest and Reports of Public International Law Cases*, Case No. 262, at p. 434.

Turkish Supreme Court 14th Civil Circuit decision dated 10/07/2003, numbered 6387/6813.

Turkish Supreme Court 15th Civil Circuit decision dated 03/18/1986, numbered 3919/1044.

Turkish Supreme Court 15th Civil Circuit decision dated 09/23/2002, numbered 4321/4067.

Turkish Supreme Court Assembly of Civil Chambers dated 07/03/1974 numbered 5/1450/810.

Turkish Supreme Court 5th Civil Circuit decision dated 05/22/1972, numbered 3513/5195.

Turkish Supreme Court Assembly of Civil Chambers dated 04/29/1972 numbered 5/247–269.

Turkish Supreme Court 15th Civil Circuit decision dated 03/23/2010 numbered 2010/1581.

Turkish Supreme Court 15th Civil Circuit decision dated 06/18/2007 numbered 2007/2680.

Turkish Supreme Court 13th Civil Circuit decision dated 6/16/1994 numbered 4390/5895.

Turkish Supreme Court 6th Civil Circuit Decision dated 3/11/1964 numbered 375/5196.

Turkish Supreme Court 6th Civil Circuit Decision dated 07/10/1970.

Turkish Supreme Court 3rd Civil Circuit Decision dated 12/02/2004 numbered 2004/13018.

Turkish Supreme Court 15th Civil Circuit decision dated 5/15/1979 numbered 1195/1130.

Turkish Supreme Court 13th Civil Circuit decision dated 6/16/1994 numbered 4390/5895.

Turkish Supreme Court 4th Civil Circuit has a decision dated 04/10/1967 numbered 2760/3075.

Turkish Supreme Court 15th Civil Circuit decision dated 05/31/1979 numbered 1195/1330.

Turkish Supreme Court 13th Civil Circuit decision dated 06/16/1994 numbered 4390/5895.

Turkish Supreme Court 11th Civil Circuit decision dated 02/04/1980 numbered 1980/448.

Turkish Supreme Court 14th Civil Circuit decision dated 10/07/2003 numbered 2003/6387.

Turkish Supreme Court 15th Civil Circuit decision dated 09/23/2002 numbered 2002/4321.

Turkish Supreme Court 15th Civil Circuit dated 11/07/1991 and numbered 1991/4163.

Turkish Supreme Court decision dated 10/23/1972 numbered 2/12.

Turkish Supreme Court Assembly of Civil Chambers' decision dated 06/21/2000 and numbered 2000/2–1051.

Turkish Supreme Court 13th Civil Circuit decision dated 6/16/1994 numbered E2012/8426 and K10349.

Turkish Supreme Court 13th Civil Circuit decision dated 6/16/1994 numbered E2012/8426 and K10349.

Turkish Supreme Court 13th Civil Circuit Decision dated 02/05/1998 numbered E.997/9703 and K.998/978.

Turkish Supreme Court 13th Civil Circuit Decision dated 09/25/2006 numbered E.2006/7789 and K.2006/12275.

Turkish Supreme Court 13th Civil Circuit Decision dated 09/25/2008 numbered E.2008/3492 and K.2008/11120.

Turkish Supreme Court 9th Civil Circuit Decision dated 01/20/2009 numbered E.2008/44630 and K.2009/537.

Constitutional Court decision numbered E2003/98, K2004/31 and dated 03.03.2004.

Constitutional Court decision numbered E2003/98, K2004/31 and dated 03.03.2004.

Turkish Supreme Court 13th Civil Circuit Decision dated 09/26/1974 and numbered 2385/2161.

Turkish Supreme Court 15th Civil Circuit decision dated 05/31/1979 numbered ≈1195/1330.

Turkish Supreme Court 2nd Civil Circuit decision dated 11/10/1960.

Turkish Supreme Court 2nd Civil Circuit decision dated 12/25/1952.

Turkish Supreme Court 11th Civil Circuit decision dated 04/05/1979.

Turkish Supreme Court Assembly of Civil Chambers' unified decision dated 10/28/1994. numbered 943/4E and 944/1K.

Turkish Supreme Court 19th Civil Circuit decision dated 05/01/2003, numbered 3763E. and 4764K.

Turkish Supreme Court 11th Civil Circuit decision dated 02/24/2006, numbered 3953/1858.

Turkish Supreme Court decision dated 4/24/1996 numbered 1995/15–1114E. and 1996/302K.

Turkish Supreme Court General Assembly on the Unification of Judgments decision dated 1/28/1994.

Turkish Supreme Court General Assembly on the Unification of Judgments decision dated 1/28/1994.

Turkish Supreme Court Commercial Circuit, 3/11/1969 dated 1969/3878E. and numbered 5118 K.

16th Commercial Court of Istanbul decision numbered 2013/157 and dated 08/20/2013.

44th Commercial Court of Istanbul, 2013/268 numbered, 12/19/2013 dated.

4th Civil Court of Ankara decision numbered 2013/273 dated 01/21/2014.

Turkish Supreme Court 11th Civil Circuit decision dated 12/05/2012 numbered 2011/13485E and 2012/19915 K.

Turkish Supreme Court 11th Civil Circuit decision dated 4/24/1981 numbered 471E and 894 K.

Turkish Supreme Court 14th Civil Circuit decision dated 06/11/2010 numbered 2010/5842E and 2010/6880K.

Turkish Supreme Court the decision dated 09/23/1975 and numbered 1975/6158E and 1975/1055K.

Turkish Supreme Court 4th Civil Circuit decision dated 09/23/1975 and numbered 1975/6158E and 1975/1055K.

VII. Appendices

Appendix I: Translations of Related Statutory Regulations

1) *Constitution of the Republic of Turkey*[1]

Article 9: Judicial power shall be used by independent courts on behalf of the Turkish nation.

Article 36: Everyone has the right to claim, defend, and receive due process as claimants or defendants before judicial authorities using legitimate methods. No court shall refuse to hear a case within its jurisdiction.

Article 48: Everyone has the freedom to work and conclude contracts in the field of his choice.

2) *Turkish Code of Contract*[2]

Article 1: A contract is concluded when both parties mutually declare their concurring assents.

Article 26: The terms of a contract may be freely determined by the parties within the limits of the law.

Article 27: Agreements that are contrary to the mandatory rules of law, morality, public policy, personal rights, or address subjects that cannot be regulated by private contract are null and void. The nullity of the terms of the agreement partly does not affect the validity of the rest of the terms. However, the contract is deemed as null and void completely if it is understood that the contract could not have been concluded without the terms considered void.

Article 262: Court of Competent Jurisdiction and Arbitration

Buyers who are Turkish residents cannot renounce the jurisdiction of the court where they live or conclude arbitration agreements for disputes arising from the contract of sale on installments.

---

1 Enacted on 11/07/1982 with the code number of 2709.

2 Numbered 6098 which was published in Official Gazette on 02/04/2011 with the number of 27836.

3) *Turkish Civil Code*[3]

Article 23: No person may waive his or her capacity to have rights or capacity to act, even partially. No person may waive his or her freedoms or restrict them against the law or morals. Upon written consent extraction, vaccination and transfer of biological substances of human origin are legitimate. However, no claim may be raised against the person under the obligation of giving biological substance, to fulfill his or her obligation; no claim may be raised for compensation of physical and spiritual damages.

4) *Cooperatives Code*[4]

Article 95: Arbitral tribunals, which are foreseen in the articles of incorporation, can hear disputes arising from the matters within the cooperatives and its organs; cooperatives and cooperative unions that they are affiliated; cooperative center unions and Turkish National Cooperative Union reserving the general provisions.

5) *Turkish Code of Civil Procedure*

Article 6:

(1) The court where the defendant real or legal person reside at the time of the filing of the case has general jurisdiction.
(2) Place of residence is determined in accordance with the Turkish Civil Code numbered 4721 and dated 11/22/2001.

Article 7:

(1) If the defendant is more than one, the case can be filed before the court where either of them resides. However, if the law designates a court having a mutual jurisdiction for all the defendants depending on the ground of the action, the case shall be heard before this court.
(2) In the event of more than one defendant, if it is understood from evidences or indications that the case is filed with the sole intent of bringing one of the defendants to another court, the court decides rejection of venue by severing the case against him on the plea of the related defendant.

---

3 Numbered 4721.

4 Numbered 1163, which is ratified on 4/24/1969 and published on 5/10/1969.

Article 9: The court in the location of the last habitual residence of the defendant in Turkey has the general jurisdiction about the ones who lack a place of residence in Turkey.

Article 11: Jurisdiction for the Cases Arising from Legacy

(1) For the following cases, the court located where the testator has most recently resided has the exclusive authority:
   a) The cases concerning the distribution of the estate, voidness of the contract of distribution, abatement and cancellation of the legacy, recovery due to legacy and the cases arising from the management of the estate among the legatees.
   b) All cases that will be filed against the legatees until the final distribution of the estate.

Article 12: Jurisdiction for the Cases Arising from In-rem Rights on Immovables

(1) The court of place of immovable has exclusive authority for the cases related to in rem rights on immovables or cases that may cause a change in the ownership of in rem rights and the cases related to possession or right of detention of the immovable.
(2) The court in the location of the immovable subject to an easement shall hear the cases related to easements.
(3) If these cases are related to more than one immovable, the case can be filed before the court in the location of one of the immovables also for others

Article 18: An agreement of jurisdiction cannot be concluded on the matters that are not subject to the will of the parties and in the event of exclusive jurisdiction.

Article 24:

(1) The judge cannot examine or rule a case ex officio without any request of either party.
(2) Unless provided in the law explicitly, no one shall be compelled to file the case in favor of him or to demand the right.
(3) Parties' right of disposition on a matter in dispute, which has a dispositive nature, remains *post litem motam*.

Article 60: The Position of Mandatory Joinder of Parties in the Case

(1) Mandatory joinder of parties can file a lawsuit together or be filed a lawsuit against together. Parties have to act together in this type of joinder or

parties. However, procedural actions taken by the parties who appear for the oral hearing shall take effect on the parties who do not appear for the oral hearing despite a due invitation.

Article 61:

(1) A party can give notice of proceedings to a third person if he believes that third person will hold him liable, or that the third person will be held liable if he loses the lawsuit until investigation is completed.

Article 62: Form of the Notice

(1) The notice is given in writing; it is required to indicate the reason of the notice with rationales and the stage of the lawsuit.
(2) The hearing cannot be adjourned due to the notice and a delay is not granted except the compulsory situations such as sequence of the notice.

Article 64: Effect of the Notice

(1) Article 69 (2) applies by analogy about the decision's effect on the person giving the notice in the case of notice of proceeding.

Article 67: Demand and Examination of Secondary Intervention

(1) Third party who demands to intervene makes an application to the court through a petition indicating the party that he wants to be at the side of, the reason for intervention and the bases of this
(2) The parties of the case shall be notified of the petition for intervention. The court invites the third party along with the parties if needed, and decides on the demand of intervention even if they don't appear.

Article 68:

(1) Intervenor can pursue the case only starting from the current stage in the event of that the demand for intervention is approved. Intervenor can use the claim and defense means in favor for the party at the side he intervened for; can take any actions not against that party's transaction and explanations.
(2) Court notifies the intervenor of the actions that the parties are informed starting from the point of intervention.

Article 69: Effect of Secondary Intervention

(1) In the main case that intervenor takes place, too, the decision is given about the parties.

(2) Secondary intervenor's claim challenging the decision given about dispute of the main case cannot be listened in recourse relation with the party. However, the intervenor can claim that the party he is at the side of conducts litigation incorrectly indicating that he has joined the case late due to not being informed of the proceeding on time; or that party has prevented the use of claim and defense means; or the intervenor could not use the facilities of claim and defense not known by him due to gross negligence of that party.

Article 166: Consolidation of Cases

(1) Cases filed before the civil courts with the same level, title and judicial locality can be consolidated under the court that the first case was filed in the event of a connection between the cases at any stage per se or upon demand. The court that the second case was filed gives the decision of consolidation and this decision binds the other court.
(2) Consolidation due to connection can be demanded from the court where the second case is filed if the cases are filed before the courts that take place in the same judicial locality with the same level and title. The court where the first case is filed is bound by this as from the approval of demand and the finalization of the decision on consolidation of cases.
(3) The court where the first case is filed shall promptly be informed of the decision of consolidation.
(4) The connection is deemed to exist in the event that the cases arise from the same or similar reasons or the decision to be rendered for one case is such as to affect the other one.
(5) The cases, appellate examinations of which are required to be made before different chambers can also be consolidated in accordance with this provision. In this case, the regional court of justice that considers the decision with regards to the main legal relationship that causes the dispute in the consolidated cases makes the appellate review.

Article 408: Disputes arising from in rem rights on immovable property or disputes that are not subject to the will of the parties' are inarbitrable.
Article 439:

(2) The award may be set aside if..
(g) the subject-matter of the dispute is not capable of settlement by arbitration under the Turkish Law
(ğ) it is in conflict with public policy.

6) *Turkish International Arbitration Code*[5]

Article 1:

(4) This Code shall not apply to disputes that concern in rem rights on immovable property located in Turkey and disputes that are not subject to the will of the parties.

Article 15: … Awards may be set aside on the following grounds:

2) If the court finds that;

a) a subject-matter of the dispute is not capable of settlement by arbitration under the Turkish Law,
b) the award is in conflict with public policy…

7) *Turkish Code of Execution and Bankruptcy*[6]

Article 154(3): If the debtor and debtee have appointed an authorized executive office with a written agreement, the executive office of that place is also considered authorized for the bankruptcy proceedings. However, parties cannot conclude a jurisdiction agreement for bankruptcy cases and can file bankruptcy cases only before the commercial court of the place of headquarter of the debtor.

8) *Code of Commercial Enterprise Pledge*[7]

Article 22: Authorized Court
Resolution of the disputes arising from the implementation of this Code is within the jurisdiction of the Commercial Court in the location of trade register.

9) *The Code on Private International Law and the Civil Procedure Code*[8].

Article 2: Application of Foreign Law

(1) Adjudicator applies Turkish conflict of laws rules and the foreign law authorized in accordance with these rules ex officio. Adjudicator may

---

5 Numbered 4686.
6 Numbered 2004 which was enacted on 06/19/1932.
7 Numbered 1447 which was approved on 07/21/197
8 Numbered 5718 and enacted on 11/27/2007 with publishing on Official Gazette dated 12/12/2007 and numbered 26728.

request the contribution of the parties to determine the content of the authorized foreign law.

(2) Turkish law will be applied in the event that related provisions of foreign law cannot be determined despite all the research.

(3) Authorizing another law by the conflict of laws rules of the law to be applied is taken into consideration only for the disputes related to law of persons and family law and set of rules of this law is applied.

(4) In the events that recourse to the law to be applied is allowed, set of rules of the law chosen is applied unless contrary is agreed.

(5) If the State, of which the law will be applied, has two or more regional unit and these regional units have different law systems, what regional law to be applied will be determined in accordance with the law of that State. In the absence of a determinative provision in the law of that State, the regional unit law that is relating most closely to the dispute applies.

Article 5: If a provision of an authorized foreign law, which is applied to a definite case, is *explicitly* contrary to Turkish public policy, this provision will not be applied; Turkish law will be applied when necessary.

Article 54: Authorized court renders the decisions of recognition on the following conditions:

(c) The order's not being explicitly on the contrary of public policy.

Article 60: *Enforcement of Foreign Arbitral Awards*

(1) Foreign arbitral awards that are final and enforceable or binding for the parties can be enforced.

(2) Enforcement of the foreign arbitral award can be requested by petition from the court of first instance agreed by the parties in writing.

If there is no such agreement between the parties, the court in the location of domicile of the person who the enforcement is requested against;

If not available, the court in the location of residence;

If not available, the court in the location of the goods which can be subject to enforcement is considered authorized.

Article 62: *Grounds of Refusal*

(1) The Court may refuse to enforce a foreign arbitral award…

(b) if the arbitral award is in conflict with the public morality and public policy,

(c) if the dispute subject to the arbitral award is inarbitrable in accordance with Turkish Law…

10) *The Legal Practitioners Act*[9]

Article 167: Resolution of Disputes through Arbitration

Any disputes arising from attorney agreements and attorney fees shall be resolved by the Arbitral Tribunal of the Bar where the legal aid is provided. Arbitral tribunal shall consist of the senior civil court of first instance judge in the judicial location of the bar and two attorneys eligible for Board of Directors to be designated by the Board of Directors of the Bar. The judge of the civil court of first instance presides at the Tribunal. The elected tribunal members serve for three years. The members whose terms expires can be re-elected.

Half of the arbitrator's fee shall be paid with the case. One copy of the decision given by the arbitral tribunal and finalized shall be sent to the bar of the attorney.

Regulations of Turkish Code of Civil Procedure numbered 1086 concerning arbitration except articles 527, 529, 532, 533/1 and 536 shall be applied to arbitral proceedings. Other issues about arbitral proceedings shall be regulated in Bar Arbitration Bylaw to be issued by Union of Turkish Bar Associations.

11) *Capital Markets Law*[10]

Article 18: Registered Capital System

(6) Members of the board of directors or shareholders, whose rights were violated, can file an action for annulment against the resolutions taken by the board of directors in accordance with the principles under this article before the commercial court in the location of the headquarters within 30 days from the announcement of the resolution.

12) *New Turkish Commercial Code*[11]

Article 18:

(2) Each merchant has to act like a prudent businessman with all the activities concerning his business.

---

9 Numbered 1136.

10 Numbered 6362 which is enacted on 12/6/2012 publishing on Official Gazette numbered 28513 and dated 12/30/2012.

11 Numbered 6102 which is enacted on 1/13/2011 publishing on Official Gazette numbered 27846 and dated 2/14/2011.

Article 219: In the event that the articles of partnership give management duty to a partner, his management right and duty cannot be restricted by other partners and he cannot be discharged from the duty either. However, the right and duty of management can be restricted or revoked 'by court order' for just cause upon the request of one of the partners.

Article 339: Content

(1) Articles of association of the joint stock corporations have to be concluded in writing; and all the founding shareholders' signatures have to be approved by the notary or the articles of association has to be signed before the trade registry manager.

(2) Following matters are written in the articles of association:
  a) Trade name of the company and the place where the headquarters will locate.
  b) Field of operation essential points of which are specified and defined.
  c) Company capital and nominal value of each share; formal requirements and conditions of their payment.
  d) Certificate of bearer share or certificate of registered share; privileges granted to specific shares; transfer restriction.
  e) Rights and assets apart from money invested; their value; number of shares to be given in return for them; value of a business or asset in the event of taking over, and the value of assets and rights bought on behalf of the company by the founder shareholders; value of payment, allowance or award to be given to the ones who serve for the foundation of the company.
  f) Dividends to be provided for the founders and members of board of directors and others.
  g) Number of the members of the board of directors, authorized signatories of them.
  h) The way to call a meeting of general assemblies; the voting rights.
  ı) Duration if the company is time-limited.
  i) The way to make the announcements of the company.
  j) Types and values of the shares undertaken by the shareholders.
  k) Accounting period of the company.

(3) First members of the board of directors are nominated by articles of association.

Article 340: Articles of association may differ from the provisions of this Code with regard to the joint stock corporations on the condition that the Code explicitly recognizes the difference. Subsidiary articles of association provisions stipulated by the other codes are exclusively applicable for those codes.

Article 356:

(1) Agreements with regard to takeover or leasing of a business organization or asset in return for a consideration exceeding ten per cent of the capital stock are not in effect within the two years from company registration unless being ratified by the general assembly and registered to the trade registry. Any type of act, which is including payments made with the purpose of their performance, prior to the ratification and registration of those agreements are invalid.

...

(4) Agreement is registered and announced by the ratification of the general assembly.

Article 376:
(3) In the event that there are indications raising doubts on the company's being deep in debt, the board of directors issues an interim financial statement of current assets on the bases of continuity of the company at the rate of possible sale price. If one can understand that the current assets fall short of the debts of the company from this financial statement, the board of directors declares this situation to the commercial court in the location of the headquarters and requests the bankruptcy of the corporation. Excepting that the creditors of the company debts, whose receivables equate to the amount that may meet the deficit of the company and eliminate the situation of being deep in debt have agreed in writing (before the decision of bankruptcy is given) that their place will be put in order after the places of all other creditors; and the experts who are appointed by the court has verified the legitimacy, literality and validness of this declaration or agreement. Otherwise, the application made to the court for expert examining is considered as a bankruptcy declaration.
Article 421: Meeting and Resolution Quorums for the Amendments of Articles of Association

(3) Following decisions on amendments to articles of association are made by affirmative votes of the shareholders or their agents of the shares that constitute at least seventy-five per cent of the capital stock:
   a) Amendment of the company's field of operation completely.
   b) Establishing privileged share.
   c) Limitation of assignment of registered shares.
(4) In the event that the quorums foreseen in sub-articles two and three are not met in the first meeting, the same quorums are sought in the following meetings.

Article 422:

(2) The board of directors is charged with giving a notarized copy of the minutes to the trade registry directorate promptly. It shall have the matters which are subject to registration and announcement in these minutes registered and announced. The minutes shall also be uploaded to the web-site of the corporation immediately.

Article 423:

(1) Resolutions issued by the general assembly are also valid for shareholders who do not attend the meeting or have dissenting vote.

Article 445: Causes for Annulment

(1) The persons identified in Article 446 can file annulment actions against general assembly resolutions that violate the law or articles of incorporation, particularly good faith, before the commercial court of first instance in the location of the company headquarters, within 3 months from the date of the decision.

Article 446: Persons Who Can File an Annulment Action

(1)

a. Shareholders who are present at the meeting, who dissented, and whose dissent is included in the minute,
b. Shareholders who claim that:

the invitation was not made in due form; the agenda was not announced properly; or

persons who are not authorized to attend the general assembly -or their agents- attended the meeting and voted;

they were unjustly not allowed to attend the general assembly and vote; and

those abovementioned violations had an impact on issuing the general assembly resolution, regardless of the shareholder's presence at the meeting or having dissented,

c. Board of directors,
d. Each member of the board of directors who will be subject to personal responsibility in the event of fulfillment of the resolution

can file annulment action.

Article 447: Nullity

(1) Resolutions of general assembly, which are especially

a. Restricting or abolishing shareholder's right to attend at the general assembly, minimum vote, sue and inalienable rights arising from law,
b. Restricting shareholder's right to demand information, investigate and audit beyond the limits of the law,
c. Infringing the fundamental structure of the joint-stock company, or are against the provisions of capital maintenance are void.

Article 448: Announcement, Security and Right to Appeal

(1) The board of directors duly announces the filing of an action for annulment or nullity, the date of the hearing, and uploads the announcement to the company web-site.
(2) In an annulment action, an oral hearing cannot commence before the time limit of three months ends. If more than one annulment action is filed, the actions shall be consolidated to be heard.
(3) The court can decide that the plaintiff must provide a security at the request of the company. The court determines the quality and quantity of the security.

Article 449: Suspending the Execution of the Resolution

(1) When an action of annulment or nullity against a general assembly resolution is filed, the court may decide to suspend the execution of the resolution subject to this action, after taking the opinion of members of the board of directors.

Article 450: Effect of the Decision

(1) A court decision pertaining to an annulment or nullity of general assembly resolution inures to the benefit of all shareholders after it is finalized. The board of directors shall immediately register a copy of this decision in the trade registry, and upload it to the company web-site.

Article 451: Liability of Persons Who File the Action for Annulment of Nullity in Bad Faith

(1) In the event that an action for annulment or nullity is filed against the resolution of general assembly in bad faith, plaintiffs are severally liable for any damages that the company incurs as a result of the action.

Article 452:

(1) The general assembly can amend all provisions of the articles of association in compliance with the conditions stipulated in the Statute unless otherwise provided, with the reservation of vested and inalienable rights.

Article 529: (Grounds for Termination) General

(1) Joint-stock corporation is terminated in the events of:
(e) the decision of its bankruptcy…

Article 530: Absence of Organs

(1) In the events that legally required organs of the company does not exist or the board of directors cannot meet for a long time, the court in the location of the headquarters sets a period of time for the company's condition to be adjusted in accordance with the law after listening to the board of directors at the request of shareholders, creditors of the company or Ministry of Customs and Trade. If the condition is not adjusted within this period of time, the court decides on the company's termination.
2) The court can take required measures at the request of one of the parties when the case is filed.

Article 538: Authorization for the Sale of Active Asset

(1) Liquidating agents may sell the company's active asset by bargain, too, unless contrary is agreed by the general assembly.
(2) For the sale of active asset at considerable amount, general assembly resolution is required. Third and fourth sub-articles of article 421 applies to this resolution.

Appendix II: Translation of Related Court Decisions

1) Turkish Supreme Court 11th Civil Circuit decision dated 12/28/1978, numbered 5258/5916:

"*The case is about the collection of 6.072.258 liras. The dispute arises from sales contract and is not a matter that is not subject to will of the parties. The arbitral clause in the contract, therefore, is valid in pursuant to articles 516,517,518 of Turkish Code of Civil Procedure* (articles 408 and 412 in the current revised version of Turkish Code of Civil Procedure)."

2) Supreme Court Assembly of Civil Chambers' rule dated 06/20/1973 numbered T/147–529:

"*The dispute is about a sales contract which is not a matter that is not subject to will of the parties. The contract between the parties or the subject matter has no aspect violating public policy. Such dispute shall be heard and settled before the arbitrator to be decided by the parties.*"

3) Turkish Supreme Court Commercial Circuit (previous name of 11th Circuit) dated 03/22/1973 and numbered 601/1210:

"*...Principally, one can agree upon damages of mental anguish similar to liquidated damages as a result of contractual liability. In an action for mental anguish, defendant's consent binds the judge. In this respect, the subject of mental anguish shall be within the content of arbitral clause...*"

4) Turkish Supreme Court 15th Civil Circuit decision dated 06/18/2007 numbered 2007/2680:

"*The lawsuit is about registration and cancellation of title arising from contract of construction and the collection of penalty clause. The Plaintiff has appealed the decision sustaining the claim of registration and cancellation of title and dismissing the claim for collection of penalty clause given by arbitrators. The jurisdiction of the court involves in public policy; therefore, it bears consideration even if the parties do not plea. The lawsuits of registration and cancellation of title, indeed, involves in public policy. Arbitrators, thus, cannot hear such cases. Hence, article 13 of Turkish Code of Civil Procedure states that the lawsuit about in-rem rights on immovables will be heard by the court of the place of the immovable. Even though an old Supreme Court decision saying that cases about in-rem rights on immovables can be heard before arbitral tribunal exists in the court file, general practice has a tendency that cases about registration and cancellation of title can be resolved by courts."*

5) Turkish Supreme Court 3rd Civil Circuit Decision dated 12/02/2004 numbered 2004/13018:

"...*Concluding an arbitration agreement is possible only for the disputes that are subject to will of the parties. This means that parties can make arbitration agreement or arbitral clause for resolution of a dispute if they are free to make an agreement to settle this dispute and this agreement is valid without any needing a court order. Considering the Supreme Court's established practices, arbitral tribunals cannot hear the declaratory actions for rental value. Because the matter of the determination of rental value involves public policy, the parties can assess the rental value only by definite standards and limitations. The will of the parties is, therefore, not unlimited. The renter, thus, is not obliged to pay the rental that the landlord asks for. In that case, arbitral tribunals cannot hear a dispute on rent because the arbitral clause about the settlement of disputes on rental value assessment, which involves public policy, will be invalid according to Turkish Code of Civil Procedure article 518."*

6) Turkish Supreme Court 13th Civil Circuit decision dated 6/16/1994 numbered 4390/5895:

"...*disputes arising from immovable properties are private law contracts and these transactions are only subject to the parties' will. The disputes arising from such contracts are arbitrable."*

7) Turkish Supreme Court 4th Civil Circuit has a decision dated 04/10/1967 numbered 2760/3075:

"...*the Law of Property Ownership has no provision impeding in arbitration of the disputes between flat owners"*

8) Turkish Supreme Court 15th Civil Circuit decision dated 05/31/1979 numbered 1195/1330:

"Turkish Code of Civil Procedure articles 516 and 536 (407–444 in the new current Code) govern the regulations about arbitration. The courts, as a general rule, have the authority to resolve any kind of dispute that is within the jurisdiction of civil or criminal judiciary and borne between the parties. It is, however, possible for the parties to a dispute, which does not involve public policy, to agree on submitting their dispute, to private persons rather than courts. Resolution of a dispute by arbitrators is a private judicial remedy in our Procedural Code. The option of

arbitration is possible in the events that it is allowed explicitly and implicitly by the laws. Whether such dispute can be resolved by an arbitral tribunal is subject to the will of the parties. In this respect, provisions of the construction contract dated 08/07/1972 about restitution of an immovable property share and having the required adjustment proceedings in the land registry are from the acts that parties are able to implement freely. These kinds of acts shall be deemed as subject to the will of the parties. Settling the dispute by way of arbitration here is shall not be regarded as a violation of law. It does not involve public policy."

9) Turkish Supreme Court 14th Civil Circuit decision dated 10/07/2003 numbered 2003/6387:

"The case requests the transfer of the ownership of an immovable property pursuant to a preliminary contract of sale. Although article –M- of the general sales specification includes the provision that 'the possible disputes between the promisor company of the sale and the promisee of the sale shall be resolved by way of arbitration', Turkish Civil Code[12] *article 706 and 1017 and Land Register Code*[13] *article 26 and 27 and the Code numbered 5519 stipulate that transfers in the land registry are possible by the declarations of the promisor and promisee in the presence of a deed officer or by 'court order'. The abovementioned articles relate to public policy and arbitration agreement is invalid regarding these matters. Therefore, the appeal claims made by the defendant's attorney in this respect are not admissible. Besides, the ownership of the immovable property, which is the subject of the dispute, has been transferred to defendant promisee during the litigation."*

10) Turkish Supreme Court 15th Civil Circuit decision dated 09/23/2002 numbered 2002/4321:

"The terms of a contract may freely be determined by the parties within the limits of the law.' pursuant to Turkish Code of Contract Article 19;[14]*however, the freedom of contract of the parties is not unlimited. Hence, lawmakers impose restriction on the subject of contracts on moral, social, and economical grounds, and on public policy in practice. The present case requested the cancellation of the construction contract between the parties in return for an apartment as well as the cancellation and registration of the title, which was transferred to contractor. In this case,*

12 Turkish Civil Code numbered 4721 which was published in Official Gazette with the number of 24607 and enacted on 12/08/2001.

13 Land Register Law numbered 2644 published in Official Gazette on 12/29/1934 with the number of 2892.

14 It is article 26 in the current Turkish Code of Contract.

because the dispute between the parties relates to in rem rights on immovable property, and also because transfer of ownership in the land registry can only be made by consensus or 'court order', arbitration of such a matter, which is against the rule legally stipulated as a matter of public policy, is not permitted. Thus, the arbitral clause for the dispute between the parties is not enforceable. The court's ruling of lack jurisdiction should be reversed. The court should hear the case."

11) The 15th Civil Circuit of Turkish Supreme Court decision dated 11/07/1991 and numbered 1991/4163:

"*... the legislator has brought an order regarding the appeal of arbitral awards. As indicated in article 533 / 1 of Turkish Code of Civil Procedure, arbitral awards may be reversed only on the grounds listed in this article where the particular circumstances match those stipulated in the article's four provisions. Arbitral awards, therefore, can be reversed on the grounds included in these provisions. To put it in a different way, it is impossible to reverse the decisions of arbitrators except for the reasons stated in the article. However, an arbitral award can be reversed in the event of breach of public policy for reasons other than those listed in article 533...*"

12) Turkish Supreme Court decision dated 10/23/1972 numbered 2/12:

"...As a result of freedom of contract principle, articles 19 and 20 of Turkish Code of Contract and article 516 of Turkish Code of Civil Procedure, it is possible for real or legal persons to prefer arbitration and conclude arbitration agreement for the disputes do not involve public policy...".

13) The 3rd Civil Circuit of Turkish Supreme Court on 12/02/2004 with the number of 2004/13018 that:

"*...Concluding an arbitration agreement is possible only for the disputes that are subject to will of the parties. This means that parties can make arbitration agreement or arbitral clause for resolution of a dispute if they are free to make an agreement to settle this dispute and this agreement is valid without any needing a court order. Considering the Supreme Court's established practices, arbitral tribunals cannot hear the declaratory actions for rental value. Because the matter of the determination of rental value involves public policy, the parties can assess the rental value only by definite standards and limitations. The will of the parties is, therefore, not unlimited. The renter, thus, is not obliged to pay the rental that the landlord asks for. In that case, arbitral tribunals cannot hear a dispute on rent because the arbitral clause about the settlement of disputes on rental value* *assessment, which involves public policy, will be invalid according to Turkish Code of Civil Procedure article 518."*

14) Supreme Court Assembly of Civil Chambers' decision, dated 06/21/2000 and numbered 2000/2–1051:

"*...Neither statute nor legal doctrine has provided an inalterable definition of public policy. However, and particularly in terms of Turkish International Private Law, the issues identified in Supreme Court decisions as against public policy include reckless conduct and uncivil manners, and actions incompatible with the fundamental rules of Turkish law and the general policies that Turkish laws are based on."*

15) Turkish Supreme Court 13th Civil Circuit decision dated 6/16/1994 numbered E2012/8426 and K10349:

"*...the entire set of rules and institutions, which protects the fundamental interests of the society and designates the fundamental structure of the society from political, social, economic, ethical and legal perspectives within a specific time period."*

"*...the intervention of public policy is essential when there is violation of imperative provisions of law, which aim to protect the public interest and public policy, morality and fundamental rights and freedoms. For instance, customs codes and tax legislations are related to public policy. Public policy would intervene in a final arbitral award which resolves a debt owed contrary to tax legislation because such award does not comply with the basic principles considered essential in Turkish law."*

16) The Turkish Constitutional Court decision in the Official Gazette dated 04/17/1964 and numbered 11685:

"*...public policy aims to secure peace and order in the country, to protect the State and State Organization; in other words, it embodies the rules that constitute the base of the regime of the community at every stage."*

17) Turkish Supreme Court 13th Civil Circuit Decision dated 09/25/2006 numbered E.2006/7789 and K.2006/12275:

"*...In accordance with article 6 of the Code numbered 4077 (currently the Code numbered 6052), contract provisions against the consumer causing instability in parties' rights and duties breach the utmost good faith principle. If the seller or provider unilaterally puts such provisions in the contract, those provisions would be unfair terms and not be binding for the consumer because they lack negotiation with the consumer. According to abovementioned article, one shall deem a contract* *provision not negotiated with the consumer if the contract provision is previously prepared and the consumer does not have an effect on that standard agreement. In the present case, it is clear that the package tour contract is a standardized contract consists of standard terms drawn up by the defendant. The defendant could not prove with an evidence that arbitral clause has been mutually agreed following a negotiation with the consumer plaintiff. Therefore, agreement eliminating the authorization of Consumer Courts for resolution of disputes arising from the contract between the plaintiff consumer and defendant has no binding effect on plaintiff…"*

18) Turkish Supreme Court 13th Civil Circuit Decision dated 09/25/2008 numbered E.2008/3492 and K.2008/11120:

"*…the purview of article 1 of the Turkish Code of Consumer Protection numbered 4077 (currently numbered 6502) states that "The purview of this Code is to take the measures maintaining health and security and economic interests of consumers in accordance with public interest; informing; educatory; compensative for damages; maintaining protection from environmental risks and incenting the attempts of consumers to protect themselves and regularizing the issues about incenting voluntary policy-making organizations in this respect". Article 2 defines the content as "This code contains any type of consumer transaction of which one party is consumer in product and service market with the purposes mentioned in Article 1". Article 3 includes definitions with regard to the application of the Code. Article 22, then, states that Arbitration Committee for Consumer Problems will be established in addition to the conditions for referring to the Committee compulsorily or voluntarily. Article 23 underlines that consumer courts shall hear any type of dispute arising from application of this Code. Reviewing the purview and provisions of the Code numbered 4077, the lawmaker has clearly drafted it in compliance with social and financial developments of contemporary law aiming at protecting the consumers who are weaker and in need of wider protection than the seller, supplier etc.*

Article 172 of Turkish Constitution, indeed, foresees that "The State shall take the measures informing and educating the consumers and incent the self-protective attempts of consumers". The State undertakes protection of health and security and economic interests of consumers and informing are firstly based on the Constitution. The Code aims at protecting public policy, providing social order, justice and harmony between consumers and sellers / suppliers etc. The Code targets maintaining public policy as well as protecting the consumer, and it is beyond doubt that this is a special Code directly related to public policy. One shall infer, therefore, that the law-maker has tacitly barred private arbitration from establishing an arbitration committee as the Arbitration Committee for Consumer Problems in accordance with Article 22 of this Code. The Code explicitly designates the authorized court, and thus, consumer courts or consumer arbitration committees shall certainly settle the disputes arising from application of this Code depending on the amount. Private arbitrators, therefore, cannot resolve any type of dispute on application of this Code considering the statement in Article 23 entitling the consumer courts. In the present case, the dispute arising from the package tour holiday contract between the parties falls within the ambit of Code numbered 4077 articles of 1,2, 3/c-f and 23. Arbitral clause in the contract, thus, is invalid because consumer courts are authorized for resolution of the dispute. Arbitrators are not entitled to resolve the dispute. The award rendered by the arbitral tribunal is, therefore, on the contrary of the proceedings and the statute shall be reversed in accordance with Turkish Code of Civil Procedure Article 533/3 as it is beyond the arbitral tribunal's jurisdiction."

19) Turkish Supreme Court 13th Civil Circuit Decision dated 09/26/1974 and numbered 2385/2161:

"...freedom of contract principle prevails in Turkish law within some exceptions such as of Turkish Code of Contract articles 19 and 20. Lawmaker has stipulated restrictive provisions on agreements of attorney's fee based on public policy and certainly forbidden the acts conflicting with these provisions. The articles 129,130, 131 of former Legal Practitioners Act numbered 3499 and articles 164, 168, 169 of current Legal Practitioners Act numbered 3499 have, thus, similar mandatory regulations. Those regulations states that the contracts about pursuing the lawsuit and any kind of consultancy fee will be in writing; no evidence will be cited except written agreement in the cases arising from the fee; minimum attorneyship fee tariff will be applied in the events that a written fee agreement does not exist, in so far as such amount will not exceed %25 of the subject of the case or decision; the fact that an attorney will not have a share in the subject matter as if he is a party and such agreements will be null and void. These provisions involve public policy and judicial review of conflicting arbitral awards by Supreme Court is not possible. Disputes about attorney's fee, therefore, cannot be resolved by arbitrators. This and other Supreme Court circuits have had the tendency in this direction since before now. The fact that the arbitrators have decided on a dispute arising from agreement of attorney's fee on the contrary of these provisions requires reversal..."

20) 16th Commercial Court of Istanbul decision numbered 2013/157 and dated 08/20/2013:

"There is no conclusive definition of public policy in legislation or doctrine. One can observe particularly in terms of Turkish International Private Law, however, in the Court of Appeals' decisions that elements such as contradiction with public morality and customs, incoherence with the fundamental rules and the general policy of Turkish laws are considered as a violation of public policy. In order for public policy to come into question, the contradiction with a rule must violate one of the fundamental principles of the local legal order or severely damage the general sense of law."

21) 4th Civil Court of Ankara decision numbered 2013/273 dated 01/21/2014:

"[*T*]*he award causing the decrease in public revenue alone cannot be considered a violation of public policy. Further merits of the award cannot be examined. The application to set the award aside, which seems to decrease public revenue…, is not approved due to the absence of a legal basis… The decrease in public revenue is not sufficient alone for such approval.*".

22) Supreme Court Commercial Circuit, 3/11/1969 dated 1969/3878E. and 5118 K. numbered decision:

"An arbitral clause inserted in the articles of incorporation for disputes arising from an unlimited liability in a company's internal affairs has a binding effect. Arbitrators can review cases in which shareholders claim that a company has not conducted the business fairly (pursuant to the provisions of the articles of incorporation). Each shareholder has the right to file a lawsuit for dissolution of the company separately or collectively based on one of the grounds listed in Article 187 of the Turkish Commercial Code…. The trial court has decided to hear the case and deny the motion to dismiss for lack of jurisdiction. This decision must be reversed. This situation does not impede another shareholder from submitting the case to arbitration; nor does it preclude the case from being heard before an arbitrator."

23) Turkish Supreme Court 4th Civil Circuit decision dated 09/23/1975 and numbered 1975/6158E and 1975/1055K:

"…Arbitral agreements have effect only on the parties of it, like any other agreement. Agreements do not have any consequences for or against the ones who are not party to them. Arbitrators are authorized to hear the cases which are between the parties of the arbitral agreement."

www.ingramcontent.com/pod-product-compliance
Ingram Content Group UK Ltd.
Pitfield, Milton Keynes, MK11 3LW, UK
UKHW021014120926
8556IPUK00040B/1127

9 783631 775721